431

HUMAN BIOLOGY AND HEALTH

Anthea Maton
Former NSTA National Coordinator
Project Scope, Sequence, Coordination
Washington, DC

Jean Hopkins
Science Instructor and Department Chairperson
John H. Wood Middle School
San Antonio, Texas

Susan Johnson
Professor of Biology
Ball State University
Muncie, Indiana

David LaHart
Senior Instructor
Florida Solar Energy Center
Cape Canaveral, Florida

Charles William McLaughlin
Science Instructor and Department Chairperson
Central High School
St. Joseph, Missouri

Maryanna Quon Warner
Science Instructor
Del Dios Middle School
Escondido, California

Jill D. Wright
Professor of Science Education
Director of International Field Programs
University of Pittsburgh
Pittsburgh, Pennsylvania

Prentice Hall
Englewood Cliffs, New Jersey
Needham, Massachusetts

Prentice Hall Science

Human Biology and Health

Student Text and Annotated Teacher's Edition
Laboratory Manual
Teacher's Resource Package
Teacher's Desk Reference
Computer Test Bank
Teaching Transparencies
Science Reader
Product Testing Activities
Computer Courseware
Video and Interactive Video

The illustration on the cover, rendered by Keith Kasnot, shows the human skeletal system in motion.

Credits begin on page 257.

FIRST EDITION

ISBN 0-13-981176-1

6 7 8 9 10   96

Prentice Hall
A Division of Simon & Schuster
Englewood Cliffs, New Jersey 07632

STAFF CREDITS

Editorial:	Harry Bakalian, Pamela E. Hirschfeld, Maureen Grassi, Robert P. Letendre, Elisa Mui Eiger, Lorraine Smith-Phelan, Christine A. Caputo
Design:	AnnMarie Roselli, Carmela Pereira, Susan Walrath, Leslie Osher, Art Soares
Production:	Suse Cioffi, Joan McCulley, Elizabeth Torjussen, Christina Burghard, Marlys Lehmann
Photo Research:	Libby Forsyth, Emily Rose, Martha Conway
Publishing Technology:	Andrew Grey Bommarito, Gwendollynn Waldron, Deborah Jones, Monduane Harris, Michael Colucci, Gregory Myers, Cleasta Wilburn
Marketing:	Andy Socha, Victoria Willows
Pre-Press Production:	Laura Sanderson, Denise Herckenrath
Manufacturing:	Rhett Conklin, Gertrude Szyferblatt

Consultants

Kathy French	National Science Consultant
William Royalty	National Science Consultant

CONTENTS

HUMAN BIOLOGY AND HEALTH

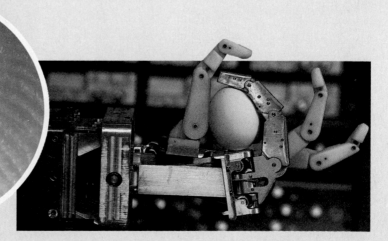

Reference Section

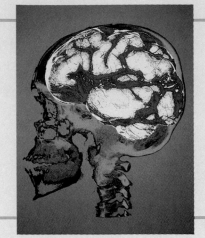

Features

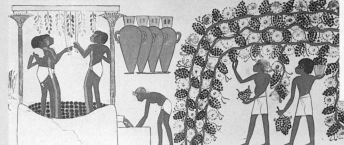

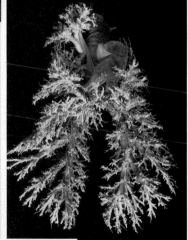

CONCEPT MAPPING

T hroughout your study of science, you will learn a variety of terms, facts, figures, and concepts. Each new topic you encounter will provide its own collection of words and ideas—which, at times, you may think seem endless. But each of the ideas within a particular topic is related in some way to the others. No concept in science is isolated. Thus it will help you to understand the topic if you see the whole picture; that is, the interconnectedness of all the individual terms and ideas. This is a much more effective and satisfying way of learning than memorizing separate facts.

Actually, this should be a rather familiar process for you. Although you may not think about it in this way, you analyze many of the elements in your daily life by looking for relationships or connections. For example, when you look at a collection of flowers, you may divide them into groups: roses, carnations, and daisies. You may then associate colors with these flowers: red, pink, and white. The general topic is flowers. The subtopic is types of flowers. And the colors are specific terms that describe flowers. A topic makes more sense and is more easily understood if you understand how it is broken down into individual ideas and how these ideas are related to one another and to the entire topic.

It is often helpful to organize information visually so that you can see how it all fits together. One technique for describing related ideas is called a **concept map**. In a concept map, an idea is represented by a word or phrase enclosed in a box. There are several ideas in any concept map. A connection between two ideas is made with a line. A word or two that describes the connection is written on or near the line. The general topic is located at the top of the map. That topic is then broken down into subtopics, or more specific ideas, by branching lines. The most specific topics are located at the bottom of the map.

To construct a concept map, first identify the important ideas or key terms in the chapter or section. Do not try to include too much information. Use your judgment as to what is really important. Write the general topic at the top of your map. Let's use an example to help illustrate this process. Suppose you decide that the key terms in a section you are reading are School, Living Things, Language Arts, Subtraction, Grammar, Mathematics, Experiments, Papers, Science, Addition, Novels. The general topic is School. Write and enclose this word in a box at the top of your map.

SCHOOL

Now choose the subtopics—Language Arts, Science, Mathematics. Figure out how they are related to the topic. Add these words to your map. Continue this procedure until you have included all the important ideas and terms. Then use lines to make the appropriate connections between ideas and terms. Don't forget to write a word or two on or near the connecting line to describe the nature of the connection.

Do not be concerned if you have to redraw your map (perhaps several times!) before you show all the important connections clearly. If, for example, you write papers for Science as well as for Language Arts, you may want to place these two subjects next to each other so that the lines do not overlap.

One more thing you should know about concept mapping: Concepts can be correctly mapped in many different ways. In fact, it is unlikely that any two people will draw identical concept maps for a complex topic. Thus there is no one correct concept map for any topic! Even though your concept map may not match those of your classmates, it will be correct as long as it shows the most important concepts and the clear relationships among them. Your concept map will also be correct if it has meaning to you and if it helps you understand the material you are reading. A concept map should be so clear that if some of the terms are erased, the missing terms could easily be filled in by following the logic of the concept map.

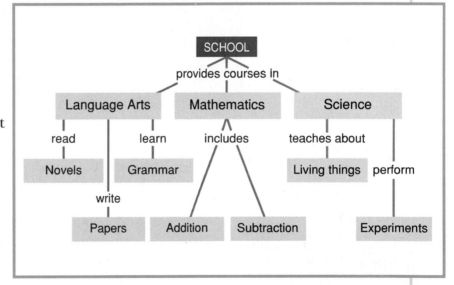

HUMAN BIOLOGY
AND HEALTH

To play soccer, all parts of the bodies of these young soccer players must work together in perfect harmony.

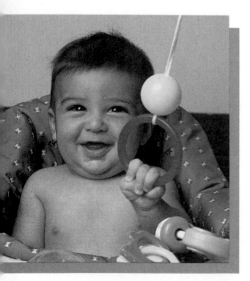

A smiling child reaching for a toy illustrates how different parts of the body—even a very young body—work together.

The day for the championship soccer game has finally arrived. The stadium is filled to capacity. The game is about to begin. The crowd quiets down as a soccer player on the attacking team prepares to kick off. The defending team members anxiously await the ball on their half of the field so that they can advance the ball into the attacking team's territory. The players on both sides have spent many years of training for this moment.

As the kicker begins to kick off, nerves carry messages to her brain, telling her body exactly what movements it must make. Her muscles move, pulling on her bones so that she kicks the ball out of the center circle. At the same time, chemicals flow through her blood, informing certain parts of her body to speed up and others to slow down.

CHAPTERS

Now comes the kickoff. She moves toward the ball, keeping her nonkicking foot next to the ball, her head down, and her eyes on the ball. Then she swings her kicking leg with the toes pointed downward and kicks the ball squarely with her instep. It's out of the center circle. The game has begun!

To help her team win the championship, all parts of the soccer player's body have to work in perfect harmony. And even though you may never compete in a championship soccer game, your body parts are also working in their own perfect harmony at this very moment. In this textbook you will discover how the different parts of your body work and how they all work together as one.

▲ *Exercise, such as running, helps to keep the body in good working condition.*

Discovery *Activity*

Yesterday, Today, and Tomorrow

1. Take a look at your classmates or a group of people who are about your age. Make a mental note of the features that you share with them.

2. Complete the same exercise with a group of adults and a group of young children.

   ■ In what ways are people of all ages the same?

   ■ What changes occur in people as they grow from children to adults?

   ■ Are all changes that occur in people easily observed?

The Human Body

Guide for Reading

After you read the following sections, you will be able to

1–1 The Body as a Whole
- Define homeostasis.
- Explain why energy is important to the human body.

1–2 Levels of Organization
- Describe the levels of organization of multicellular living things.
- Classify the four basic types of tissues.

All objects, including the human body, give off infrared rays. Infrared rays cannot be seen, but they can be felt as heat. You have felt infrared rays in the form of heat from the sun or a glowing light bulb. A thermograph, which looks like a small television camera, converts the body's invisible infrared rays into a visible picture called a thermogram. So an object that appears to be invisible in the dark becomes visible with the help of a thermograph.

As a thermograph converts the invisible heat rays given off by the body into thermograms, it creates heat maps. Look carefully at the thermogram, or heat map, of a young boy and his dog. Notice that different areas of the body show various colors. The warmest areas of the body appear white. The coolest areas appear purple or black. What does the color of the dog's nose tell you about its temperature?

Thermograms are useful in medicine because they help doctors "see" what is happening inside the body. In some cases, they help doctors diagnose certain illnesses. As you turn the pages that follow, you too will be able to "see" what is happening inside the human body. Why not take a look.

Journal *Activity*

You and Your World In your journal, draw a picture of yourself performing your favorite activity. Below your drawing, describe what you are doing and what parts of your body are involved in the activity. Which actions occur automatically? Which actions do you have to think about?

◀ *In this thermogram, the warmest areas appear white and the coolest areas appear black.*

1–1 The Body as a Whole

Every minute of the day, even when you are asleep, your body is busily at work. Blood is being pumped through blood vessels by your heart. Air is being pushed in and out of your body by your lungs. Your intestines are giving off chemicals that break down the food you have eaten into smaller parts. Your nerves are sending out signals from the brain to all parts of your body. Chemical messengers are regulating all kinds of processes.

To you these activities probably seem quite different—and in many ways they are. However, all these activities have the same purpose: to delicately control the body's internal environment. This internal environment must remain stable, or constant, even during extreme changes in the activities of the body or in its surroundings.

For example, you may eat a large amount of sweets (foods containing mainly sugar) on one day and none at all on the next day. The amount of sugar that goes into your body is quite different on the two days. But the amount of sugar in your blood

Figure 1–1 *No matter what the weather is outside, the human body is able to maintain homeostasis, or a stable internal environment.*

remains remarkably stable, or unchanged. **The process by which the body's internal environment is kept stable in spite of changes in the external environment is called homeostasis** (hoh-mee-oh-STAY-sihs). Put another way, **homeostasis** is the process by which the delicate balance between the activities occurring inside your body (amount of sugar in the blood) and those occurring outside your body (amount of sweets you eat) is maintained.

In order to perform all the life activities, humans, like all living things, need energy. Even homeostasis needs energy. After all, the body works hard to keep its internal environment stable. Where does the body get the energy to do all of this work? Just as an engine uses gasoline as its energy source, living things use food as the source of energy for all their activities.

1–1 Section Review

1. What is homeostasis?
2. What is the body's source of energy?

Critical Thinking—*Applying Concepts*
3. Explain why it is important for all living things to maintain homeostasis.

1–2 Levels of Organization

Here's a riddle for you: What do you and an ameba have in common? The answer: Both of you are made of cells. Actually, the whole "body" of the ameba is made up of one cell. Your body, however, is made up of many cells. Living things that are composed of only one cell are called unicellular; those that are composed of many cells are called multicellular.

In multicellular living things—humans, birds, trees, turtles, and hamsters, to name just a few—the work of keeping the living thing alive is divided among the different parts of its body. Each part has

Guide for Reading

Focus on this question as you read.

▶ *What are the levels of organization in the human body?*

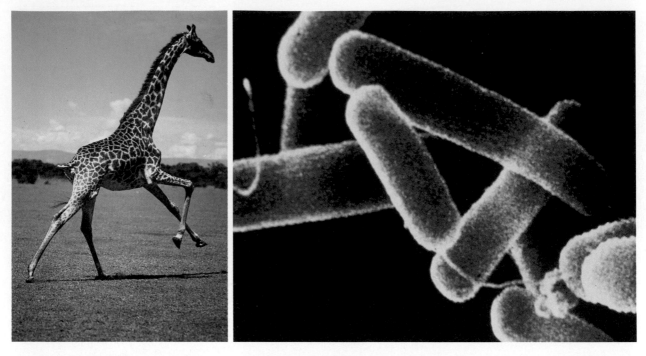

Figure 1–2 *All living things are made of cells. Bacteria are unicellular, whereas the giraffe is multicellular. Does the giraffe have bigger cells than a bacterium or just more of them?*

a specific job to do. And as the part does its specific job, it works in harmony with all the other parts to keep the living thing healthy and alive.

The groupings of these specific parts within a living thing are called levels of organization. **The levels of organization in a multicellular living thing include cells, tissues, organs, and organ systems.**

Cells

Your body is made up of different **cells,** which are the building blocks of living things. Just as a house is made up of many bricks, so your body is made up of many cells—trillions of cells, in fact! And each of the trillions of cells in your body has its own special job. For example, some cells work to continuously provide fuel for your body. Other cells are involved in sensing external conditions for your body. And still other cells aid in the job of the organization and control of your entire body.

Cells come in all shapes and sizes. There are box-shaped cells, cells that resemble giant balls, and cells that look like tiny strands of wool. Regardless of its particular job or shape, a cell works in harmony with other cells to keep the body alive. Let's take a look at three different kinds of cells, each specialized for a particular job.

FIND OUT BY CALCULATING

How Many Cells?

There are 5 million red blood cells in every milliliter of blood. How many red blood cells are there in 5 milliliters of blood? How many milliliters of blood will contain 7.5 million red blood cells? Ten million red blood cells?

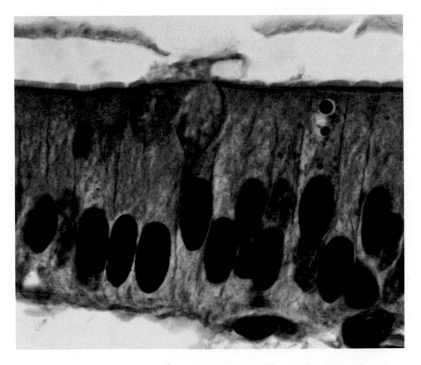

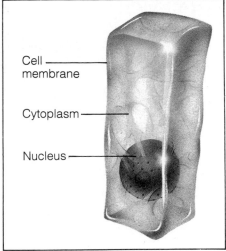

Figure 1–3 *The illustration shows some of the basic parts of a typical cell. Can you find the corresponding parts in the photograph of cells of the small intestine?*

ABSORBING CELLS The small intestine is a tube-like structure located below the liver and the stomach. The small intestine plays an important role in the process of digestion. Lining the inside of the small intestine are cells that absorb digested food and then transport it to the bloodstream. The bloodstream (also made of cells) delivers the digested food to all parts of the body. Remember, food provides the body with the energy it needs to stay alive. In order to do this, the food must come into contact with huge numbers of absorbing cells.

Figure 1–4 *Each of these "hills" in the small intestine contains blood vessels ready to carry digested food throughout the body. Why is a "hilly" small intestine better suited to absorbing digested food than a smooth small intestine would be?*

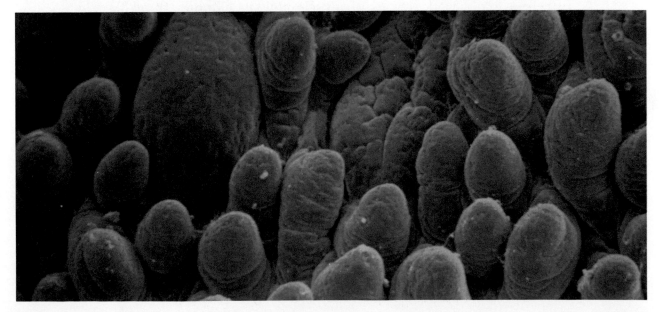

If you were to look at the lining inside the small intestine under a microscope, you would see that it is covered by structures resembling tiny and even tinier hills. See Figure 1–4 on page 17. In just 6.5 square centimeters of the small intestine, there are 20,000 tiny hills and 10 billion tinier hills!

Within each hill is a network of tiny blood vessels. As digested food passes through these hill-like structures, it is absorbed by these cells. Then it is passed on to the tiny blood vessels, which carry the digested food to all parts of the body.

ASSEMBLY CELLS The body contains millions of cells that are responsible for assembling, or putting together, important chemical substances. The pancreas, a fish-shaped structure located just behind the stomach, contains a variety of these assembly cells. Some of them are specialized to produce enzymes. Enzymes are chemicals that help to break down food into simpler substances. Others are specialized to produce hormones. Hormones are chemical messengers that help to regulate certain activities of the body.

CELLS FOR MOVEMENT Every move you make—from the twitch of an eyebrow to the powerful stride of running to the lifting of this textbook—depends on muscle cells. A muscle cell is like no other type of cell in the body because a muscle cell is able to contract, or shorten. In doing so, a muscle cell causes movement. You will read more about the different types of muscle cells in Chapter 2.

Tissues

Your body is a masterpiece of timing and organization. Its trillions of cells work together to keep you alive. To help you accomplish this task, the cells that make up your body are organized into **tissues.** A tissue is a group of similar cells that perform the same function. **There are four basic types of tissues in the human body: muscle, connective, nerve, and epithelial** (ehp-ih-THEE-lee-uhl). Observing these tissues under a microscope, you might be surprised to see how different they are from one another.

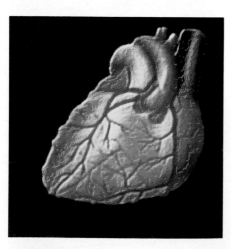

Figure 1–5 *The heart contains muscle tissue, epithelial tissue, connective tissue, and nerve tissue.*

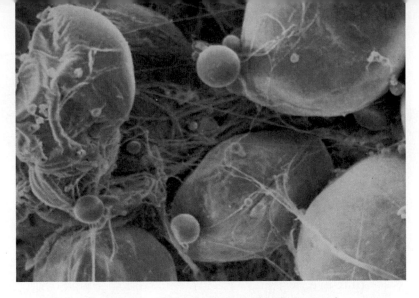

Figure 1–6 *Notice how these human fat cells vary in size, depending on the amount of fat they are storing. Why is fat considered a type of connective tissue?*

MUSCLE TISSUE   The only kind of tissue in your body that has the ability to contract, or shorten, is muscle tissue. By contracting and thus pulling on bones, one type of muscle tissue makes your body move. Another type of muscle tissue lines the walls of structures inside your body. This muscle tissue does jobs such as moving food from your mouth to your stomach. A third type of muscle tissue is found only in the heart. This muscle tissue enables the heart to contract and pump blood.

CONNECTIVE TISSUE   The tissue that provides support for your body and connects all its parts is called connective tissue. Bone is an example of connective tissue. Are you surprised to learn that bone is a tissue? Not all tissues need to be soft. Without bone, your body would lack support and definite shape. In other words, without bone you would just be a blob of flesh! Blood is another example of connective tissue. One of the blood's most important jobs is to bring food and oxygen to body cells and carry away wastes. A third kind of connective tissue is fat. Fat keeps the body warm, cushions structures from the shock of a sudden blow, and stores food.

NERVE TISSUE   The third type of tissue is nerve tissue. Nerve tissue carries messages back and forth between the brain and spinal cord and every other part of your body. And it does so at incredible speeds. In the fraction of a second it takes for you to feel the cold of an ice cube you are touching, your nerve tissue has carried the message from your finger to your brain. Next time you have a chance to hold an ice cube, think about this.

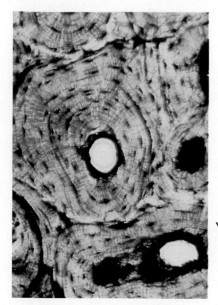

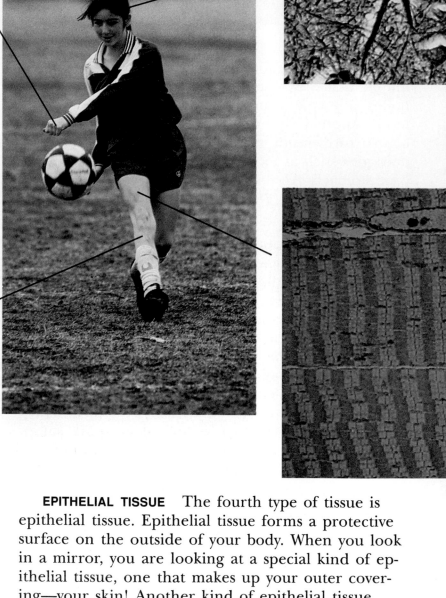

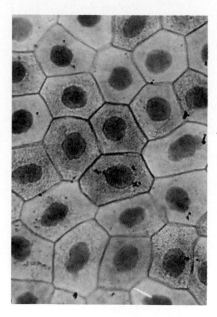

Figure 1–7 *Tissues are groups of similar cells that work together. How do connective tissue (top left), nerve tissue (top right), muscle tissue (bottom right), and epithelial tissue (bottom left) allow for the delicate movements needed to kick a soccer ball?*

EPITHELIAL TISSUE The fourth type of tissue is epithelial tissue. Epithelial tissue forms a protective surface on the outside of your body. When you look in a mirror, you are looking at a special kind of epithelial tissue, one that makes up your outer covering—your skin! Another kind of epithelial tissue lines the cavities, or hollow spaces, of the mouth, throat, ears, stomach, and other body parts.

Organs

Just as cells join together to form tissues, different types of tissues combine to form **organs.** An organ is a group of different tissues with a specific job. The heart, stomach, and brain are familiar examples of organs. But did you know that the eye, skin, and tongue are also organs? The heart is an example of an organ made up of all four kinds of tissues. Although the heart consists mostly of muscle tissue, it is covered and protected by epithelial tissue and also contains connective and nerve tissues.

Organ Systems

Many times even a complicated organ is not adequate enough to perform a series of specialized jobs in the body. In these cases, an **organ system** is needed. An organ system is a group of organs that work together to perform a specific job. Your body can work as it does because it is made up of many organ systems. The organ systems and their functions are shown in Figure 1–9 on page 22. Although each system performs a special function for the body, no one system acts alone. Each organ system contributes to the constant "teamwork" that keeps you, and most multicellular living things, alive.

To help you better understand how organ systems, organs, tissues, and cells are related, try this: Think of an organ system as an automobile manufacturing company. The organs would be represented by the different company divisions that are responsible for a particular model of automobile. Within each division, there are many departments— for example, accounting, assembly, design, and sales. Each department would represent the tissues that form each organ. And the people that work in each of the various departments would represent the cells that make up each type of tissue.

So whether it's in the automobile manufacturing company or in the body, it should now be clear to you that each level has its own specialized job to do. Yet each level is dependent on the activities of the other levels to either build an automobile or keep a body alive.

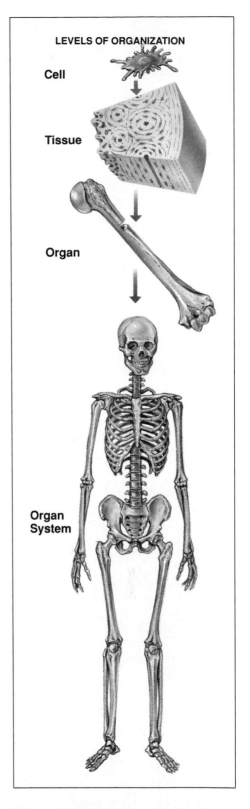

Figure 1–8 *Notice how bone cells are organized to form a tissue, an organ, and an organ system.*

Figure 1–9 *The 11 organ systems of the human body are shown in the chart. Which of these systems are you using right now?*

SYSTEMS OF THE HUMAN BODY

System	Functions
Skeletal	Protects, supports, allows movement, produces blood cells, and stores minerals
Muscular	Allows body movement and maintains posture
Digestive	Breaks down food and absorbs nutrients
Circulatory	Transports nutrients, wastes, and other materials and plays a role in the immune response
Respiratory	Exchanges oxygen and carbon dioxide between blood and air
Excretory	Removes solid and liquid wastes
Nervous	Detects sensation and controls most functions
Endocrine	Plays a part in the regulation of metabolism, reproduction, and many other functions
Reproductive	Performs reproduction and controls male and female functions and behaviors
Immune	Controls the immune response and fights disease
Integumentary (skin)	Protects, regulates temperature, prevents water loss

FIND OUT BY
WRITING

Organs and Organ Systems

On a sheet of paper, copy the following chart.

Organ   Organ System
lung
small intestine
kidney
brain
rib
heart
thyroid gland
biceps
skin
pancreas

Using books in the library, find out the name of the organ system to which each organ belongs. Write the name of the organ system next to the proper organ. Now expand this list by adding other organs you have heard of or read about. Find out to which organ system each of these organs belongs.

1–2 Section Review

1. List the levels of organization in humans.
2. What are the four basic types of human tissues?
3. List the organ systems of the human body.

Connection—*You and Your World*
4. Using a bicycle or any type of machine as an example, explain how each part of the machine works with every other part so that the machine can do its job. Compare this with the way the systems of the body work together.

22 ■ H

Artificial Body Parts

Thanks to *chemical technology,* many worn-out or damaged body parts can be replaced totally or in part by plastics. Plastics can be stronger than steel or lighter than a sheet of paper. Plastics are synthetic materials that can be shaped into any form, from a transparent bag to a football helmet. In fact, the word plastics comes from the Greek word *plastikos,* which means able to be molded.

Plastics are made from chemicals. These chemicals come from such raw materials as coal, petroleum, salt, water, and limestone. Because plastics have a variety of special properties, they can do some jobs better than other materials.

Two special properties—harmless to the human body and unaffected by chemicals in the body —make certain plastics useful in medicine. For example, if a hip, knee, elbow, or shoulder joint breaks because of an accident or wears out from a disease (such as arthritis), it can be replaced with an artificial joint made of plastics. Plastics have also been used to replace parts of the intestines and faulty valves in the heart. Whenever surgeons do these

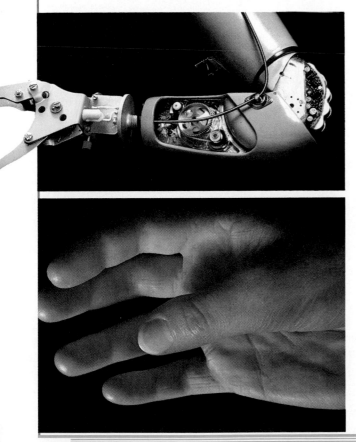

or other types of body repair, they use threads made of plastics to sew all the parts into place. Strong, lightweight plastics are also used to make artificial body parts. Some artificial hands have "skin" made of plastics, complete with fingerprints and a partial sense of touch!

As you might imagine, the list of uses for plastics in medicine is almost endless. In fact, the day of a bionic person— once a figment of the imagination of a television scriptwriter—may soon become a reality.

Laboratory Investigation

Looking at Human Cheek Cells

Problem

What are the characteristics of some typical human cells?

Materials *(per pair of students)*

microscope	medicine dropper
glass slide	methylene blue
coverslip	paper towel
toothpick	

Procedure 🧪 📷 👁

1. Place a drop of water in the center of the slide.
2. Using the flat end of the toothpick, gently scrape the inside of your cheek. Although you will not see them, cells will come off the inside of your cheek and stick to the toothpick.
3. Stir the scrapings from the same end of the toothpick into the drop of water on the slide. Mix thoroughly and cover with the coverslip.
4. Place the slide on the stage of the microscope and focus under low power. Examine a few cells. Focus on one cell. Sketch and label the parts of the cell. (Refer to Figure 1–3 for the basic parts of the cell.)
5. Switch to high power. Sketch and label the cell and its parts.
6. Remove the slide from the stage of the microscope. With the medicine dropper, put one drop of methylene blue at the edge of the coverslip. **CAUTION**: *Be careful when using methylene blue because it may stain the skin and clothing.* Place a small piece of paper towel at the opposite edge of the coverslip. The stain will pass under the coverslip. Use another piece of paper towel to absorb any excess stain.
7. Place the slide on the stage of the microscope again and find an individual cell under low power. Sketch and label that cell and the cell parts that you see.
8. Switch to high power and sketch and label the cell and its parts.

Observation

How are cheek cells arranged with respect to one another?

Analysis and Conclusions

1. What is the advantage of staining the cheek cells?
2. Explain why the shape of cheek cells is suited to their function.
3. Based on your observations, to which tissue type do cheek cells belong?
4. **On Your Own** Examine some other types of human cells, such as muscle, blood, or nerve, under the microscope. Sketch and label the parts of the cell. How does this cell compare with the cheek cell?

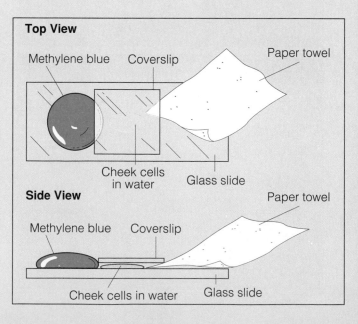

Top View
Methylene blue   Coverslip   Paper towel
Cheek cells in water   Glass slide

Side View
Methylene blue   Coverslip   Paper towel
Cheek cells in water   Glass slide

Study Guide

Summarizing Key Concepts

1–1 The Body as a Whole

▲ The process by which the body's internal environment is kept stable in spite of changes in the external environment is called homeostasis.

▲ Humans, like all living things, need energy to do work.

1–2 Levels of Organization

▲ The levels of organization in a multicellular living thing include cells, tissues, organs, and organ systems.

▲ Cells come in all shapes and sizes. Regardless of its job or shape, a cell works in harmony with other cells to keep the body alive.

▲ Cells are the building blocks of living things.

▲ A tissue is a group of similar cells that perform the same function.

▲ There are four types of tissues in the human body: muscle, connective, nerve, and epithelial.

▲ Muscle tissue has the ability to contract, or shorten. By contracting and thus pulling on bones, one type of muscle tissue makes the body move. Another type of muscle tissue lines the walls of structures inside the body. A third type of muscle tissue enables the heart to contract and pump blood to all parts of the body.

▲ Connective tissue provides support for the body and connects all its parts.

▲ Nerve tissue carries messages back and forth between the brain and the spinal cord and every other part of the body.

▲ Epithelial tissue forms a protective surface on the outside of the body and lines its internal cavities.

▲ An organ is a group of different tissues with a specific function.

▲ An organ system is a group of organs that work together to perform a specific job.

Reviewing Key Terms

Define each term in a complete sentence.

1–1 The Body as a Whole
homeostasis

1–2 Levels of Organization
cell
tissue
organ
organ system

Chapter Review

Content Review

Multiple Choice

Choose the letter of the answer that best completes each statement.

1. The term most closely associated with homeostasis is
   a. growth.   c. regulation.
   b. stability.   d. energy.
2. To do work, living things must have
   a. growth.   c. energy.
   b. green plants.   d. oxygen.
3. A group of similar cells that perform a similar function is called a(an)
   a. tissue.   c. organ system.
   b. organ.   d. living thing.
4. A tissue that has the ability to contract is
   a. muscle tissue.
   b. connective tissue.
   c. nerve tissue.
   d. epithelial tissue.
5. Which type of tissue is blood?
   a. muscle tissue
   b. connective tissue
   c. nerve tissue
   d. epithelial tissue
6. An organ made up of all four kinds of tissues is the
   a. brain.   c. heart.
   b. blood.   d. spinal cord.

7. A tissue that protects the surface of the body is
   a. muscle tissue.
   b. connective tissue.
   c. nerve tissue.
   d. epithelial tissue.
8. From smallest to largest, the levels of organization in a multicellular living thing are
   a. tissues, cells, organs, organ systems.
   b. cells, organs, tissues, organ systems.
   c. organ systems, organs, tissues, cells.
   d. cells, tissues, organs, organ systems.
9. Which is an example of a unicellular living thing?
   a. ameba   c. human
   b. tree   d. turtle
10. Which system removes wastes from the body?
    a. skeletal   c. digestive
    b. nervous   d. excretory

True or False

If the statement is true, write "true." If it is false, change the underlined word or words to make the statement true.

1. <u>Homeostasis</u> is the process by which the body's internal environment is kept stable in spite of changes in the external environment.
2. All living things need <u>energy</u> to do work.
3. A group of different tissues that have a specific function is called a (an) <u>organ</u>.
4. <u>Muscle</u> tissue provides support for the body and connects its parts.
5. Fat is an example of <u>connective</u> tissue.

Concept Mapping

Complete the following concept map for Section 1–1. Refer to pages H8–H9 to construct a concept map for the entire chapter.

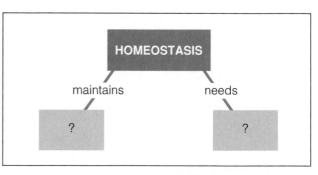

Concept Mastery

Discuss each of the following in a brief paragraph.

1. List and describe the four types of tissues in the body.
2. Explain the relationship between cells, tissues, organs, and organ systems.
3. Name three systems of the body and give the function of each.
4. Why is homeostasis important to the survival of a living thing?
5. Explain why the human body needs energy.

Critical Thinking and Problem Solving

Use the skills you have developed in this chapter to answer each of the following.

1. **Making inferences** What role does homeostasis play in the existence of a living thing?
2. **Applying concepts** How does wearing a heavy coat in winter help to maintain homeostasis?
3. **Relating concepts** When exercising on a hot day, you begin to sweat a lot and you become thirsty. How do sweating and becoming thirsty illustrate homeostasis?

4. **Relating facts** Although the structures of the body are grouped into separate organ systems, they are not independent of one another. Explain how a bad cold, which affects the respiratory system, can keep you from playing a good game of softball.
5. **Developing a model** Design a new organ for the human body. The function of this organ will be storage of air for long periods during swimming and space travel. Which tissues might be needed? What will the function of each tissue be? What cells will make up each tissue? What will the cells look like? Include a sketch of this organ.
6. **Relating facts** Provide two examples of body activities in which two or more organ systems work together.
7. **Using the writing process** Develop an advertising campaign for the use of antacids. An antacid is a substance that helps to calm an upset stomach. In your campaign, show how an upset stomach affects not only the digestive system, of which the stomach is a part, but other organ systems as well.

Skeletal and Muscular Systems

Guide for Reading

After you read the following sections, you will be able to

2–1 The Skeletal System

- List the functions of each part of the skeletal system.
- Describe the characteristics and structure of bone.
- Describe three types of movable joints.

2–2 The Muscular System

- Classify the three types of muscle tissues.
- Explain how muscles cause movement.

2–3 Injuries to the Skeletal and Muscular Systems

- List the three most common injuries to the skeletal and muscular systems.

Slowly, the young man climbs up the ladder toward the top of the circus tent. The crowd grows quiet. You feel your heart beginning to beat faster. You tilt your head back. Your eyes follow the man in the glistening costume. As he grabs the trapeze, the muscles in his arms bulge. Suddenly, he leaps and is flying through space. Then he lets go of the trapeze and does a somersault in midair . . . once, twice, three times. You gasp and then gaze in disbelief as, incredibly, the man does another somersault—a quadruple! It has never been done before!

How, you wonder, has the trapeze artist been able to perform such a daring feat? Part of the answer lies in the hundreds of hours he has spent training and practicing. And part of the answer lies in the dedication he has brought to his work. But certainly he could never have performed this spectacular act if it were not for his finely coordinated body. Working together with many of his other organs, the trapeze artist's bones and muscles have made the "impossible" happen. In the pages that follow, you will discover how your skeletal and muscular systems work for you—making the ordinary to the almost impossible possible.

Journal *Activity*

You and Your World Perform one type of movement with each of the following parts of your body: finger, wrist, arm, and neck. In your journal, describe the motion of each body part. What allows you to move these body parts? How is each motion different?

◄ *A trapeze artist performs a daring feat—a quadruple somersault!*

Guide for Reading

Focus on these questions as you read.
- ▶ What are the five functions of the skeletal system?
- ▶ What is the structure of bone?

FIND OUT BY DOING

Bones as Levers

Using books in the library, find out about the three classes of levers. How do bones act as levers? On posterboard, draw one class of levers. Next to the drawing, draw an example of the bones that act like that lever. In the drawing, label the effort, load, and fulcrum. At the bottom of the posterboard, define effort, load, and fulcrum.

■ What are the two other classes of levers? Give an example for each of these levers in the body.

2–1 The Skeletal System

The skeletal system is the body's living framework. This complicated structure contains more than 200 **bones**—actually, about 206. The bones are held together by groups of stringy connective tissues called **ligaments.** Another group of connective tissues called **tendons** attach bones to muscles. Together, the bones, ligaments, and tendons make up most of the skeletal system.

Functions of the Skeletal System

The skeletal system has five important functions: It provides shape and support, allows movement, protects tissues and organs, stores certain materials, and produces blood cells. The first of these important functions—giving shape and support to the body—should be pretty clear to you. Imagine that you did not have a skeletal system. What would you look like? A formless mass? A blob of jelly? The answer is yes to both descriptions! In fact, if the skeletal system did not perform this vital role, it would be meaningless to consider any of its other functions.

The skeletal system helps the body move. Almost all your bones are attached to muscles. As the muscles contract (shorten), they pull on the bones,

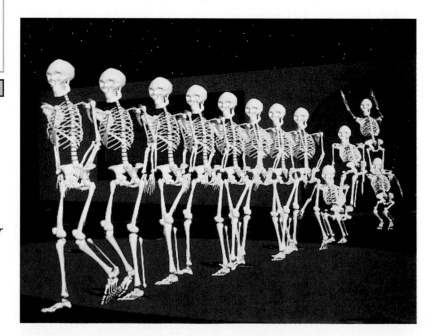

Figure 2–1 *As a result of computer graphics, the jumping and walking movements of a human skeleton take on a ghostly appearance. What type of connective tissue holds the bones of the skeleton together?*

causing the bones to move. By working together, the actions of the bones and muscles enable you to walk, sit, stand, and do a somersault.

Bones protect the tissues and organs of your body. If you move your fingers along the center of your back, you will feel your backbone, or vertebral column. Your backbone protects your spinal cord, which is the message "cable" between the brain and other body parts. As you may recall from Chapter 1, the spinal cord is made up of nerve tissue. Nerve tissue is extremely soft and delicate and, therefore, easily damaged. So you can see why it is important that the spinal cord is protected from injury.

Bones are storage areas for certain substances. Some of these substances give bones their stiffness. Others play a role in blood clotting, nerve function, and muscle activity. If the levels of these substances in the blood should fall below their normal ranges, the body will begin to remove them from where they are stored in the bones.

The long bones in your body (such as those in the arms and legs) produce many blood cells. One type of blood cell carries oxygen. Another type destroys harmful bacteria.

Parts of the Skeleton

Suppose you were asked to make a life-size model of the human skeleton. Where would you start? You might begin by thinking of the human skeleton as consisting of two parts. The first part covers the area that runs from the top of your head and down your body in a straight line to your hips. This part includes the skull, the ribs, the breastbone, and the vertebral column. The vertebral column contains 26 bones, which are called vertebrae (VER-tuh-bray; singular: vertebra, VER-tuh-bruh).

The second part of the skeletal system includes the bones of the arms, legs, hands, feet, hips, and shoulders. There is a total of 126 bones in this part of the skeletal system.

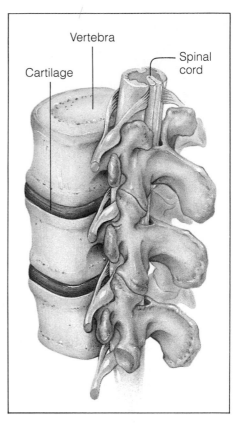

Figure 2–2 *The vertebral column consists of a series of small bones stacked one on top of the other. Together, these bones protect the delicate spinal cord and also form a strong support for the body. What are the individual bones of the vertebral column called?*

Figure 2–3 *Unlike humans, the king crab has a hard external skeleton. What are some advantages of having an internal skeleton?*

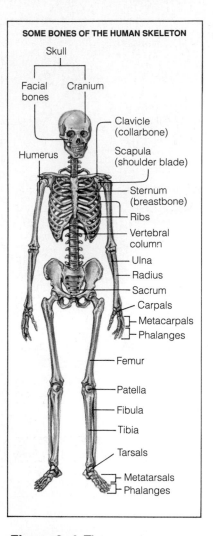

SOME BONES OF THE HUMAN SKELETON

Skull
- Facial bones
- Cranium

- Clavicle (collarbone)
- Humerus
- Scapula (shoulder blade)
- Sternum (breastbone)
- Ribs
- Vertebral column
- Ulna
- Radius
- Sacrum
- Carpals
- Metacarpals
- Phalanges
- Femur
- Patella
- Fibula
- Tibia
- Tarsals
- Metatarsals
- Phalanges

Figure 2–4 *There are approximately 206 bones in the human skeletal system. What is another name for the collarbone?*

Development of Bones

Many bones are formed from a type of connective tissue called **cartilage** (KAHRT-'l-ihj). Cartilage is a dense material that contains fibers. Although cartilage is strong enough to support weight, it is also flexible enough to be bent and twisted. You can prove this to yourself by moving your nose back and forth and by flapping your ears. The tip of your nose and your ears are made of cartilage.

Many bones in the skeleton of a newborn baby are composed almost entirely of cartilage. The process of replacing cartilage with bone starts about seven months before birth and is not completed until a person reaches the age of about 25 years. At this time, a person "stops growing." However, some forming and reforming of bone still occurs even in adulthood, primarily where bone is under a great deal of stress.

Although most of your body's cartilage will eventually be replaced by bone, there are a few areas where the cartilage will remain unchanged, such as in the knee, ankle, and elbow. These areas are usually found where bone meets bone. Here the cartilage has two jobs. One job is to cushion the bones against sudden jolts, such as those that occur when you jump or run. The other job is to provide a slippery surface for the bones so that they can move without rubbing against one another. Because cartilage is three times more slippery than ice, it is the ideal material for this task.

Figure 2–5 *X-rays of the hands of a 2-year-old (top left) and a 3-year-old (bottom left) show that the cartilage in the wrist has not yet been replaced by bone. In the X-ray of a 14-year-old's hand (center), the replacement of cartilage by bone is almost complete, as it is in the hand of a 60-year-old (right). What type of tissue is cartilage?*

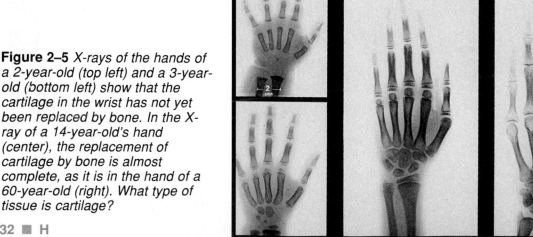

Structure of Bones

Bone is not only one of the toughest materials in the body, it is also one of the lightest. You may be surprised to learn that the 206 bones of your skeletal system make up barely 14 percent of your body's mass! Because of bone's strength, you may have thought of bone as nonliving. On the contrary, bones are alive. They contain living tissue—nerves, bone-forming cells, and blood vessels.

Bones, however, are similar in some ways to such nonliving things as rocks. Can you think of a few reasons why? Two obvious similarities are hardness and strength. Both bones and rocks owe their hardness and strength to chemical substances called minerals. Rocks contain a wide variety of minerals; bones are made up mainly of mineral compounds that contain the elements calcium and phosphorus. As you may already know, dairy products, such as milk and cheese, are good sources of calcium and phosphorus. So next time someone suggests that you drink lots of milk "to keep your bones strong and healthy," you will know why this suggestion makes sense.

Let's take a close look at the longest bone in the body to see what it (and other bones) is made of. This bone, called the femur (FEE-mer), links your hip to your knee. Probably the most obvious part of this bone is its long shaft, or column. The shaft, which is shaped something like a hollow cylinder, contains compact bone. Compact bone is dense and similar in texture to ivory. Within the shaft of a long bone are hollow cavities, or spaces. Inside these

FIND OUT BY DOING

Examining a Bone

1. Obtain a turkey or chicken leg bone.

2. Clean all the meat off the bone. Using a knife, cut off one end of the leg bone. **CAUTION:** *Be careful when using a knife.* Examine the bone carefully.

What is the name of this bone? Describe what the bone looks like inside and out. Identify as many parts of the bone as you can. What is this bone called in the human skeleton?

■ The bones of birds are very light. Why do you think this is so?

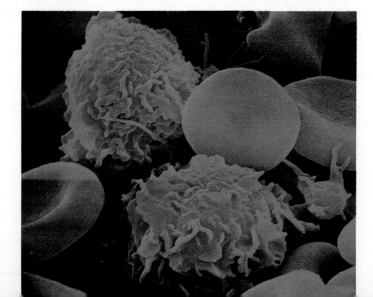

Figure 2–6 *The red marrow of bones such as the skull and ribs produces the body's red blood cells and white blood cells. As seen through an electron microscope, red blood cells are beret-shaped structures and white bloods cells are furry-looking structures. What does yellow marrow contain?*

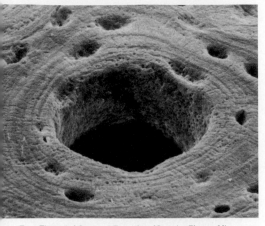

From *Tissues and Organs: A Text-Atlas of Scanning Electron Microscopy.*
By Richard G. Kessel and Randy H. Kardon. Copyright © 1979 by W.H.
Freeman and Company. Reprinted by permission.

Figure 2–7 *As the diagram illustrates, the most obvious feature of a long bone is its long shaft, or center, which contains dense, compact bone. Running through compact bone is a system of canals that bring materials to the living bone cells. One such canal is seen in the center of the photograph. What materials are carried through the canals?*

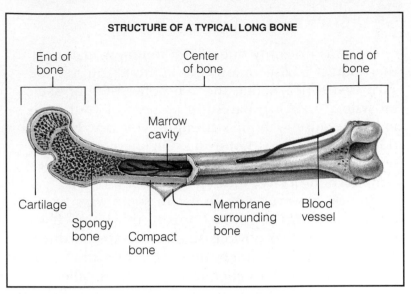

STRUCTURE OF A TYPICAL LONG BONE

End of bone   Center of bone   End of bone

Marrow cavity

Cartilage   Spongy bone   Compact bone   Membrane surrounding bone   Blood vessel

cavities is a soft material called yellow **marrow.** Yellow marrow contains fat and blood vessels. Another type of marrow called red marrow produces the body's blood cells. Red marrow is found in the cavities of such places as the skull, ribs, breastbone, and vertebral column.

Surrounding the shaft of the femur is a tough membrane that contains bone-forming cells and blood vessels. This membrane aids in repairing injuries to the bone and also supplies food and oxygen to the bone's living tissue. Muscles are attached to this membrane's surface. At each end of the shaft is an enlarged knob. The knobs are made of a type of bone called spongy bone. Spongy bone is not soft and spongy, as its name implies, but is actually quite strong. Because spongy bone resembles the supporting girders of a bridge, its presence at the ends of long bones adds strength to bone without adding mass. Figure 2–7 shows these basic parts of a bone.

Running through the bone is a system of pipelike canals that bring food and oxygen to the living bone cells. These canals also contain nerves. The nerves send messages through the canals to living parts of the bone.

Skeletal Joints

Imagine that you are pitching your first baseball game of the season. The catcher signals you to throw a fast ball. You know that the batter is a powerful hitter, so you shake your head no. The catcher

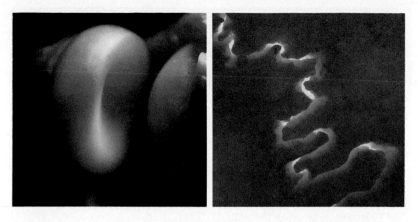

Figure 2–8 *Joints, or places where two bones meet, allow bones to move without damaging each other. The ball-and-socket joint in the shoulder (left) permits the greatest range of movement, whereas the joints in the skull (right) do not move at all. What type of joint is found at the elbow?*

changes the signal to a curve ball. You agree and nod. And then you wind up and send your curve ball sailing over the plate. "Strike one!" the umpire shouts.

You could not make any of these simple movements—shaking and nodding your head or winding up and pitching the ball—if it were not for structures in your skeletal system called **joints.** A joint is any place where two bones come close together. Generally, a joint is responsible for keeping the bones far enough apart so that they do not rub against each other as they move. At the same time, a joint holds the bones in place.

There are several different kinds of joints. Some joints allow the bones they connect to move. Other joints permit little or no movement. Examples of joints that permit no movement are the joints found in the skull. Although these joints permit no movement, they enable the bones in the skull to fuse (join) as you grow. In the pitching example you just read about, the pivot joint, which is located between the first two vertebrae in your neck, enabled you to shake and nod your head in response to the catcher's signals. A pivot joint allows for rotation of one bone around another.

When you wound up to pitch your curve ball, the ball-and-socket joint of your shoulder allowed you to swing your arm in a circle. Ball-and-socket joints, which provide for the circular motion of bones, consist of a bone with a rounded head that fits into the cuplike pocket of another bone. Can you think of

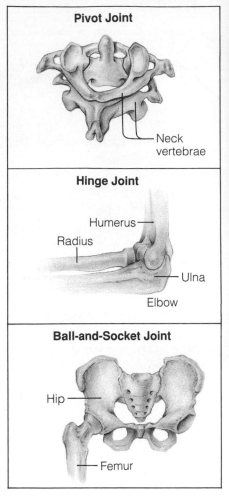

Pivot Joint

Neck vertebrae

Hinge Joint

Humerus
Radius
Ulna
Elbow

Ball-and-Socket Joint

Hip
Femur

Figure 2–9 *The actions involved in pitching a ball require the use of many types of joints. What movement does the ball-and-socket joint allow for?*

another location in your body where you would find a ball-and-socket joint?

As you moved your arm forward, the bend at your elbow straightened out and you whipped the ball toward the batter. The elbow is a hinge joint. A hinge joint, which is also found at the knee, allows for movement in a forward and backward direction. However, it allows for little movement from side to side. Figure 2–9 shows where the hinge joint and the other joints you just read about are located in the body.

2–1 Section Review

1. What are the five functions of the skeletal system?
2. What is a ligament? A tendon?
3. List three places in the body where cartilage is found.
4. What is marrow?
5. Compare the movements of three types of movable joints.

Critical Thinking—*Relating Facts*
6. Suggest an advantage of having the ribs attached to the breastbone by cartilage.

PROBLEM Solving

What Kind of Joint Is This?

The pivot, ball-and-socket, and hinge joints that you have read about in the chapter are not the only types of movable joints in the body. There are several other movable joints.

The accompanying drawings illustrate six types of movable joints. Notice the motion that each joint is capable of producing. On a separate sheet of paper, copy the following list of activities.

- Pushing a door open
- Lifting a book from a desk
- Kneeling
- Giving the "thumbs up" signal
- Waving the hand
- Shrugging the shoulders
- Shaking the head from side to side

Applying Concepts

Now compare the motion of each joint with each activity. Determine which type of joint or joints is needed to perform each activity and write the name of the joint next to its appropriate activity.

SIX TYPES OF MOVABLE JOINTS

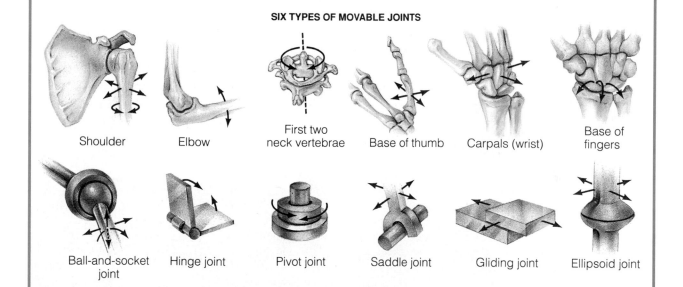

Shoulder Elbow First two neck vertebrae Base of thumb Carpals (wrist) Base of fingers

Ball-and-socket joint Hinge joint Pivot joint Saddle joint Gliding joint Ellipsoid joint

2–2 The Muscular System

It is three o'clock in the morning, and you have been asleep for several hours. All day you walked, ran, and played, using your muscles in a variety of ways. Now that you are asleep, all the muscles in your body are also at rest. Or are they?

Guide for Reading

Focus on this question as you read.

▶ *What are the three types of muscles?*

Without waking you, many of the more than 600 muscles in your body are still working to keep you alive. The muscles in your heart are contracting to pump blood throughout your body. Your chest muscles are working to help move air in and out of your lungs. Perhaps last night's dinner is still being moved through your digestive system by muscles.

Most muscles, or muscle tissue, are composed of muscle fibers that run beside, or parallel to, one another and are held together in bundles of connective tissue. Each muscle fiber is actually a single cylinder-shaped cell. Recall from Chapter 1 that a tissue is a group of similar cells that work together to perform a specific function. In the case of muscle tissue, that function is to contract, or shorten.

Types of Muscles

In the human body, there are three types of muscle tissue: skeletal muscle, smooth muscle, and cardiac muscle. Each type of muscle tissue has a characteristic structure and function. The muscle tissue that attaches to and moves bones is called **skeletal muscle.** This is an appropriate name for this type of muscle tissue because it is associated with the bones of the body, or the skeletal system. By contracting, skeletal muscle causes your arms, legs, head, and other body parts to move.

Figure 2–10 *Like an American toad and an impala, a human can perform many types of movements as a result of the actions of muscles pulling on bones.*

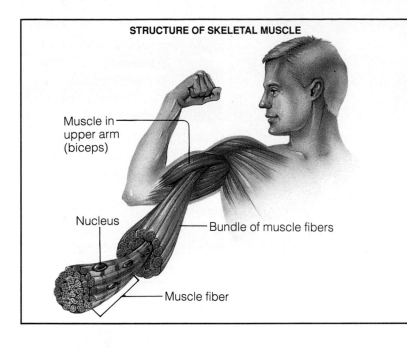

STRUCTURE OF SKELETAL MUSCLE

Muscle in upper arm (biceps)

Nucleus

Bundle of muscle fibers

Muscle fiber

Figure 2–11 *Muscle tissue is composed of muscle fibers that run parallel to one another and are held together in bundles of connective tissue. The biceps muscle, which is located in the upper arm, is an example of skeletal muscle tissue. Why is the biceps classified as a skeletal muscle?*

If you were to look at skeletal muscle under a microscope, you would see that it is striated (STRIGH-ayt-ehd), or banded. For this reason, skeletal muscles are called striated muscles. Figure 2–12 on page 40 shows the bands associated with skeletal muscle. And because skeletal muscles move only when you want them to, they are also called voluntary muscles.

To appreciate how some of the voluntary (skeletal) muscles in your body work, think of the movements you make in order to write your name on a sheet of paper. The instant you want it to, your arm stretches out to pick up the paper and pencil. You grasp the pencil and lift it. Then you press the pencil down on the paper and move your hand to form the letters in your name. Your eyes move across the page as you write. To do all of this, you have to use more than 100 muscles. Now suppose you did this little task 100 times. Do you think the muscles in your hand would ache? Probably so. For although skeletal muscles react quickly when you want them to, they also tire quickly. Perhaps you might want to actually try this.

A second type of muscle tissue is called **smooth muscle.** Unlike skeletal muscle, smooth muscle does not have bands. Hence, its name is smooth. In general, smooth muscles can contract without your actively causing them to. Thus, smooth muscles are also called involuntary muscles. The involuntary

Voluntary or Involuntary?

1. Blink your eyes three times.

2. Then try not to blink. Time how long you are able to keep yourself from blinking. Record your data.

3. Repeat step 2. Determine the average time you can keep from blinking.

How does your average time compare with that of your classmates? Are the eye muscles involved with blinking voluntary or involuntary muscles? Explain.

■ Using a mirror, observe what happens to your pupils in bright light and in dim light. Are the muscles that are involved in these actions voluntary or involuntary? How does the action of these muscles differ from those involved in blinking?

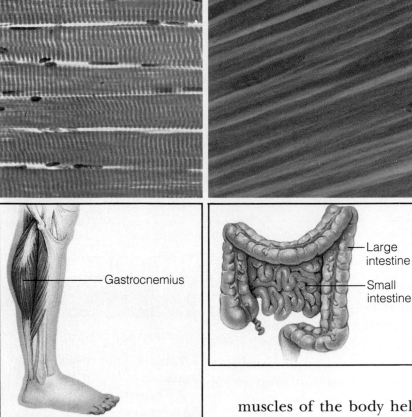

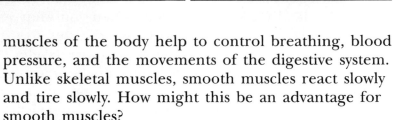

Figure 2–12 *There are three types of muscle tissue: skeletal muscle tissue (left), smooth muscle tissue (center), and cardiac muscle tissue (right). Where in the body are these muscle tissues found?*

muscles of the body help to control breathing, blood pressure, and the movements of the digestive system. Unlike skeletal muscles, smooth muscles react slowly and tire slowly. How might this be an advantage for smooth muscles?

A third type of muscle tissue, **cardiac muscle,** is found only in the heart. Branching out in many directions, cardiac muscle fibers weave a complex mesh. The contractions of these muscle fibers make the heart beat. Like smooth muscles, cardiac muscles are involuntary. Heart muscle, as you may have guessed, does not tire.

Action of Skeletal Muscles

As you have learned, muscles do work only by contracting, or shortening. In order for skeletal muscles to bring about any kind of movement, the action of two muscles or two groups of muscles is needed. Put another way, muscles always work in pairs.

For example, if you were to raise your lower arm at the elbow, you would notice that a bulge appears in the front of your upper arm. This bulge is caused by the contraction of a muscle called the biceps. At the same time the biceps contracts, a muscle called the triceps, which is located at the back of your upper arm, relaxes. Now suppose you wanted to straighten your arm. To perform this simple feat, your triceps would have to contract and your biceps would have to relax at the same time. Figure 2–13 shows how these two muscles (the biceps and the triceps) work together to help you bend and straighten your arm.

The mechanism by which muscles contract is actually a bit more complex than what you have just read. For it is not only muscles that are involved in this action. Nerve tissue is also involved. Skeletal

Figure 2–13 *When you "make a muscle," the biceps muscle and the triceps muscle work together. According to the diagram, which muscle relaxes when the arm is bent? When the arm is straightened?*

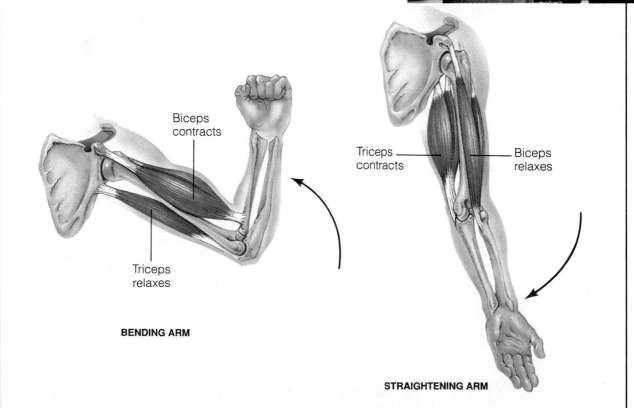

Biceps contracts

Triceps relaxes

BENDING ARM

Triceps contracts

Biceps relaxes

STRAIGHTENING ARM

FIND OUT BY DOING

Muscle Action

1. Obtain a spring-type clothespin.

2. Count how many times you can click the clothespin in two minutes using your right hand. Record the information.

3. Rest for one minute and repeat step 2. Then rest for another minute and repeat step 2 again. Determine the average number of clicks for the right hand.

4. Using your left hand, repeat steps 2 and 3.

Was there a difference in the number of clicks per minute between the right and the left hand? Explain.

■ Why do you think you were able to click the clothespin faster at the beginning of the investigation than you were near the end?

muscles, you see, contract only when they receive a message from a nerve to do so. The nerves carry messages from the brain and spinal cord to the muscles, signaling them to contract.

You may be surprised to learn that there is no such thing as a weak or strong contraction of a muscle fiber. When a fiber receives a message to contract, it contracts completely or not at all. The strength of a muscle contraction is determined by the number of fibers that receive the message to contract at the same time. Strong muscle contractions, such as those that are involved in hitting a ball with a bat, require the contractions of more muscle fibers than would be needed to open a textbook.

2–2 Section Review

1. List the three types of muscle tissue.
2. Compare the structure of a voluntary muscle and an involuntary muscle.
3. Describe how muscles work in pairs.

Critical Thinking—*You and Your World*
4. If your biceps were paralyzed, what movement would you be unable to make?

Guide for Reading

Focus on this question as you read.

▶ What are the three most common injuries involving the skeletal and muscular systems?

2–3 Injuries to the Skeletal and Muscular Systems

Supported by bone and activated by muscle, your body can perform a wide range of movement—from hammering a nail to blinking an eye. The same foot that can stand on tiptoe can kick a soccer ball. The same hand that can pat a puppy's head can pound a desk. Based on these activities, you may be inclined to think that the bones and muscles—components of the skeletal and muscular systems—are invincible. But are they?

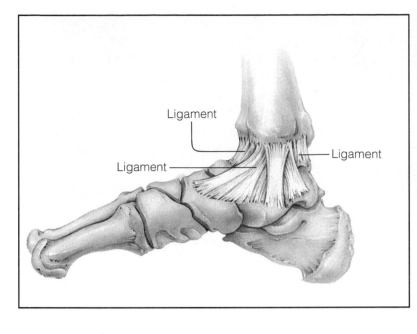

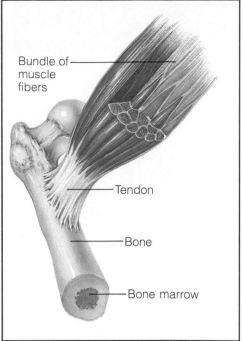

Although bones and muscles are able to withstand quite a bit of wear and tear, they are vulnerable to injuries. **Some injuries that affect the skeletal and muscular systems are sprains, fractures, and dislocations.** In a **sprain,** the ligaments or tendons, such as those in the ankle, get torn or pulled beyond their normal stretching range. Although a sprained ankle may be painful, you can move your ankle because the injured ligaments and tendons are still able to function.

The most common type of injury to the skeletal system is a **fracture.** A fracture is a break in a bone. Fortunately, because a bone is made up of living tissue, it begins to heal almost as soon as the fracture occurs. A bone's self-healing process takes place in an orderly sequence of events. First the broken blood vessels at the fracture area form a blood clot. In a few days, minerals from the sharp ends of the broken bone are absorbed into the bloodstream. At the same time, fibers of connective tissue grow out of the bone to hold the fractured ends together with a type of bone-making "glue." In as short a time as a few weeks, some bones have healed so well that even X-rays cannot show where the fracture occurred.

Sometimes a blow to the skeleton causes a bone to be forced out of its joint. This type of injury is called a **dislocation.** Dislocations can be serious, but fortunately they can be corrected easily in most cases.

Figure 2–14 *In a sprain, tendons or ligaments get torn or pulled beyond their normal reaching range. What structures are joined by tendons? Ligaments?*

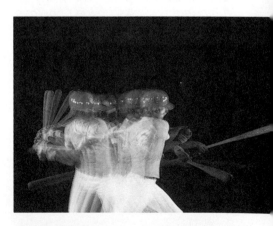

Figure 2–15 *Although the skeletal and muscular systems are able to withstand a lot of wear and tear, they are vulnerable to injuries. What injuries might this baseball player develop from swinging at the ball too hard?*

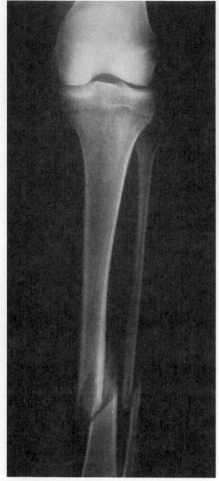

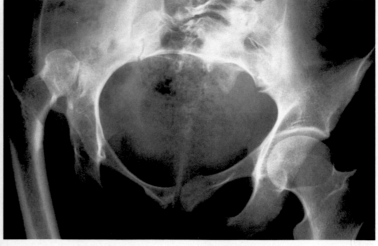

Figure 2–16 *In the X-ray of a lower leg (left), you can see breaks in the tibia and fibula. The X-ray of a hip (right) shows how a bone can be forced out of its joint in a dislocation. What is another name for a break in a bone?*

The dislocated bone can be pushed back into position by a doctor.

As scientists learn more about the skeletal and muscular systems, they continue to develop new techniques for repairing or replacing damaged parts. One technique for healing fractures involves applying weak electrical currents to broken bones. In most cases, electricity causes the bones to heal more quickly. Sometimes badly damaged joints, such as the hip or the knee, can be replaced with artificial joints made of plastics or metal.

2–3 Section Review

1. List the three most common injuries to the skeletal and muscular systems.
2. Compare a sprain and a fracture.
3. Describe the repair of a broken bone.
4. Why do you think a sprained ankle is so painful?

Connection—*Chemistry*

5. Artificial hips are generally made of plastics and alloys (substances that are mixtures of metals or metals and other elements), which are lightweight and do not react with other materials. Explain why these characteristics make plastics and alloys useful in the replacement of human body parts.

CONNECTIONS

Turning on Bone Growth

What has *electricity* got to do with the growth of bone? According to researchers Clinton Rubin and Kenneth McLeod at the State University of New York at Stony Brook, low, painless doses of electricity can prevent or treat osteoporosis. Osteoporosis is a disorder that causes a loss and a weakening of bone tissue. Affecting up to half of all women over the age of 45, osteoporosis can lead to spinal deformities and broken hips.

In one study, Rubin and McLeod experimented on turkeys because, like humans, turkeys lose bone tissue as they age. Rubin and McLeod sped up the loss of bone by immobilizing (preventing the movement of) one wing in each of about 40 turkeys. The immobilized bones in these turkeys wasted away significantly within a period of two months. Another group of turkeys wore small electric coils that set up electromagnetic (having to do with electricity and magnetism) fields that produced an electric current that traveled through the wing. The wing bones of these birds showed no wasting away. In fact, they actually showed an increase in

bone mass! In other studies, researchers have shown that cells zapped with electricity absorb greater amounts of calcium, which, as you may recall, is necessary for bone growth.

Although it may seem to you that scientists can turn on bone growth with the flip of a switch, it is not quite as simple as that. To begin with, scientists will have to prove that they are not causing one health problem while fixing another. At present, there is concern about the relationship between electromagnetic fields (which are produced by almost everything from high-power wires to household appliances) and the risk of cancer.

Scientists are now trying to find out just what the relationship and possible dangers are. Meanwhile, the bone researchers point out that they use electromagnetic waves that are different from those generated by power lines and electrical appliances. They also have proof that for the past 20 years, doctors have used currents of electricity to repair bone fractures.

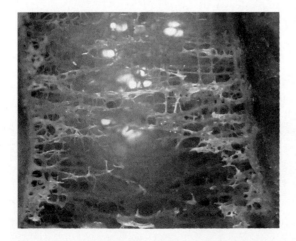

Notice that the bone tissue from an 80-year-old man with osteoporosis (bottom) has larger empty spaces than the bone tissue from a healthy 31-year-old man (top).

Laboratory Investigation

Observing Bones and Muscles

Problem

What are the characteristics of bones and muscles?

Materials (per group)

2 chicken leg bones	vinegar
tiny piece of raw, lean beef	medicine dropper
	water
2 dissecting needles	2 glass slides
methylene blue	coverslip
2 jars with lids	microscope
knife	paper towel

Procedure

Part A

1. Place one chicken leg bone in each of the two jars.

2. Fill one of the jars about two-thirds full with vinegar. Cover both jars.

3. After five days, remove the bones from the jars. Rinse each bone with water.

4. With the knife, carefully cut each of the bones in half. **CAUTION:** *Be careful when using a knife.* Examine the inside of each bone.

Part B

1. Place the tiny piece of raw beef on one of the glass slides. With a medicine dropper, place a drop of water on top of the beef.

2. With the dissecting needles, carefully separate, or tease apart, the fibers of the beef. **CAUTION:** *Be careful when using dissecting needles.*

3. Transfer a few fibers to the second slide. Add a drop of methylene blue. **CAUTION:** *Be careful when using methylene blue because it may stain the skin and clothing.* Cover with a coverslip. Use the paper towel to absorb any excess stain.

4. Examine the slide under the microscope.

Observations

1. How do the two bones differ in texture and flexibility? Describe the appearance of the inside of each bone.

2. Describe the appearance of the beef under a microscope.

Analysis and Conclusions

1. What has happened to the minerals and the marrow within the bone that was put in vinegar? How do you know this?

2. Why was one bone put in an empty jar?

3. What type of muscle tissue did you observe under the microscope?

4. How does the structure of the muscle tissue aid in its function?

5. **On Your Own** Repeat this investigation using substances other than vinegar.

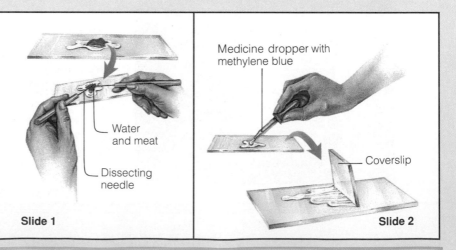

Slide 1 — Water and meat; Dissecting needle

Slide 2 — Medicine dropper with methylene blue; Coverslip

Summarizing Key Concepts

2–1 The Skeletal System

▲ Bones are fastened together by connective tissues called ligaments. Tendons are connective tissues that connect muscles to bones.

▲ The skeletal system has five important functions: It provides shape and support, allows movement, protects tissues and organs, produces blood cells, and stores certain materials.

▲ The human skeleton is divided into two parts. One part consists of the skull, the ribs, the breastbone, and the vertebral column. The other part is made up of the bones of the arms, legs, hands, feet, shoulders, and hips.

▲ Cartilage is a flexible connective tissue that supports, acts as a shock absorber, and cushions other skeletal parts.

▲ A joint is a place where two bones come close together.

2–2 The Muscular System

▲ Muscle tissue is made of fibers bundled together by connective tissue. Muscle tissue moves only by contracting, or shortening.

▲ There are three types of muscle tissue: skeletal, smooth, and cardiac. Skeletal muscles permit voluntary movement and are connected to bone. Smooth muscles help control breathing, blood pressure, and movements of the digestive system. Cardiac muscles make the heart beat.

▲ All skeletal muscles work in pairs. When one contracts, the other relaxes.

2–3 Injuries to the Skeletal and Muscular Systems

▲ The most common injuries to the skeletal and muscular systems are sprains, fractures, and dislocations.

▲ A tearing or pulling of a ligament or a tendon beyond its normal stretching range is called a sprain.

▲ A fracture is a break in a bone.

▲ When a bone is forced out of its joint, the injury is called a dislocation.

Reviewing Key Terms

Define each term in a complete sentence.

2–1 The Skeletal System
bone
ligament
tendon
cartilage
marrow
joint

2–2 The Muscular System
skeletal muscle
smooth muscle
cardiac muscle

2–3 Injuries to the Skeletal and Muscular Systems
sprain
fracture
dislocation

Chapter Review

Content Review

Multiple Choice

On a separate sheet of paper, write the letter of the answer that best completes each statement.

1. Approximately how many bones are there in the skeletal system?
   a. 126   b. 26   c. 206   d. 96
2. Bones are held together by stringy connective tissue called
   a. cartilage.   c. ligaments.
   b. joints.   d. tendons.
3. The nose and ears contain a flexible connective tissue called
   a. marrow.   c. muscle.
   b. bone.   d. cartilage.
4. Two minerals that make up the nonliving part of bones are
   a. sodium and chlorine.
   b. calcium and iron.
   c. magnesium and phosphorus.
   d. calcium and phosphorus.
5. A place where two bones come close together is called a
   a. dislocation.   c. tendon.
   b. joint.   d. ligament.
6. The longest bone in the body is the
   a. vertebra.   c. femur.
   b. collarbone.   d. breastbone.
7. An example of a ball-and-socket joint is the
   a. shoulder. b. neck.   c. elbow. d. knee.
8. The elbow is an example of a
   a. ball-and-socket joint.
   b. hinge joint.
   c. pivot joint.
   d. bone.
9. Skeletal muscles are also known as
   a. involuntary muscles.
   b. smooth muscles.
   c. cardiac muscles.
   d. voluntary muscles.
10. Which of the following occurs when a bone is forced out of its joint?
    a. dislocation   c. fracture
    b. contraction   d. sprain

True or False

If the statement is true, write "true." If it is false, change the underlined word or words to make the statement true.

1. <u>Tendons</u> join muscles to bones.
2. Bone is an example of <u>nerve</u> tissue.
3. Cartilage is a flexible <u>muscle</u> tissue.
4. Bones contain the minerals calcium and <u>iron</u>.
5. A <u>joint</u> is a place where two bones come close together.
6. The elbow is an example of a <u>ball-and-socket</u> joint.
7. Skeletal muscle is also called <u>involuntary</u> muscle.
8. <u>Smooth</u> muscle tissue is found only in the heart.

Concept Mapping

Complete the following concept map for Section 2–1. Refer to pages H8–H9 to construct a concept map for the entire chapter.

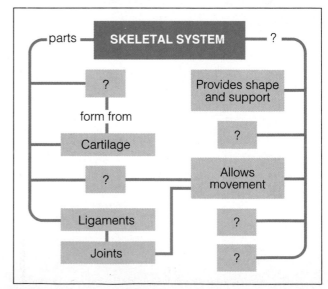

Concept Mastery

Discuss each of the following in a brief paragraph.

1. What are the two major parts of the human skeletal system? Which bones belong to each part?
2. Use Figure 2–4 on page 32 to identify the following bones with their scientific names.
   a. thigh
   b. finger
   c. toe
   d. kneecaps
   e. breastbone
   f. shoulder blade
3. Explain the differences among ligaments, tendons, and cartilage.
4. Name the three types of muscle tissue. Discuss their functions.
5. Describe the structure of the femur.
6. List three movable joints. Describe the actions of each joint.
7. Explain how the biceps and triceps enable you to bend and straighten your arm.
8. Compare a voluntary muscle and an involuntary muscle. Give an example of each type of muscle.

Critical Thinking and Problem Solving

Use the skills you have developed in this chapter to answer each of the following.

1. **Relating concepts** What is the advantage of having some joints, such as the knee and elbow, covered by a fluid-filled sac?
2. **Applying concepts** Bones heal faster in children than they do in adults. Why do you think this is so?
3. **Interpreting photographs** Because cartilage does not appear on X-ray film, it is seen as a clear area between the shaft and the knobs of individual bones. Examine the photographs showing the X-rays of two hands. Which hand belongs to the older person? Explain.

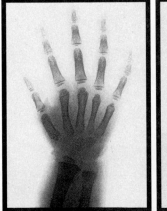 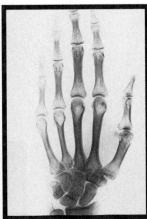

4. **Applying concepts** Suggest a reason why there are more joints in the feet and hands than in most other parts of the body.
5. **Relating concepts** What role does good posture play in maintaining healthy muscles and tendons?
6. **Relating facts** Explain why you feel pain when you fracture, or break, a bone.
7. **Relating cause and effect** Osteoporosis is a disease that usually occurs in older people. It involves a loss and a weakening of bone tissue. Doctors recommend that people over the age of 45 eat more foods that contain calcium. How is this helpful in preventing osteoporosis?
8. **Using the writing process** Choose a five-minute segment out of your day. In a journal, record all the activities that you performed during this time. Then try to identify all the muscles, bones, and joints you used. Use the figures in this chapter to help you, and don't forget those involuntary muscles, too!

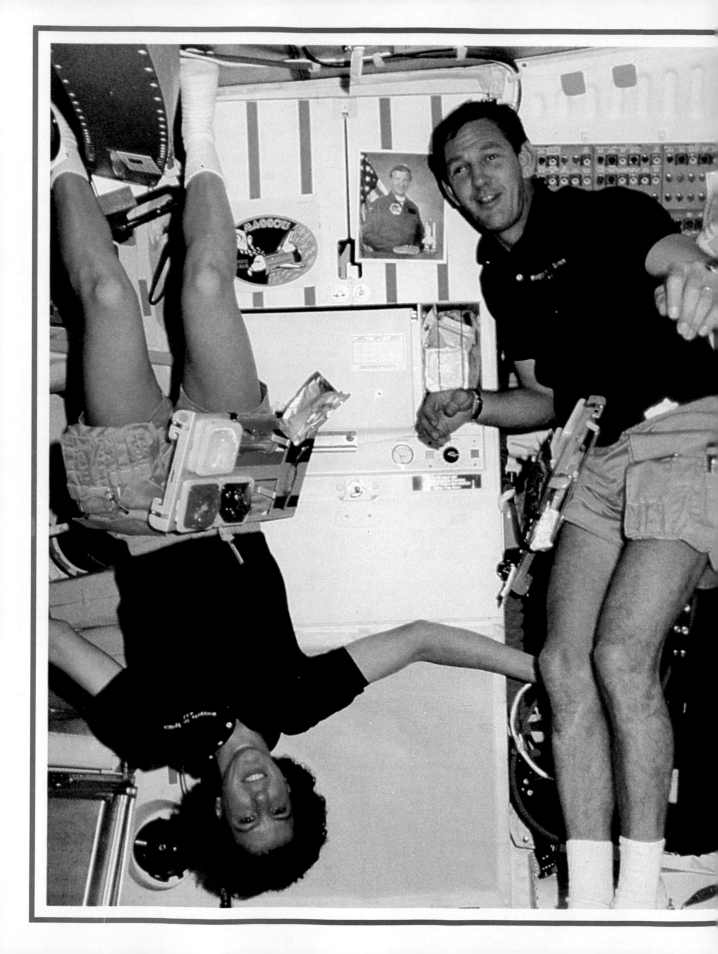

Digestive System

Guide for Reading

After you read the following sections, you will be able to

3–1 The Importance of Food
- Define nutrients.

3–2 Digestion of Food
- Describe how food is digested in the mouth, stomach, and small intestine.
- Compare mechanical digestion and chemical digestion.

3–3 Absorption of Food
- Describe how nutrients are absorbed in the digestive system.

3–4 Maintaining Good Health
- Describe the roles weight control and proper exercise habits play in maintaining good health.

Eating a meal in space is no ordinary event! Mistakes can produce strange and funny scenes. A dropped fork may fall up instead of down. Spilled milk is just as likely to end up on the ceiling as on the floor. And a banana left unattended may float away from an open mouth—or toward one. These "tricks" produced by weightlessness are conditions of space travel to which all astronauts must adjust.

Would you like to live in space? Before you answer, take a moment to consider this: What must it be like to live in a place where every spoonful of pudding is in danger of escaping and lettuce leaves in a salad fly away like butterflies? Perhaps you have never thought seriously about the experience of eating and swallowing food in space. What happens to the food after it is swallowed? Without gravity, will it move up instead of down? And what about food that is already in the stomach? In the pages that follow, you will learn how your body digests and absorbs food—right here on Earth! Then you will be better able to answer the questions about eating in space.

Journal *Activity*

You and Your World What did you have for dinner last night? What did you eat for lunch today? Who was with you, and where did you eat these meals? In your journal, explore the thoughts and feelings you had during these mealtimes.

◀ *Astronauts eating a meal in space*

3–1 The Importance of Food

Throughout the world, more than 5 billion very special chemical factories are in operation both day and night. From basic raw materials, these factories produce a great variety of chemicals. What goes on in these factories could not occur anywhere else. These factories can discover and correct their own faulty work. They can reproduce and repair some of their parts. And they can also control their own growth. Have you already guessed what these factories are? If not, you can find out by simply looking in a mirror. Yes, you and all humans are, in a way, chemical factories.

Like any factory, you need raw materials to build new products, repair old parts, and produce the energy that keeps the factory going. Where do you get

Figure 3–1 *A balanced diet consists of nutrients from each of the four basic food groups. These groups are the milk group (top left), the vegetable and fruit group (top right), the meat and protein group (bottom left), and the grain and grain products group (bottom right). What foods other than meat are found in the meat and proteins group?*

these raw materials? The raw materials are provided by the **nutrients** (NOO-tree-ehnts) that are in the foods you eat. **Nutrients are the usable portions of food. Nutrients include proteins, carbohydrates, fats, vitamins, minerals, and water.**

You can get all the nutrients your body needs for proper functioning by drinking water and by eating the right amounts of foods from the four basic food groups. You are probably familiar with these groups. They are the milk group, the meat and proteins group, the fruits and vegetables group, and the grain and grain products group. Figure 3–1 contains some examples of the foods in each of the four basic food groups.

As you have just read, nutrients are the body's source of energy. The amount of energy that can be obtained from nutrients is measured in units known as **Calories.** A Calorie is the amount of energy needed to raise the temperature of 1 kilogram of water by 1 degree Celsius. Some foods are high in Calories, whereas others are quite low. For example,

Figure 3–2 *Nutrients provide the body with energy for studying, sledding, playing basketball, and raking leaves—to name just a few activities. In what unit is the amount of energy obtained from nutrients measured?*

FIND OUT BY CALCULATING

Determining Your Metabolic Rate

Basal metabolic rate, or BMR, is the energy needed (in Calories) to keep your awake but restful body functioning.

To determine your BMR, multiply 1 Calorie by your weight in kilograms (2.2 lbs = 1 kg). Then multiply this number by 24 hours. You now have your basal metabolic rate in Cal/kg/day. What is your BMR? Would you need more or fewer Calories when you are doing some type of activity? Explain your answer.

100 grams (4 ounces) of lettuce contain about 20 Calories. The same quantity of peanuts contains about 650 Calories. Notice that the amount of food is the same (100 grams), but the number of Calories is not. The number of Calories a person needs daily depends on the person's size, body build, occupation, and age.

Proteins

The nutrients that are used to build and repair body parts are called **proteins.** Proteins are made of chains of **amino** (uh-MEE-noh) **acids.** In fact, amino acids are sometimes called the building blocks of proteins. In order for your body to use proteins, they must first be broken down into their amino acid parts. Then they can enter the cells of your body, where they are reassembled into the proteins that make up your muscles, skin, and other organs inside your body.

Amazingly enough, the thousands of different proteins in your body are built from only 20 or so different amino acids. Your body can make 12 of these amino acids; the other 8 must be obtained from your diet (the foods you eat every day). These 8 amino acids are called essential amino acids because it is essential (necessary) that they are included in the foods you eat.

Foods that contain all 8 essential amino acids are red meat, fish, poultry, dairy products, and eggs. Because these foods contain all the essential amino acids, they are called complete proteins. Most plant proteins (rice, cereals, and vegetables), on the other hand, are missing one or more of the essential amino acids. Thus, these proteins are called incomplete proteins. If any essential amino acids are missing from the diet, the manufacture of important proteins stops completely. For this reason, people who are vegetarians must be sure that their diet includes different plant foods so that they obtain all the essential amino acids.

Figure 3–3 *The photograph shows a hair penetrating the outer layer of skin. Both hair and skin are made mainly of proteins. What are the building blocks of proteins called?*

THE SIX BASIC NUTRIENTS

Substances	Sources	Needed For
Proteins	Soybeans, milk, eggs, lean meats, fish, beans, peas, cheese	Growth, maintenance, and repair of tissues Manufacture of enzymes, hormones, and antibodies
Carbohydrates	Cereals, breads, fruits, vegetables	Energy source Fiber or bulk in diet
Fats	Nuts, butter, vegetable oils, fatty meats, bacon, cheese	Energy source
Vitamins	Milk, butter, lean meats, leafy vegetables, fruits	Prevention of deficiency diseases Regulation of body processes Growth Efficient biochemical reactions

Mineral salts
  Calcium and
  phosphorus
  compounds
	Whole-grain cereals, meats, milk, green leafy vegetables, vegetables, table salt	Strong bones and teeth
		Blood and other tissues

Iron compounds	Meats, liver, nuts, cereals	Hemoglobin formation
Iodine	Iodized salt, seafoods	Secretion by thyroid gland
Water	All foods	Dissolving substances Blood Tissue fluid Biochemical reactions

Figure 3–4 *Nutrients are grouped into six categories in this chart. Which nutrient prevents vitamin-deficiency diseases?*

Carbohydrates

It is three o'clock in the afternoon, and you are beginning to feel tired and somewhat lazy. You really need to eat some type of food that will bring your body up to its working level again. Suddenly you remember the orange tucked neatly away in your knapsack. Like all fruits, oranges contain energy-rich substances called **carbohydrates.** Carbohydrates are also found in vegetables and grain products.

There are two types of carbohydrates: starches and sugars. A starch is made of a long chain of sugars. In order to digest a starch, the body must first break the connections between each of the sugars in the chain. Once this is done, the sugars can be used to provide much-needed fuel for the body. Sugars,

Figure 3–5 *Carbohydrates are substances that supply the body with its main source of energy. If you are a human, a muffin may be a good source of carbohydrates. If you are an iguana, however, a cactus leaf may be more to your liking as a source of carbohydrates.*

on the other hand, can be used for fuel almost immediately.

What happens if you eat more carbohydrates than your body can use for fuel? The excess carbohydrates are stored in your muscles and liver in the form of starch. Unfortunately, these stored carbohydrates add mass to the body. So a diet containing too many carbohydrates can cause a person to gain weight.

Fats

Like carbohydrates, **fats** supply the body with energy. In fact, fats supply the body with twice as much energy (and twice as many Calories!) as do equal amounts of proteins and carbohydrates. In addition to providing energy for the body, fats help to support and cushion vital organs, protecting them from injury. Fats also insulate the body against heat loss.

Foods that are rich in fats come from both plants and animals. You may be surprised to learn that any plant or animal fat that is liquid at room temperature is called an oil. That is why the liquid fat in which you cook your French fries is called an oil and not a fat, even though it is 100 percent fat. The word fat, on the other hand, is used to describe any oil that is solid at room temperature. Some sources of fats are nuts, butter, and cheeses.

Figure 3–6 *Like carbohydrates, fats supply the body with energy. Any fat that is a liquid at room temperature is called an oil. Whether a fat is a solid or a liquid at room temperature, however, it is still a fat—and 100 percent fat! Which has more Calories: a gram of carbohydrates or a gram of fat?*

Vitamins and Minerals

In addition to proteins, carbohydrates, and fats, your body also needs **vitamins** and **minerals.** Because they are required in only small amounts, vitamins and minerals are sometimes called micronutrients.

What role do vitamins and minerals have in the body? Vitamins help to regulate the growth and normal functioning of your body. There are two groups of vitamins—fat-soluble vitamins and water-soluble vitamins. The fat-soluble vitamins are so named because they can be stored in fat tissue. Vitamins A, D, E, and K are fat-soluble vitamins. The water-soluble

Figure 3–7 *According to this chart, which vitamin is important for proper vision? For blood clotting?*

VITAMINS

Vitamin	Source	Use
A (carotene)	Yellow and green vegetables, fish-liver oil, liver, butter, egg yolks	Important for growth of skin cells; important for vision
D (calciferol)	Fish oils, liver, made by body when exposed to sunlight, added to milk	Important for the formation of bones and teeth
E (tocopherol)	Green leafy vegetables, grains, liver	Proper red blood cell structure
K	Green leafy vegetables, made by bacteria that live in human intestine	Needed for normal blood clotting
B_1 (thiamine)	Whole grains, liver, kidney, heart	Normal metabolism of carbohydrates
B_2 (riboflavin)	Milk products, eggs, liver, whole grain cereal	Normal growth
Niacin	Yeast, liver, milk, whole grains	Important in energy metabolism
B_6 (pyridoxine)	Whole grains, meats, poultry, fish, seeds	Important for amino acid metabolism
Pantothenic acid	Many foods, yeast, liver, wheat germ, bran	Needed for energy release
Folic acid	Meats, leafy vegetables	Proper formation of red blood cells
B_{12} (cyanocobalamin)	Liver, meats, fish, made by bacteria in human intestine	Proper formation of red blood cells
C (ascorbic acid)	Citrus fruits, tomatoes, green leafy vegetables	Strength of blood vessels; important in the formation of connective tissue; important for healthy gums

MINERALS

Mineral	Source	Use
Calcium	Milk products, green leafy vegetables	Important component of bones and teeth; needed for normal blood clotting and for normal cell functioning
Chlorine	Table salt, many foods	Important for fluid balance
Magnesium	Milk products, meat, many foods	Needed for normal muscle and nerve functioning; metabolism of proteins and carbohydrates
Potassium	Grains, fruits, many foods	Normal muscle and nerve functioning
Phosphorus	Meats, nuts, whole grains, many foods	Component of DNA, RNA, ATP, and many proteins; part of bone tissue
Sodium	Many foods, table salt	Nerve and muscle functioning; water balance in body
Iron	Liver, red meats, grains, raisins, nuts	Important part of hemoglobin molecule
Fluorine	Water (natural and added)	Part of bones and teeth
Iodine	Seafood, iodized table salt	Part of hormones that regulate rate of metabolism

Figure 3–8 *Minerals help to keep the body functioning normally. Which minerals provide for normal nerve and muscle functioning?*

FIND OUT BY WRITING

Vitamin-Deficiency Diseases

Use reference materials in the library to find out about a vitamin-deficiency disease, such as scurvy, pellagra, or rickets. Write a brief report on your findings. In your report, make sure that you answer the following questions: What causes the disease? What are the symptoms of the disease? How can the disease be prevented?

vitamins include vitamin C and vitamins B_1, B_2, B_6, and B_{12} (which are also known as the B complex). Water-soluble vitamins cannot be stored in fat tissue and are thus constantly washed out of the body. Therefore, water-soluble vitamins should be included in a balanced diet every day. The chart in Figure 3–7 on page 57 gives the sources and uses of some important vitamins.

Like vitamins, minerals help to keep your body functioning normally. Hemoglobin, the protein in red blood cells that carries oxygen, contains the mineral iron. Calcium, another important mineral, makes up a major part of teeth and bones. The sources and uses of some important minerals are listed in Figure 3–8.

Water

Although you can survive many days without food, several days without water can be fatal. Why is water so important? There are several reasons. Most chemical reactions that take place in the body can do so only in the presence of water. Water carries nutrients and other substances to and from body organs through the bloodstream. Water also helps your body maintain its proper temperature, 37°C.

On the average, the human body is approximately 55 to 75 percent water. Under normal conditions, you need about 2.4 to 2.8 liters of water daily (that is about 10 to 12 8-ounce glasses). By drinking the proper amount of fluids (about 2 liters) and eating a balanced diet, you can provide your body with its much-needed supply of water.

Figure 3–9 *Water is essential for our survival. However, if people do not use existing water resources wisely, fertile land may soon become sandy desert.*

3–1 Section Review

1. What are nutrients? Describe the six types of nutrients.
2. What is a Calorie?
3. How do water-soluble and fat-soluble vitamins differ?
4. Why is water important to the body?

Critical Thinking—*Relating Concepts*
5. Explain how it is possible for a person to be overweight and suffer from improper nutrition at the same time.

PROBLEM Solving

Reading Food Labels

Carmen has been asked by her teacher to determine the most nutritious breakfast cereal in her local market. Upon her arrival at the market, Carmen heads for the aisle containing the breakfast cereals and picks up the first cereal box. As a health-conscious and well-informed consumer, Carmen reads the list of ingredients and the nutrition labeling on the box of cereal. She knows that this information will help her compare similar foods on the basis of their share of nutrients to Calories.

Carmen knows that in order to burn up 1 gram of carbohydrate or protein, her body needs to use 4 Calories. For 1 gram of fat, her body needs to use 9 Calories. She realizes that it takes more than twice the number of Calories to burn up 1 gram of fat than it does to burn up 1 gram of carbohydrate or protein. That is one reason why Carmen tries to limit the amount of fats that she eats.

Carmen also knows that an ideal diet should get no more than 30 percent of its Calories from fats. Of the remaining Calories, 50 to 55 percent should come from carbohydrates and 15 to 20 percent from proteins. The carbohydrates should be in the form of starches rather than sugars.

Thanks to Carmen, you are on your way to becoming a more-informed consumer. Now look at a typical cereal box and determine if the dry cereal is high in nutrition and low in Calories.

1. To determine the percentage of fat Calories, multiply the grams of fat (in this case, 2) by 9 (the number of Calories

---

NUTRITION INFORMATION PER SERVING

SERVING SIZE . . . . 1 OUNCE (1¼ CUPS)
SERVINGS PER PACKAGE 15

	1 ounce cereal	plus ½ cup vitamin A & D fortified skim milk*
CALORIES	110	150
PROTEIN, g	4	8
CARBOHYDRATE, g	20	26
FAT, g	2	2
CHOLESTEROL, mg	0	0
SODIUM, mg	290	350
POTASSIUM, mg	105	310

PERCENTAGE OF U.S. RECOMMENDED DAILY ALLOWANCES (U.S. RDA)

PROTEIN	6	15
VITAMIN A	25	30
VITAMIN C	25	25
THIAMIN	25	30
RIBOFLAVIN	25	35
NIACIN	25	25
CALCIUM	4	20
IRON	45	45
VITAMIN D	10	25
VITAMIN B$_6$	25	25
FOLIC ACID	25	25
PHOSPHORUS	10	20
MAGNESIUM	10	15
ZINC	6	8
COPPER	6	6

*PLUS ½ CUP 2% MILK CONTAINS 170 CALORIES, 4 GRAMS FAT AND 10 MILLIGRAMS CHOLESTEROL. ALL OTHER NUTRIENTS REMAIN AS LISTED.

INGREDIENTS: WHOLE OAT FLOUR (INCLUDES THE OAT BRAN), WHEAT STARCH, SUGAR, SALT, CALCIUM CARBONATE, TRISODIUM PHOSPHATE.

VITAMINS AND MINERALS: VITAMIN C (SODIUM ASCORBATE), IRON (A MINERAL NUTRIENT), A B VITAMIN (NIACIN), VITAMIN A (PALMITATE), VITAMIN B$_6$ (PYRIDOXINE HYDROCHLORIDE), VITAMIN B$_2$ (RIBOFLAVIN), VITAMIN B$_1$ (THIAMIN MONONITRATE), A B VITAMIN (FOLIC ACID) AND VITAMIN D.

CARBOHYDRATE INFORMATION

	1 ounce	with ½ cup milk
COMPLEX CARBOHYDRATES, g . . .	19	19
STARCH, g 17		
DIETARY FIBER, g 2*		
SUCROSE AND OTHER SUGARS, g	1	7
TOTAL CARBOHYDRATES, g	20	26

*1g SOLUBLE AND 1g INSOLUBLE FIBER

in 1 gram of fat). Then divide the result (18 Calories) by the total number of Calories (110). The resulting percentage of fat Calories is 16, which is to be expected, because grains, of which cereals are made, are low in fat.

2. To determine the percentage of carbohydrate Calories, multiply the grams of carbohydrate (20) by 4 (the number of Calories in 1 gram of carbohydrate). Then divide the result (80 Calories) by the total number of Calories (110). The resulting percentage of carbohydrate Calories is 73. This is normal for a cereal because it is high in carbohydrates and well above the 50 to 55 percent recommended as the maximum in a healthful diet.

3. To determine the percentage of protein Calories, multiply the grams of protein (4) by 4 (the number of Calories in 1 gram of protein). Then divide the result (16) by the total number of Calories (110). The resulting percentage of protein Calories is 15, which is within the recommended 15 to 20 percent.

Now it is your turn to play consumer. You can use a calculator or computer to help you with your calculations.

1. What is the percentage of fat, carbohydrate, and protein Calories in the cereal to which one-half cup of skim milk has been added? (Refer to information that appears in the column headed Plus 1/2 cup skim milk.)

2. What is the percentage of fat, carbohydrate, and protein Calories in the cereal to which 2% milk has been added? (See information next to *.)

3. Based on your results, is it more healthful to use skim milk or 2% milk?

4. In the dry cereal, how many grams of carbohydrates are in the form of starch? In the form of sugars?

3–2 Digestion of Food

Most foods that you eat cannot be used immediately by your body. They must first be broken down into the usable forms you have just learned about. **Food must be broken down into nutrients by a process called digestion. The breaking down of food into simpler substances for use by the body is the work of the digestive system.** Once food has been digested, or broken down into nutrients, the nutrients are carried to all the cells of the body by the blood. There, in the cells, the nutrients can be used to provide energy and the raw materials for cell growth and repair. In the following sections, you will discover the path that food takes through the digestive system.

Guide for Reading

Focus on these questions as you read.

▶ *What happens to food during the process of digestion?*

▶ *What are the parts of the digestive system?*

Figure 3–10 *The breaking down of food into simpler substances that can be used by the body is the work of the digestive system. The digestive system consists of a number of different organs. Through which organ does food enter the digestive system?*

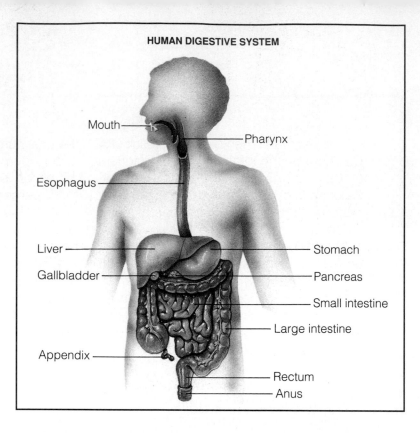

HUMAN DIGESTIVE SYSTEM

Mouth
Pharynx
Esophagus
Liver
Stomach
Gallbladder
Pancreas
Small intestine
Large intestine
Appendix
Rectum
Anus

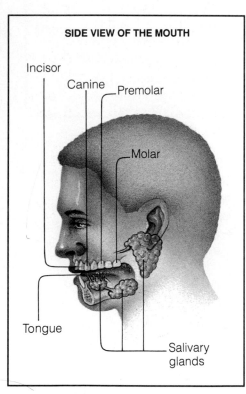

SIDE VIEW OF THE MOUTH

Incisor
Canine
Premolar
Molar
Tongue
Salivary glands

Figure 3–11 *Salivary glands, which are found in the mouth, produce saliva. Saliva contains the enzyme ptyalin. Which nutrient does ptyalin break down?*

The Mouth

Close your eyes and imagine your favorite food. Did your mouth water as you pictured something really delicious? Probably so. This response occurs because the mouth contains salivary (SAL-uh-vair-ee) glands. Salivary glands produce and release a liquid known as saliva (suh-LIGH-vuh). Seeing, smelling, or even thinking about food can increase the flow of saliva.

As you know from experience, saliva helps to moisten your food. But saliva has another important function. Saliva contains a chemical substance called **ptyalin** (TIGH-uh-lihn). Ptyalin breaks down some of the starches in food into sugars. You can actually detect this process by trying the following activity. Put a small piece of bread into your mouth and chew it for a few minutes. What happens? The bread begins to taste sweeter. Why? Bread is made mainly of starches, and starches are made of long chains of sugars. When ptyalin comes into contact with a starch, it begins to digest the starch, or break it down into sugars. The presence of these sugars makes the bread taste sweeter.

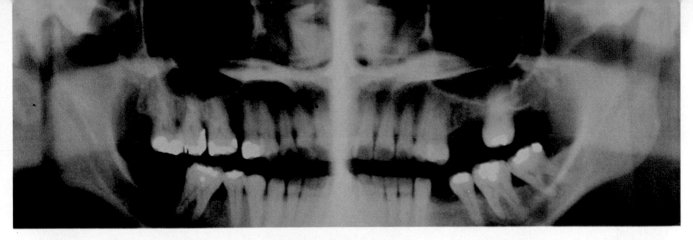

Figure 3–12 *The X-ray of the mouth shows the location of the four types of teeth: incisors, canines, premolars, and molars. The brighter areas in the teeth are the fillings. Where are the incisors located?*

Ptyalin belongs to a group of chemicals in your body known as **enzymes.** An enzyme helps to control a wide variety of chemical reactions, including the breaking down of foods into simpler substances. The digestion of foods by enzymes, such as ptyalin, is called chemical digestion. So although you may not have realized it, chemical digestion actually begins in your mouth!

Chemical digestion is not the only type of digestion that occurs in the mouth. Mechanical digestion, which is the physical action of breaking down food into smaller parts, also begins in the mouth. When you bite into your food, your incisors (ihn-SIGH-zerz), or front teeth, cut off a piece of the food. You then pull the food into your mouth with your lips and use your tongue to push it farther along into your mouth. Here the canines (KAY-nighnz), or eyeteeth, tear and shred the food while the flat-headed premolars and molars, or back teeth, grind and crush the food into small pieces.

Now that you have imagined your favorite food, think of the one you dislike most. The moment this food is in your mouth, something happens that makes you want to spit it out. If someone asked you why, you would probably say that the food tastes bad. Food tastes good or bad to you because there are taste buds on your tongue. Without taste buds, you would not be able to tell the difference between the food you dislike and the food you like.

Covering the surface of your tongue are small projections that give parts of the tongue a velvety

FIND OUT BY DOING

How Sweet It Is

1. Obtain two baby-food jars with lids. Label one jar A and the other B.

2. Fill each jar with equal amounts of water.

3. Place a whole sugar cube into jar A and a crushed sugar cube into jar B.

4. Place the lid on each jar and carefully shake each jar about five times.

5. Place the jars on a flat surface where they can remain undisturbed. Observe the rate of solution, or the time it takes for the sugar to dissolve completely, in each jar.

Which jar had the faster rate of solution? Can you think of any other factors that would affect the rate of solution? How would you test for these factors?

■ Relate the results of your investigation to the importance of mechanical digestion.

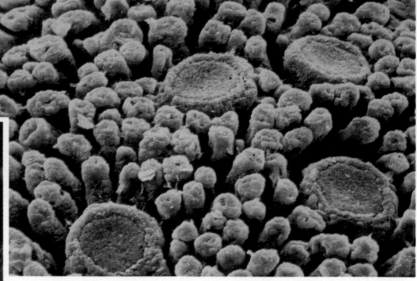

Figure 3–13 *Covering the tongue's surface are tiny projections that give it a velvety appearance (top). Located along the sides of these projections are the taste buds (left). The taste buds can detect four different kinds of tastes produced by the chemicals in food. What are these four tastes?*

appearance. See Figure 3–13. Your taste buds are found along the sides of these projections. There are four types of taste buds, each of which reacts to a different group of chemicals in food. The reactions between taste buds and food chemicals produce four kinds of tastes: sweet, sour, bitter, and salty. The flavor of food, however, does not come from taste alone. Flavor is a mixture of taste, texture, and odor. Anyone who has ever had a stuffed nose caused by a cold knows how important the sense of smell is to the flavor of food.

What happens once you have finished chewing your food? You swallow it, of course! When you swallow, smooth muscles near the back of your throat begin to force the food downward. As you may recall from Chapter 2, smooth muscles are involuntary muscles. This means that they can contract without your actively causing them to. As you swallow, a small flap of tissue called the epiglottis (ehp-uh-GLAHT-ihs) automatically closes over your windpipe. The windpipe is the tube through which the air you breathe reaches your lungs. When the epiglottis closes over the windpipe, it prevents food or water from moving into the windpipe—or "down the wrong pipe," as we say. After swallowing, the epiglottis moves back into place to allow air into the windpipe.

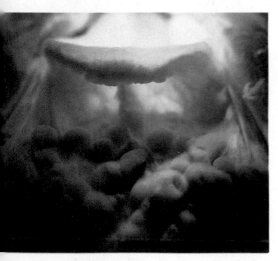

Figure 3–14 *The epiglottis, which is a flap of tissue, folds over the windpipe to keep food or water from going "down the wrong pipe."*

The Esophagus

After you swallow, smooth muscles force the food into a tube called the **esophagus** (ih-SAHF-uh-guhs). The word esophagus comes from a Greek word that means to carry what is eaten. And that is exactly what this 25-centimeter-long tube does as it transports food down into the next organ of the digestive system.

The esophagus, like most of the organs in your digestive system, is lined with slippery mucus. The mucus helps food travel through the digestive system easily. The movement of food through your esophagus takes about seven seconds. However, mucus alone is not responsible for the speed of this trip. Waves of rhythmic muscular contractions, which begin as soon as food enters the esophagus, push food downward. These waves of contractions are called **peristalsis** (per-uh-STAHL-sihs). Peristalsis is so strong that it can force food through parts of your digestive system even if you are lying down. Because of peristalsis, a person can digest food even while floating upside down in the weightlessness of space.

FIND OUT BY DOING

Simulating Peristalsis

1. Obtain a 40-cm piece of clear plastic tubing.

2. Hold the tubing vertically and insert a small bead into the top opening of the tubing. The bead should fit snugly into the tubing.

3. Pinch the tubing above the bead so that the bead is pushed down along the length of the tubing.

How does this action compare with peristalsis?

■ What action would you be simulating if you were to pinch the tubing below the small bead?

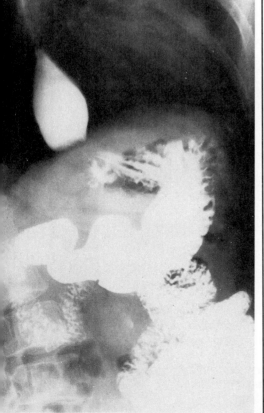

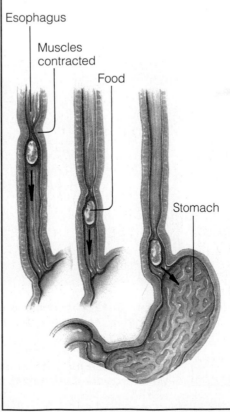

Esophagus

Muscles contracted

Food

Stomach

Figure 3–15 *Peristalsis is the waves of contractions that push food through parts of the digestive system. Use the diagram to identify the parts of the digestive system shown in the X-ray. Notice the vertebral column in the background.*

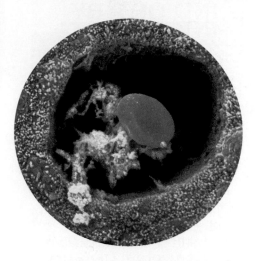

Figure 3–16 *To protect the stomach from the effects of hydrochloric acid, tiny pits secrete a layer of mucus, which appears yellow in the photograph. The single red blood cell floating out of the pit is thought to be a sign that the stomach has been irritated by a substance such as alcohol.*

The Stomach

After leaving the esophagus, the food enters a J-shaped organ called the **stomach.** Cells in the stomach wall release a fluid called gastric juice. Gastric juice contains the enzyme **pepsin,** hydrochloric acid, and thick, slippery mucus. If you were studying chemistry, you would learn that hydrochloric acid is a strong acid. This means that it is very reactive. In fact, the hydrochloric acid in your stomach is so reactive that if you could remove a drop of it and place it on a rug, it would burn a hole in the rug! The mucus, on the other hand, coats and protects the stomach wall. Can you see why such protection is necessary?

While food is in the stomach, it undergoes both mechanical digestion and chemical digestion. The contractions of the stomach muscles provide a kind of mechanical digestion as they churn the food and mix it with gastric juice. With the help of hydrochloric acid, pepsin breaks down some of the complex proteins in the food into simpler proteins. The action of pepsin on the proteins is a form of chemical digestion. Both of these types of digestion occur as peristalsis pushes the food toward the stomach's exit.

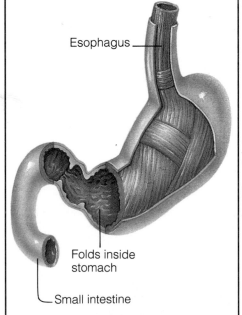

Esophagus

Folds inside stomach

Small intestine

Figure 3–17 *The stomach wall consists of several layers of smooth muscles (left). When these muscles contract, food and gastric juice within the stomach are mixed together. Notice that the stomach's inner lining contains many folds (right). These folds will smooth out as the organ fills with food. What enzyme does gastric juice contain?*

The Small Intestine

The food moving out of your stomach is quite a bit different from the food that you placed in your mouth. After three to six hours in your stomach, muscle contractions and enzymes have changed the food into a soft, watery substance. In this form, the food is ready to move slowly into another organ of the digestive system—the **small intestine.** Although this organ is only 2.5 centimeters in diameter, it is more than 6 meters long. As in the esophagus and the stomach, food moves through the small intestine by peristalsis.

Although some chemical and mechanical digestion has already taken place in the mouth and the stomach, most digestion takes place in the small intestine. The cells lining the walls of the small intestine release an intestinal juice that contains several types of digestive enzymes.

Most chemical digestion that occurs in the small intestine takes place within the first 0.3 meter of this organ. Here, intestinal juice helps to break down food arriving from the stomach. This juice, however, does not work alone. It is helped by juices that are produced by two organs located near the small intestine. These organs are the **liver** and the **pancreas** (PAN-kree-uhs). Because food never actually passes

Enzymes

Enzymes speed up the rate of certain body reactions that would otherwise occur very slowly. During these reactions, the enzymes are not used up or changed in any way. Using reference materials in the library, look up the meaning of "substrate" and the "lock-and-key hypothesis." Using posterboard and colored construction paper, make a labeled diagram of this hypothesis. Present the diagram to the class.

■ What is the relationship between an enzyme and a substrate?

SOME DIGESTIVE ENZYMES

Digestive Juice	Digestive Enzyme	Works on	Changes It to
Saliva	Ptyalin	Starch	Complex sugars
Gastric	Pepsin	Protein	Simpler proteins
Pancreatic	Amylase Trypsin Lipase	Starch Proteins Fats	Complex sugars Simpler proteins Fatty acids and glycerol
Intestinal	Lactase, maltase, sucrase Peptidase Lipase	Complex sugars Simpler proteins Fats	Simple sugars Amino acids Fatty acids and glycerol

Figure 3–18 *According to this chart, which enzymes work on proteins? Which work on fats?*

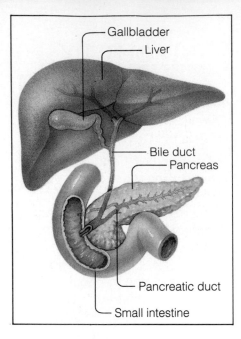

Figure 3-19 *The liver, pancreas, and gallbladder produce and store substances that are released into the small intestine to aid in the digestion of food.*

FIND OUT BY DOING

Do Oil and Water Mix?

1. Obtain two baby-food jars with lids. Place 5 mL of vegetable oil and 5 mL of water in each jar.

2. Cover both jars and gently shake them a few times. Then place the jars on a flat surface and observe what happens in each jar.

3. Remove the lid from one of the jars and add a few drops of liquid soap to the oil-and-water mixture. Repeat step 2.

Under what circumstances do oil and water mix?

■ How does the action of liquid soap resemble the action of bile?

through the liver and the pancreas, these organs are considered to be digestive helpers.

THE LIVER Located to the right of the stomach is the liver, the body's largest and heaviest organ. One of its many important functions is to aid digestion by producing a substance called bile. Once bile is produced in the liver, it moves into the gallbladder, where it is stored until needed.

As food moves into the small intestine from the stomach, the gallbladder releases bile through a duct (tubelike structure) into the small intestine. Because bile is not an enzyme, it does not chemically digest foods. It does, however, help to break up large fat particles into smaller ones in much the same way a detergent breaks up grease. These smaller fat particles can then be digested easily by enzymes in the small intestine.

THE PANCREAS The pancreas is a soft triangular organ located between the stomach and the small intestine. The pancreas produces a substance called pancreatic juice, which is a mixture of several enzymes. These enzymes move into the small intestine at the same time the bile does and help to break down proteins, starches, and fats.

The pancreas also produces a substance called insulin, which is important in controlling the body's use of sugar. You will read more about the pancreas and insulin in Chapter 6.

3-2 Section Review

1. Describe the process of digestion.
2. Compare mechanical and chemical digestion.
3. What is peristalsis? Why is it important?
4. Where does most of the digestion of food take place?
5. Why are the liver and the pancreas called digestive helpers rather than digestive organs?

Connection—*You and Your World*
6. Why is it important to chew your food thoroughly before swallowing it?

3–3 Absorption of Food

Guide for Reading

Focus on this question as you read.

What is the process of absorption?

After a period of 3 to 5 hours, most of the food that is in the small intestine is digested. Proteins are broken down into individual amino acids. Carbohydrates (starches and sugars) are broken down into simple sugars. And fats are broken down into substances called fatty acids and glycerol. But before these nutrients can be used for energy, they must first be absorbed (taken in) by the bloodstream through the walls of the small intestine.

Absorption in the Small Intestine

The small intestine has an inner lining that looks something like wet velvet. This is because the inner lining of the small intestine is covered with millions of tiny fingerlike structures called **villi** (VIHL-igh; singular: villus, VIHL-uhs).

Digested food is absorbed through the villi into a network of blood vessels that carry the nutrients to all parts of the body. The presence of villi helps to increase the surface area of the small intestine, enabling more digested food to be absorbed faster than would be possible if the small intestine's walls were smooth. The villi contain tiny blood vessels that absorb and carry away the nutrients.

By the time the food is ready to leave the small intestine, it is basically free of nutrients, except for water. All the nutrients have been absorbed. What remains are undigested substances that include water and cellulose, a part of fruits and vegetables.

As the undigested food leaves the small intestine, it passes by a small finger-shaped organ called the appendix (uh-PEHN-diks). The appendix, which leads nowhere, has no known function. However, scientists suspect it may play a role in helping the body resist disease-causing bacteria and viruses. The only time that you may be aware of the appendix is when it becomes irritated, inflamed, or infected, causing appendicitis (uh-pehn-duh-SIGHT-ihs). The only cure for appendicitis is to remove the appendix by surgery as soon as possible.

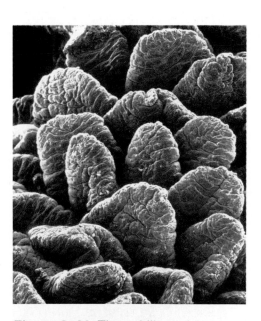

Figure 3–20 *These hills and ridges, which resemble part of a mountain range on the Earth's surface, are actually part of the small intestine. The tiny structures, called villi, line the inside of the small intestine. What is the function of the villi?*

Absorption in the Large Intestine

After leaving the small intestine, the undigested food passes into the **large intestine.** The large intestine is shaped like a horseshoe that fits over the coils of the small intestine. The large intestine is about 6.5 centimeters in diameter but only about 1.5 meters long. How do you think the large intestine got its name?

After spending about 18 to 24 hours in the large intestine, most of the water that is contained in the undigested food is absorbed. At the same time, helpful bacteria living in the large intestine make certain vitamins, such as K and two B vitamins, that are needed by the body.

Materials that are not absorbed in the large intestine form a solid waste. This solid waste is made up of dead bacteria, some fat and protein, undigested food roughage, dried-out parts of digestive juices, mucus, and discarded intestinal cells. A short tube at the end of the large intestine called the **rectum** stores this waste. Solid wastes are eliminated from the body through an opening at the end of the rectum called the **anus.**

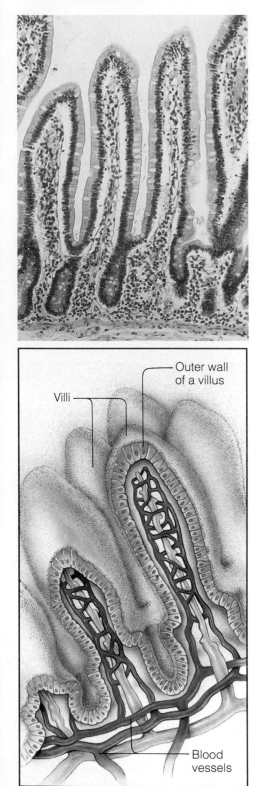

Villi — Outer wall of a villus

Blood vessels

Figure 3–22 *The large intestine forms an upside-down horseshoe that fits over the small intestine (left). Lining the inside of the large intestine are many tunnels that contain mucus-making cells (right).*

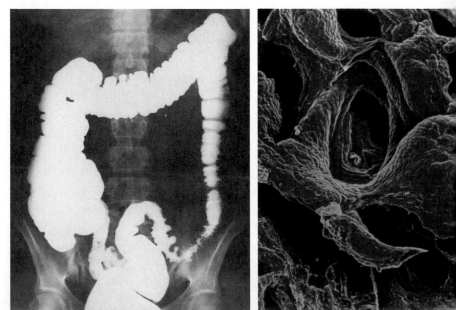

3–3 Section Review

1. Describe the process of absorption in the small intestine.
2. What is the function of the villi?
3. Describe the process of absorption in the large intestine.
4. What is the function of the rectum? The anus?

Critical Thinking—*Relating Facts*
5. Gallstones, which are crystals of minerals and salts that form in bile, sometimes block the entrance to the small intestine. What effect would this blockage have on the digestion of food?

3–4 Maintaining Good Health

As you have already learned, you can supply your body with the materials it needs for growth, repair, and energy by eating a balanced diet. **You can also keep your body healthy and running smoothly by controlling your weight and by getting proper amounts of exercise.**

Exercise

Activities such as swimming, jogging, bicycling, hiking, and walking briskly are good ways to exercise. Regular exercise helps to strengthen the heart. Exercise also results in firmer muscles, better posture, greater strength, increased endurance, and an improved sense of balance.

Weight Control

When a person eats more food than is needed, the body stores the excess energy in the form of fat. This fat is deposited mainly in a layer of tissue under the skin. In order to get rid of this stored fat, the person must use up more energy than is provided in the foods he or she eats. In this way, the body

Guide for Reading

Focus on this question as you read.

▶ *What are two important factors in maintaining good health?*

Figure 3–23 *When a person eats more food than is needed by the body, the body stores the excess food in the form of fat. This fat is deposited mainly in a layer of tissue under the skin. How can a person get rid of this stored fat?*

Figure 3–24 *In order to maintain good health, most people — including older people—need moderate exercise. What are some of the benefits of exercise?*

will break down the stored fat to release the needed energy.

When a person is overweight, all the organs of the body, especially the heart, must work harder to bring materials to and remove wastes from the excess fat tissue. Some people who are overweight may choose to go on a weight-loss diet. It is important that the diet chosen is a balanced one—one that contains the proper amounts of nutrients needed by the body. Before starting any weight-loss diet, a person should go to a doctor. The doctor will give the person a complete checkup and discuss a sensible diet. Once a person loses the excess weight, he or she can maintain a steady weight by taking in only as many Calories in food as are used up.

3–4 Section Review

1. Explain how exercise and weight control contribute to good health.
2. List four activities that are good forms of exercise.
3. What must be included in any balanced diet?
4. How can you maintain a steady weight?

Connection—*You and Your World*
5. Imagine that you have put on a little weight. Design a balanced diet that will help you get rid of the weight.

What's Cooking?

Recall the last time you cooked an egg or boiled some water. Did you use a gas stove or an electric stove? Or did you use a microwave oven? Whichever appliance you used, they had one thing in common: They are all sources of heat. Heat, which is a form of energy, cannot be seen. However, you can see the work that heat does by observing what happens to food when you cook it. In a way, cooking can be defined as the transfer of heat from its source to food. The various cooking methods, such as boiling, frying, and baking, bring about their effects by using different materials—water, oil, air—and different methods of *heat transfer*.

Heat is transferred by three methods: conduction, convection, and radiation. In conduction, heat is transferred through a material without carrying any of the material with it. For example, heat from a gas or an electric burner passes through a pan to the food inside it. In convection, heat is transferred as a liquid or a gas moves from a warm area to a cooler one. In a pan of cold water that has been placed on a hot burner, for example, the water nearer the burner will heat up and move to the top. This will cause the cooler water nearer the top of the pan to

sink. This process will continue until all the water reaches the same temperature.

Unlike the processes of conduction and convection, the process of radiation can occur through a vacuum. In radiation, waves of energy are used to heat materials. This energy is absorbed by the particles in the material, causing them to vibrate. In microwave ovens, for example, the microwaves produced by powerful electromagnetic (electric and magnetic) fields cause the water in food to vibrate. This action releases heat into the food. Because all of the energy is absorbed by the food and not wasted on heating the surrounding air or the oven itself, microwave cooking is quicker and more economical than other types of cooking methods.

Laboratory Investigation

Measuring Calories Used

Problem

How many Calories do you use in 24 hours?

Materials (per student)

pencil and paper	scale

Procedure

1. Look over the chart of Calorie rates. It shows how various activities are related to the rates at which you burn Calories. The Calorie rate shown for each activity is actually the number of Calories used per hour for each kilogram of your body mass.

2. Using a scale, note your weight in pounds. Convert your weight into kilograms (2.2 lb = 1 kg). Record this number.

3. Classify all your activities for a given 24-hour period. Record the kind of activity, the Calorie rate, and the number of hours you were involved in that activity.

4. For each of your activities, multiply your weight by the Calorie rate shown in the chart. Then multiply the resulting number by the number of hours or fractions of hours you were involved in that activity. The result is the number of Calories you burned during that period of time. For example, if your weight is 50 kilograms and you exercised strenuously, perhaps by running, for half an hour, the Calories you burned during that activity would be equal to 50 x 10.5 X 0.5 = 262.5 Calories.

5. Add together all the Calories you burned in the entire 24-hour period.

Observations

How many Calories did you use in the 24-hour period?

Analysis and Conclusions

1. Explain why the values for the Calorie rates of various activities are approximate rather than exact.

2. What factors could affect the number of Calories a person used during exercise?

3. Why do young people need to consume more Calories than adults?

4. **On Your Own** Determine the number of Calories you use in a week. In a month.

Activity	Average Calorie Rate
Sleeping	1.1
Awake but at rest (sitting, reading, or eating)	1.5
Very slight exercise (bathing, dressing)	3.1
Slight exercise (walking quickly)	4.4
Strenuous exercise (dancing)	7.5
Very strenuous exercise (running, swimming rapidly)	10.5

Average Caloric Needs Chart		
	Age	Calories
Males	9–12 12–15	2400 3000
Females	9–12 12–15	2200 2500

Study Guide

Summarizing Key Concepts

3–1 The Importance of Food

▲ The six groups of nutrients are proteins, carbohydrates, fats, vitamins, minerals, and water.

3–2 Digestion of Food

▲ Digestion is the process of breaking down food into simple substances.

▲ The salivary glands release saliva, which contains the enzyme ptyalin. Ptyalin breaks down some starches into simple sugars.

▲ The changing of food into simple substances by the action of enzymes is called chemical digestion.

▲ Mechanical digestion occurs when food is broken down by chewing and by the churning movements of the digestive tract.

▲ After leaving the mouth, food enters the esophagus and is pushed downward into the stomach by peristalsis.

▲ The stomach releases gastric juice, which contains hydrochloric acid, mucus, and pepsin. Pepsin is an enzyme that breaks down proteins into amino acids.

▲ In the stomach, food undergoes both mechanical and chemical digestion.

▲ After leaving the stomach, food enters the small intestine, where it is acted upon by intestinal juice that digests proteins, starches, and fats.

▲ In the small intestine, bile, which is produced by the liver and stored in the gallbladder, aids in the digestion of fats .

▲ Pancreatic juice travels to the small intestine and digests proteins, starches, and fats.

3–3 Absorption of Food

▲ Nutrients are absorbed into the bloodstream through fingerlike structures called villi located on the inner lining of the small intestine.

▲ The large intestine absorbs most of the water from the undigested food.

▲ Undigested food substances are stored in the rectum and then eliminated from the body through the anus.

3–4 Maintaining Good Health

▲ A regular exercise program helps to strengthen the heart, develop better posture, firm up muscles, build a stronger body, and increase endurance.

Reviewing Key Terms

Define each term in a complete sentence.

3–1 The Importance of Food

nutrient
Calorie
protein
amino acid
carbohydrate
fat
vitamin
mineral

3–2 Digestion of Food

ptyalin
enzyme
esophagus
peristalsis
stomach
pepsin
small intestine
liver
pancreas

3–3 Absorption of Food

villus
large intestine
rectum
anus

Chapter Review

Content Review

Multiple Choice

Choose the letter of the answer that best completes each statement.

1. The nutrients that are used to build and repair body parts are
   - a. proteins.
   - b. minerals.
   - c. carbohydrates.
   - d. vitamins.
2. Which is not found in the mouth?
   - a. pepsin
   - b. saliva
   - c. ptyalin
   - d. taste buds.
3. The tube that connects the mouth and the stomach is the
   - a. small intestine.
   - b. pancreas.
   - c. esophagus.
   - d. epiglottis.
4. Gastric juice contains the enzyme
   - a. bile.
   - b. pepsin.
   - c. ptyalin.
   - d. mucus.
5. The digestion of proteins begins in the
   - a. mouth.
   - b. liver.
   - c. small intestine.
   - d. stomach.

6. In the digestive system, proteins are broken down into
   - a. fatty acids.
   - b. glycerol.
   - c. simple sugars.
   - d. amino acids.
7. The liver produces
   - a. pepsin.
   - b. bile.
   - c. hydrochloric acid.
   - d. ptyalin.
8. The fingerlike structures that form the inner lining of the small intestine are called
   - a. cilia.
   - b. villi.
   - c. enzymes.
   - d. nutrients.
9. Water is absorbed in the
   - a. small intestine.
   - b. pancreas.
   - c. large intestine.
   - d. liver.
10. Regular exercise helps a person have
    - a. good posture.
    - b. firm muscles.
    - c. a stronger heart.
    - d. all of these.

True or False

If the statement is true, write "true." If it is false, change the underlined word or words to make the statement true.

1. The nutrients that supply the greatest amount of energy are the fats.
2. A chemical that breaks down food into simple substances is called an enzyme.
3. Starches and sugars are examples of proteins.
4. Vitamin K is an example of a water-soluble vitamin.
5. Pepsin is the enzyme in saliva.
6. Undigested food substances are stored in the epiglottis.
7. The enzyme pepsin digests proteins.
8. The small, finger-shaped organ located where the small intestine and large intestine meet is the appendix.

Concept Mapping

Complete the following concept map for Section 3–1. Refer to pages H8–H9 to construct a concept map for the entire chapter.

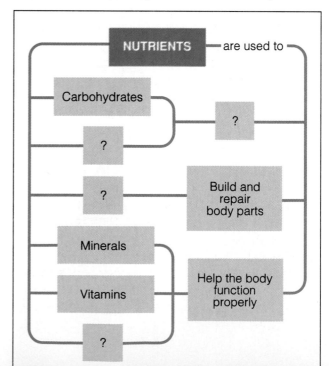

Concept Mastery

Discuss each of the following in a brief paragraph.

1. If you were to eat a slice of bread (starch) with butter (fat) and drink a glass of milk (protein), what would happen to each of these foods during digestion?
2. Food does not really enter your body until it is absorbed into the blood. Explain why. *Hint:* Think of the digestive system as a tube passing through your body.
3. Appendicitis is usually treated by removing the appendix. Explain why this treatment does not interfere with the functioning of a person's digestive system.
4. Describe the structure of villi and their role in absorption.
5. Describe the location and function of the epiglottis.
6. Where does mechanical digestion occur? Chemical digestion?
7. Compare absorption in the small intestine with absorption in the large intestine.
8. Why can talking with food in your mouth be a dangerous thing to do?
9. Explain why vomiting can be considered reverse peristalsis.

Critical Thinking and Problem Solving

Use the skills you have developed in this chapter to answer each of the following.

1. **Making inferences** Suppose your doctor prescribed an antibiotic that killed all the bacteria in your body. What effect would this have on your digestive system?
2. **Making comparisons** Compare the human digestive system to an "assembly line in reverse."
3. **Making diagrams** Draw a diagram of the human digestive system and label all the organs. Use a red pencil to color the organs through which food passes. Use a blue pencil to color the organs through which food does not pass.
4. **Applying concepts** Fad diets have become popular in the United States. Some of these diets involve eating only a limited variety of food. Explain why some fad diets may be an unhealthy way to lose weight.
5. **Making comparisons** Compare the process of digestion to the process of absorption.
6. **Relating concepts** Following surgery, most patients are fed a glucose, or simple sugar, solution intravenously. Intravenously means into a vein. Why do you think this is done?
7. **Sequencing events** Trace the path of a piece of hamburger on a bun through the digestive system. Name each digestive organ and describe what happens in each organ.
8. **Using the writing process** Carbohydrate loading is a technique used by athletes to help them reach their peak of efficiency. To find out the benefits and potential problems of this practice, prepare a list of questions that you might ask a doctor and a coach during an interview on this subject.

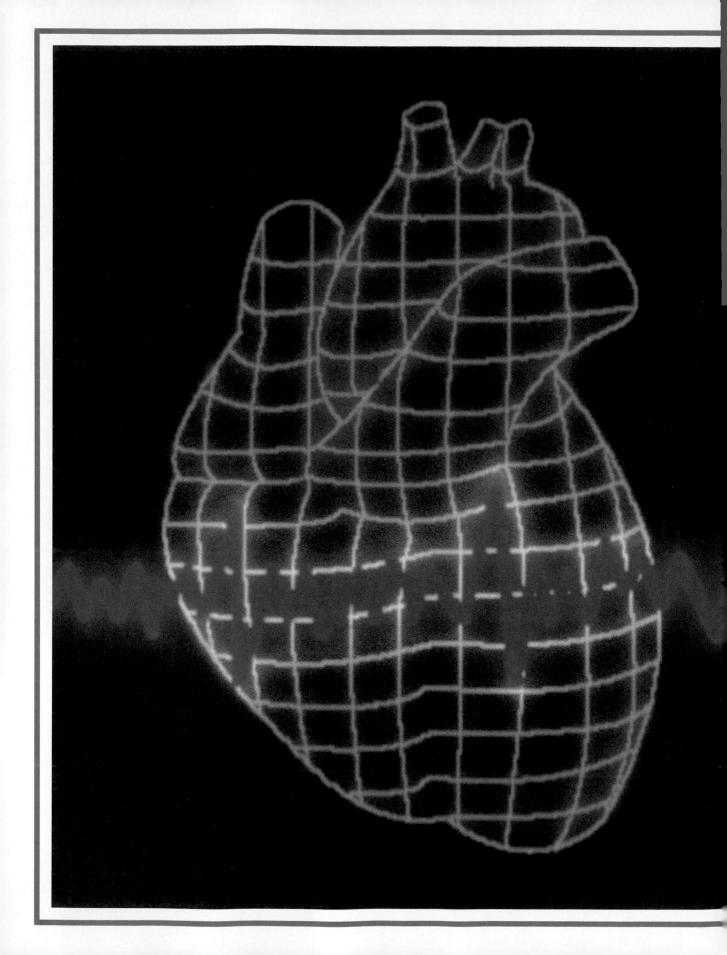

Circulatory System

Guide for Reading

After you read the following sections, you will be able to

4–1 The Body's Transportation System
- Identify the main function of the circulatory system.

4–2 Circulation in the Body
- Trace the path of blood through the body.
- Relate the structures of the heart and blood vessels to their functions.

4–3 Blood—The River of Life
- Compare the four main components of blood.
- Identify the two main human blood groups.

4–4 Cardiovascular Diseases
- Relate cardiovascular diseases to the circulatory system.

At 6:24 AM, the first call of the day came in. A 73-year-old man who lived 120 kilometers away was having severe chest pains. "Strap yourself in, we're taking off!" shouted the pilot to the chief flight nurse over the roar of the helicopter. The chief flight nurse is one of several highly trained members of Survival Flight, a special medical unit that comes to the aid of people who are having heart attacks.

By 8:12 AM, the nurse had given the patient an injection of a drug that dissolves blockages in the blood vessels near the heart. Such blockages can prevent the heart from receiving an adequate supply of blood. By 8:23 AM, the Survival Flight team was loading the patient onto the helicopter and preparing to rush him to a hospital.

The Survival Flight team's helicopter is equipped with a stretcher, medical instruments, and medicine. But the team's greatest strength is the knowledge possessed by its members. They all know how the heart works and what to do when something goes wrong. By reading the pages that follow, you too will discover some of this special knowledge.

Journal *Activity*

You and Your World In your journal, list all the activities that you do that affect your circulatory system. Then on a new page in your journal, make two columns with the headings Helpful and Harmful. Place the activities from your list in the appropriate column.

 Superimposed on this computer graphic of the heart is a part of an electrocardiogram, or record of the electrical activities of the heart.

4–1 The Body's Transportation System

The main task of the circulatory system in all organisms is transportation. **The circulatory system delivers food and oxygen to body cells and carries carbon dioxide and other waste products away from body cells.** The power behind this pickup-and-delivery system is the heart. The heart pumps blood to all parts of the body through a network of blood vessels. This network is so large that if it could be unraveled, it would wrap around the Earth more than twice!

As you may already know, oxygen combines with food inside your body cells to produce usable energy. Without energy, body cells would soon die. Thus, one of the most important jobs of the circulatory system is delivering oxygen to the cells. The cells

Figure 4–1 *The disk-shaped red objects in this photograph are red blood cells. Notice how densely packed the red blood cells are as they squeeze through the tiniest of blood vessels—the capillaries.*

that use the most oxygen—and the first to die without oxygen—are brain cells.

When cells combine oxygen and food to produce energy, they also produce a waste product called carbon dioxide. Removing carbon dioxide from cells is another important job of the circulatory system.

Still another important job of the circulatory system is to transport food to all body cells. At the same time, wastes produced by the cells are carried away by the blood. If the blood did not remove such wastes, the body would poison itself with its own waste products!

Sometimes the body comes under attack from microscopic organisms such as bacteria and viruses. At such times, another transporting function of the circulatory system comes into play: supplying the body with defenses against invaders. The defenses take the form of disease-fighting cells and chemicals. When invading organisms attack areas of the body, the circulatory system rushes the disease-fighting cells and chemicals to the area under attack.

Disease-fighting chemicals are not the only types of chemicals transported by the circulatory system. The circulatory system carries chemical messengers as well. Chemical messengers bring instructions from one part of the body to another. For example, a chemical messenger produced in the pancreas is carried by the blood to the liver. Its message is "Too much sugar in the blood. Remove some and store it."

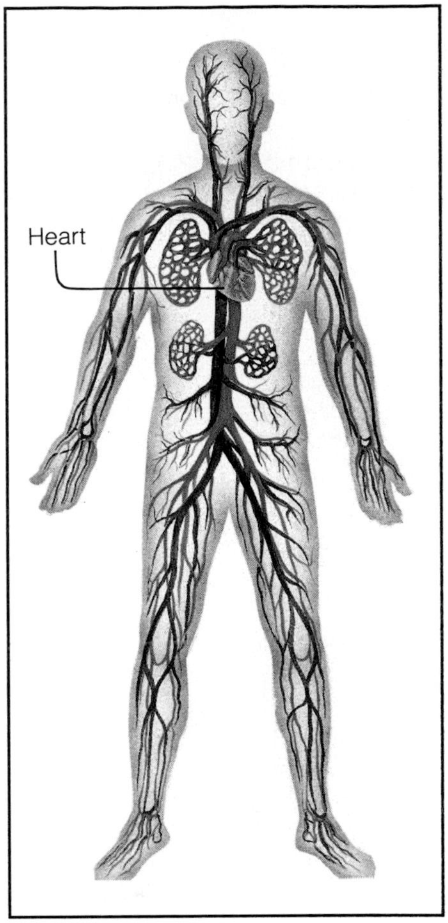

Figure 4–2 *The function of the circulatory system is to deliver food and oxygen to body cells and carry carbon dioxide and other waste products away from body cells. What organ pumps blood throughout the body?*

4–1 Section Review

1. What are the functions of the circulatory system?
2. Why is it important that wastes produced by the cells are carried away by the blood?

Critical Thinking—*Making Calculations*
3. The heart of an average person pumps about 5 liters of blood per minute. How much blood is pumped out of the heart per hour? Per day? Per week?

Guide for Reading

Focus on this question as you read.

▶ *What path does blood take through the circulatory system?*

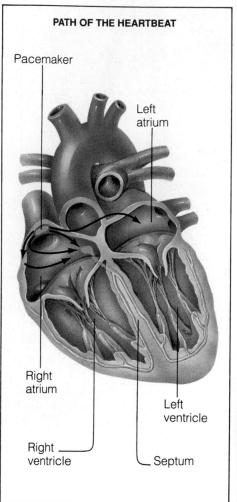

PATH OF THE HEARTBEAT

Pacemaker

Left atrium

Right atrium

Right ventricle

Left ventricle

Septum

Figure 4–3 *The heartbeat is controlled by an area of nerve tissue within the heart called the pacemaker. In the illustration, you can see the path a message from the pacemaker takes as it spreads through the heart. The photograph shows a network of nerves lining a section of a ventricle.*

4–2 Circulation in the Body

In a way, the entire circulatory system is like a vast maze that starts at the heart. Unlike most mazes, however, this one always leads back to the place where it began. **In the circulatory system, blood moves from the heart to the lungs and back to the heart. Blood then travels to all the cells of the body and returns again to the heart.** In the next few pages, you will follow the blood on its journey through the circulatory maze. You will begin, of course, at the heart.

You may be surprised to learn that the heart is a muscle that rests only between beats. Even when you are asleep, about 5 liters of blood is pumped through your body every minute. During an average lifetime, the heart beats more than 2 billion times and pumps several hundred million liters of blood through the many thousands of kilometers of blood vessels in the body.

Not much larger than a fist, the heart is located slightly to the left of the center of your chest. If you place your fingers there and gently press down, you probably will be able to feel your heart beating. The heartbeat, or the heart's rhythm, is controlled by an area of nerve tissue within the heart. Because this

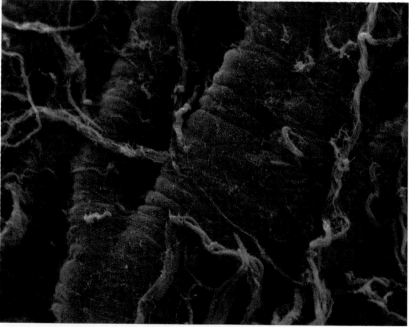

area regulates the heart's pace, or rate of beating, it is called the pacemaker. Located in the upper-right side of the heart, the pacemaker sends out signals to heart muscle, causing it to contract. For a variety of reasons, the body's pacemaker may fail to operate properly. If this happens, an artificial pacemaker, complete with a battery, can be inserted into the body or worn outside the body.

The Right Side of the Heart

Most people think of the heart as a single pump, but it is actually two pumps. One pump is located on the right side of the heart. The second pump is located on the left side of the heart. A thick wall of tissue called the septum separates the heart into a right side and a left side. Each side has two chambers. Your journey through the circulatory maze begins in the right upper chamber, called the right **atrium** (AY-tree-uhm; plural: atria). Figure 4–4 shows the location of the right atrium.

FIND OUT BY DOING

Catch the Beat

How does temperature affect heartbeat rate? Design an experiment to find the answer to this question by using the following materials:

Daphnia culture
2 glass depression slides
coverslip
microscope
stopwatch
ice cube

As you plan your experiment, keep in mind that it must contain only one variable. Remember to include a control.

■ What effect would warm (not hot) water have on the *Daphnia*'s heartbeat rate?

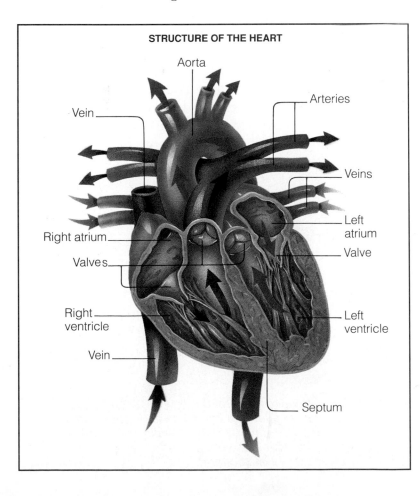

STRUCTURE OF THE HEART

Aorta
Arteries
Vein
Veins
Left atrium
Right atrium
Valve
Valves
Right ventricle
Left ventricle
Vein
Septum

Figure 4–4 *The heart is divided into a right side and a left side by a septum, or wall. Each side of the septum contains two chambers: an upper chamber and a lower chamber. The upper chambers are called atria, and the lower chambers are called ventricles. What is the function of the atria?*

Inside the right atrium, you find yourself swirling in a dark sea of blood. A great many red blood cells surround you. Red blood cells carry oxygen throughout the body. When the red blood cells join up with oxygen molecules, the blood turns bright red. Such blood is said to be oxygen-rich. The blood in which you are swimming in the right atrium, however, is dark red, not bright red at all. This can only mean that these red blood cells are not carrying much oxygen. Rather, they are carrying mostly the waste gas carbon dioxide. This blood, then, is oxygen-poor. And that makes sense. For the right atrium is a collecting chamber for blood returning from its trip through the body. Along the way, the red blood cells have dropped off most of their oxygen and picked up carbon dioxide.

Suddenly the blood begins to churn, and you feel yourself falling downward. You are about to enter the heart's right lower chamber, called the right **ventricle.** But before you do, you must pass through a small flap of tissue called a valve. The valve opens to allow blood to go from the upper chamber to the lower chamber. Then it closes immediately to prevent blood from backing up into the upper chamber.

You now find yourself in the right ventricle. Your stay here will be quite short. The ventricles, unlike the atria, are pumping chambers. Before you know it, you feel the power of a heartbeat as the ventricle contracts and blood is forced out of the heart through a large blood vessel.

To the Lungs and Back

Now your journey has really begun. Because you are surrounded by oxygen-poor blood, your first stop should be obvious. Do you know what it is? The right ventricle is pumping you toward the lungs. The trip to the lungs is a short one. In the lungs, the red blood cells drop off the waste gas carbon dioxide. As the carbon dioxide enters the lungs, it is immediately

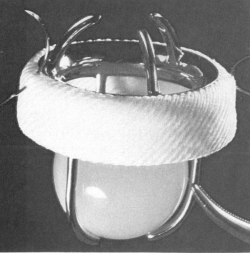

Figure 4–5 *Heart valves control the flow of blood through the heart. A heart valve called the bicuspid valve (top) is found between the left atrium and the left ventricle. Sometimes when a natural heart valve does not work properly, it must be replaced by an artificial heart valve (bottom).*

exhaled (breathed out). At the same time, the red blood cells are busy picking up oxygen, which has been brought into the lungs as a result of inhaling (breathing in). What is the color of the blood now?

As you leave the lungs, you might be expecting to travel with the oxygen-rich blood to all parts of the body. But to your surprise, you discover this is not the case. The oxygen-rich blood you are traveling in must first return to the heart so that it can be pumped throughout the body. Your next stop is the hollow chamber known as the left atrium.

The Left Side of the Heart

The left atrium, like the right atrium, is a collecting chamber for blood returning to the heart. The left atrium, however, collects oxygen-rich blood as it returns from the lungs. Once again, the blood quickly flows downward through a valve and enters the left ventricle.

The left ventricle has a lot more work to do than the right ventricle does. The right ventricle has to pump blood only a short distance to the lungs. But the left ventricle has to pump blood to every part of the body. In fact, the left side of the heart works about six times harder than the right side. That is why you feel your heartbeat on the left side of your chest.

Arteries: Pipelines From the Heart

As the left ventricle pumps the oxygen-rich blood out of the heart, the blood passes through the largest blood vessel in the body. This blood vessel is called the aorta (ay-OR-tuh). The aorta is an **artery,** or a blood vessel that carries blood away from the heart.

Soon after leaving the heart, the aorta branches into smaller arteries. Some of these smaller arteries return immediately to the heart, supplying the heart muscle with food and oxygen. Others branch again and again, like the branches of a tree. These branching arteries form a network that connects all parts of the body.

As you pass through the aorta and enter a smaller artery, you notice that the inner wall of the artery is

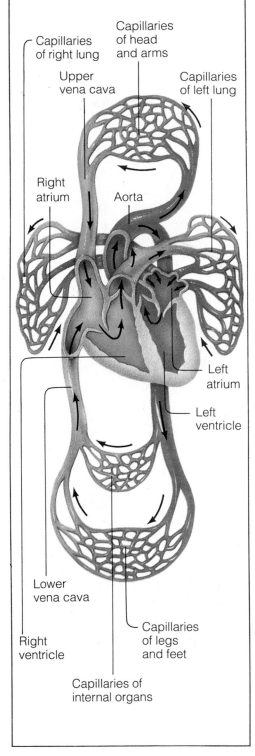

Figure 4–6 *Blood travels through the body in a continuous path. The path of oxygen-rich blood is shown in red, and the path of oxygen-poor blood is shown in blue.*

Circulation

Human circulation is divided into two types of circulation: pulmonary circulation and systemic circulation.

Use reference books to find out the structures that are involved in each type of circulation. Draw a labeled diagram of the human circulatory system, using two different-colored pencils to illustrate the structures that make up each type of circulation.

■ Why do you think these two types of circulation are so named?

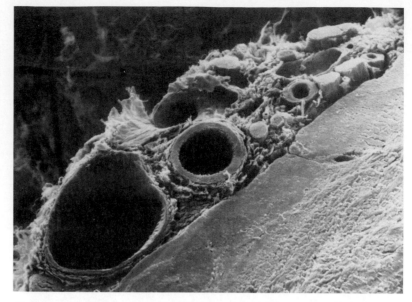

Figure 4–7 *This photograph shows that the wall of a small artery (right) is thicker than the wall of a medium-sized vein (left).*

quite smooth. The smooth inner wall allows blood to flow freely. Around the smooth inner wall is an elastic middle layer that is made mainly of smooth muscle tissue. Much of the flexibility of arteries comes from this elastic middle layer. The flow of blood in an artery is controlled by the contraction and relaxation of the smooth muscle tissue. As the artery contracts, large amounts of blood are sent to an area. When the artery relaxes, the amount of blood flowing to the area is lessened. The outer wall of the artery contains flexible connective tissue. Connective tissue allows arteries to stretch and return to normal size with each heartbeat.

Your trip continues as you travel to smaller branching arteries. Where you go from here depends on many factors. For example, if a meal has recently been eaten, much of the blood will be directed toward the intestines to pick up food. If the body is exercising, the blood supply to the muscles will probably be increased. If there are a great many wastes in the blood, you may be sent to the liver, where certain wastes are changed into substances that are not poisonous to the body. Or you may travel to one of the kidneys, where other wastes are removed from the blood. No matter where you are sent, however, one thing is sure. You will find the brain one of your primary destinations. For whether it is thinking very hard or not, the brain always gets priority over any other part of the body.

Capillaries: The Unseen Pipelines

The artery network carries blood all over the body. But arteries cannot drop off or pick up any materials from body cells. Can you think of a reason why not? *Hint:* Recall the description of the structure of an artery. The walls of arteries are too thick for oxygen and food to pass through. In order for the blood to do its main task—delivering and picking up materials—it must pass from the thick-walled arteries into very thin-walled blood vessels. Extremely thin-walled blood vessels are called **capillaries.**

You will probably have a hard time squeezing through the capillary in which you now find yourself. Don't feel bad. In most capillaries, there is only enough room for the red blood cells to pass through in single file. It is here in the capillaries that the basic work of the blood—giving up oxygen and taking on wastes—is carried out. Food and oxygen leak through the thin walls of the capillaries and enter the body cells. Wastes pass out of the body cells and enter the blood in the capillaries. Other materials transported by the blood can also leave and enter body cells at this time.

Figure 4–8 *The three types of blood vessels that make up the circulatory system are the arteries, capillaries, and veins. What is the function of each type of blood vessel?*

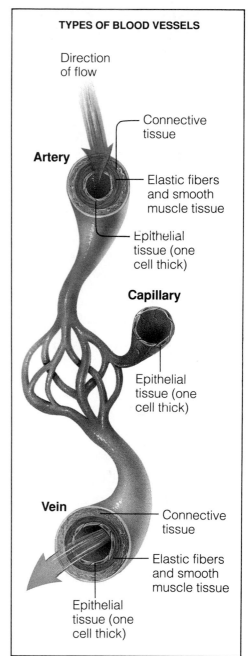

TYPES OF BLOOD VESSELS

Direction of flow

Artery

Connective tissue

Elastic fibers and smooth muscle tissue

Epithelial tissue (one cell thick)

Capillary

Epithelial tissue (one cell thick)

Vein

Connective tissue

Elastic fibers and smooth muscle tissue

Epithelial tissue (one cell thick)

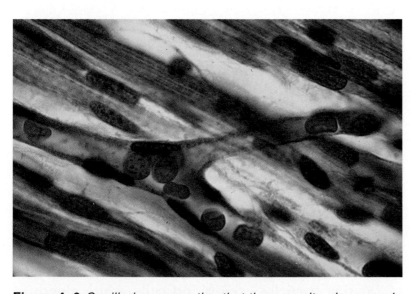

Figure 4–9 *Capillaries are so tiny that they permit only one red blood cell to squeeze through at a time. What is the function of a red blood cell?*

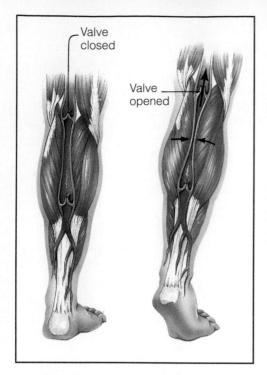

Figure 4–10 *Valves in the walls of veins prevent the backflow of blood and keep it moving in one direction—back to the heart. The contraction of nearby skeletal muscles such as those in the leg help the valves in performing this function.*

Focus on this question as you read.

▶ *What are the four main components of blood?*

Veins: Pipelines to the Heart

Once the work of giving up oxygen and taking on wastes is completed in the capillaries, your trip through the circulatory maze is just about over. Because the blood has given up its oxygen, it is dark red again. The blood now starts back to the heart, trickling from the capillaries into blood vessels called **veins.** Veins carry blood back to the heart.

As you might expect, veins are much larger than capillaries. And unlike arteries, veins have thinner walls as well as tiny one-way valves. These valves help to keep the blood from flowing backward.

4–2 Section Review

1. Trace the path of blood through the circulatory system.
2. List the four chambers of the heart.
3. Describe the three types of blood vessels.
4. Explain why the walls of the ventricles are much thicker than the walls of the atria.

Critical Thinking—*Relating Facts*
5. Why is it important that veins contain valves?

4–3 Blood—The River of Life

If you were to look at blood under a microscope, you would see that it is made up of tiny particles floating in a fluid. This makes blood a fluid tissue—one of the body's two fluid tissues. Lymph (LIHMF) is the other. Recall from Chapter 1 that a tissue is a group of cells that work together for a specific function.

The fluid portion of the blood is called **plasma.** And the tiny particles floating in the plasma are different types of blood cells and cell fragments—three different types, to be exact. **The three different types of floating particles—red blood cells, white blood cells, and platelets—and the plasma in which they float, are the four main components of blood.**

Plasma

Plasma is a yellowish fluid that is about 90 percent water. The remaining 10 or so percent is made up of sugars, fats, salts, gases, and plasma proteins. The plasma proteins, which have a number of vital functions, are divided into three groups. One group of plasma proteins helps to regulate the amount of water entering and leaving the blood. The second group includes antibodies, which are special proteins

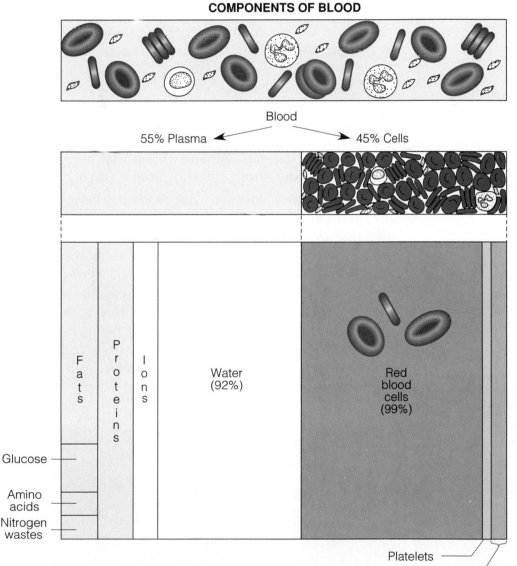

COMPONENTS OF BLOOD

Blood

55% Plasma   45% Cells

Fats

Proteins

Ions

Water (92%)

Glucose

Amino acids

Nitrogen wastes

Red blood cells (99%)

Platelets

White blood cells

Figure 4–11 *Blood is composed of a fluid portion called plasma and three different types of blood particles. Of what substance is plasma mainly composed?*

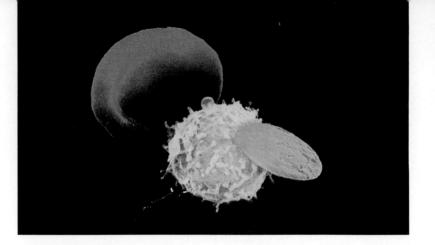

that help to fight off tiny invaders such as bacteria, viruses, and foreign substances. And the third group is responsible for blood clotting. The plasma also carries digested food, hormones (chemical messengers), and waste products.

Red Blood Cells

The most numerous cells in the blood are the **red blood cells.** Under a microscope, red blood cells look like round, flattened hats with thickened rims and flat centers—almost like tiny berets. The centers of these flexible red disks are so thin that they seem clear. This characteristic thinness enables red blood cells to bend at the center, a useful trick when trying to squeeze through a narrow capillary.

Red blood cells are produced in the bone marrow. A young red blood cell, like all living body cells, contains a nucleus. However, as the red blood cell matures, this nucleus grows smaller and smaller until it vanishes. Red blood cells pay a price for life

Figure 4–13 *In the bone marrow, a young red blood cell begins its life by filling up with hemoglobin and then getting rid of its nucleus (left). As the red blood cell moves into the bloodstream, it takes on its familiar disk shape (right).*

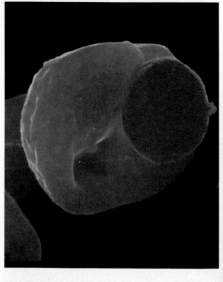

without a nucleus. They are very delicate and have a life span of only 120 days. Red blood cells in your body are at this moment dying at a rate of about 2 million per second. Fortunately, new red blood cells are being formed in the bone marrow at the same rate. When a red blood cell wears out or is damaged, it is broken down in the liver and the spleen, an organ just to the left of the stomach. So many red blood cells are destroyed in the spleen each day that this organ has been called the "cemetery" of red blood cells.

Have you ever heard people complain that they have "iron-poor" blood? That phrase refers to a shortage of an iron-containing protein called **hemoglobin** (HEE-muh-gloh-bihn), which is found in red blood cells. In fact, it is the buildup of hemoglobin in the red blood cells that forces out the nucleus. As blood flows through the lungs, oxygen in the lungs binds to hemoglobin in the red blood cells. As blood is transported throughout the body, oxygen is delivered to all body cells. Hemoglobin also helps to carry some carbon dioxide wastes back to the lungs.

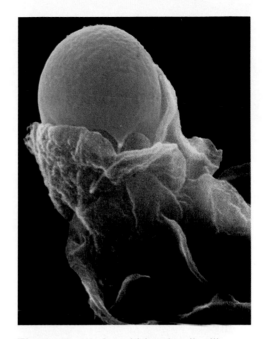

Figure 4–14 *A red blood cell will remain in the bloodstream for about 120 days, at which time the red blood cell will be digested by a white blood cell.*

White Blood Cells

Outnumbered almost 500 to 1 by red blood cells, **white blood cells** make up in their size and life span what they lack in their numbers. White blood cells are larger than red blood cells—some are even twice the size of red blood cells. And although certain kinds of white blood cells live for only a few hours, most can last for months or even years!

Figure 4–15 *White blood cells are larger than red blood cells (left). The main function of white blood cells is to protect the body against attack by invaders such as bacteria, which are the two small rod-shaped structures in this photograph (right).*

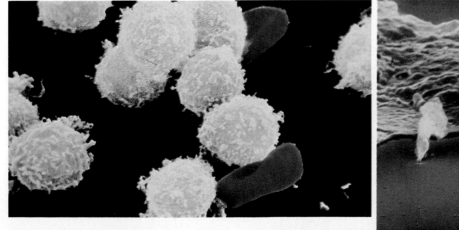

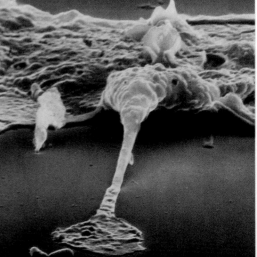

Like red blood cells, most white blood cells develop in the bone marrow. However, unlike red blood cells, white blood cells do not lose their nuclei when they mature. The main function of white blood cells is to protect the body against attack by tiny invaders such as bacteria, viruses, or other foreign substances. Quickly carried by blood to areas under seige, white blood cells can attack invaders in a variety of ways. Some white blood cells surround and digest the invaders. Others make antibodies. Still others produce special chemicals that help the body fight off disease. You will learn more about white blood cells and their role in protecting the body against invaders in Chapter 8.

Platelets

Have you ever wondered what happens inside a blood vessel when you cut yourself? Why doesn't all your blood ooze out of your body? The answer has to do with the third kind of blood particle, **platelets.** As soon as a blood vessel is cut, platelets begin to collect around the cut. When they touch the rough surface of the torn blood vessel, they burst apart, releasing chemicals that set off a series of reactions. One of these reactions produces a chemical called

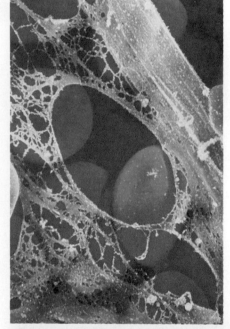

Figure 4–16 *When a blood vessel is punctured (bottom right), blood particles called platelets (bottom left) release chemicals that set off a series of reactions to help stop the flow of blood from the body. One of these reactions produces a threadlike chemical called fibrin that forms a net over the cut to trap blood particles and plasma (top).*

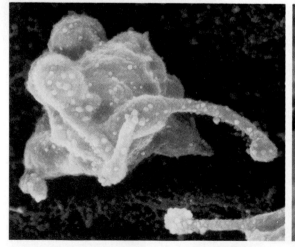

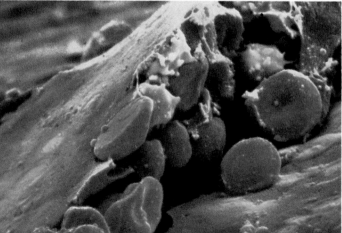

fibrin (FIGH-brihn). Fibrin gets its name from the fact that it weaves tiny fibers across the cut in the blood vessel. These fibers act as a net to trap blood cells and plasma. See Figure 4–16.

Eventually, the plasma hardens and forms a clot. Although you may not realize it, you are probably quite familiar with blood clots and the clotting process. Anytime your body forms a scab in response to a cut or a scrape, you are experiencing the clotting process. A scab, you see, is a clot that forms on the surface of your skin.

Platelets are so named because they resemble tiny plates. Actually, platelets are not cells but rather fragments of cells. They have no nucleus or color. These fragments break away from large cells, which are produced in bone marrow, and enter the bloodstream. There they remain for no more than ten days. But in that short time, these cell fragments may save a life by helping to form leak-sealing clots!

Blood Groups

In the seventeenth century, the French scientist Jean-Baptiste Denis tried to transfer blood from lambs to humans. This process of transferring blood from one body to another is called a transfusion.

Were Denis's transfusions successful? No, they were not. But it was not until 300 years later that the American scientist Karl Landsteiner learned why Denis's transfusions failed. By mixing the plasma of one person with the red blood cells of another, Landsteiner discovered that in some cases the two blended smoothly. However, in other cases, the cells did not mix but instead clumped (stuck together). As you might expect, such clumping inside the body clogs the capillaries—a dangerous and sometimes deadly situation. Landsteiner found that the clue to the behavior was the way human red blood cells containing certain proteins on their outer coats reacted to plasma containing different proteins. These proteins in the plasma are called clumping chemicals. Lansteiner identified the proteins in the red blood cells as A and B, and those in the plasma as anti A and anti B. Anti A and anti B were so named because of their reactions against the presence of protein A and/or protein B.

FIND OUT BY
WRITING

Blood Donating Center

Visit a local blood donating center. Interview a nurse or doctor to find out what techniques are used to screen potential donors. In a written report, include this information as well as what happens to the blood after it is donated.

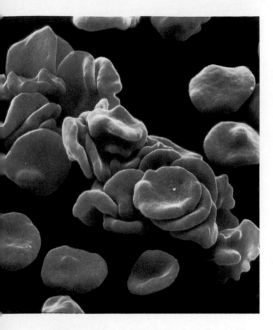

Figure 4–17 *When a person with group B blood receives a transfusion of, for example, group A blood, anti-A chemicals in the group B plasma recognize the group A red cells as foreign. As a result, the red blood cells from the group A blood will clump, or stick together, and possibly clog some of the body's important blood vessels.*

The presence or absence of protein A and/or protein B on the outer coat of every red blood cell in a person's blood determines the person's blood group. People with group A blood have red blood cells that contain protein A. People with group B blood have red blood cells that contain protein B. People with group AB blood have red blood cells that contain both proteins. And, as you might expect, people with group O blood have red blood cells that contain neither protein. On the basis of whether one or both of these proteins were present or absent in the blood, Landsteiner classified human blood into four basic groups, or types: A, B, AB, and O. He named this the ABO blood group.

Why are blood groups so important? Sometimes as a result of injury or illness a person loses quite a bit of blood and is too weak to produce more. In such instances, a blood transfusion is needed. But before a blood transfusion can be performed, blood from the donor (person giving blood) and the recipient (person receiving blood) must be tested to determine if the blood groups are compatible (similar to each other).

If blood groups that are not compatible are mixed, the red blood cells of the dissimilar blood group will clump together. Such clumps can cause fatal blockages in blood vessels. This is where the clumping chemicals (anti A and anti B) in the plasma come in. Refer to Figure 4–18 as you read about each blood group.

The plasma of people with group O blood, for example, contains both the anti-A and the anti-B chemical. The anti-A chemical causes red blood cells containing protein A to clump together, whereas the anti-B chemical causes red blood cells containing protein B to clump together. Thus people with group O blood can safely receive only group O blood. People with group A blood produce the anti-B chemical. The anti-B chemical causes red blood cells containing protein B to clump together. So people with group A blood can safely receive group A blood. The plasma of people with group AB blood does not contain either the anti-A or the anti-B chemical. Therefore, people with group AB blood can safely receive groups A, B, and O blood, as well as group AB blood.

ABO BLOOD SYSTEM

Blood Group	Proteins on Red Blood Cells	Clumping Chemicals in Plasma	Can Accept Transfusions from Group(s)
A	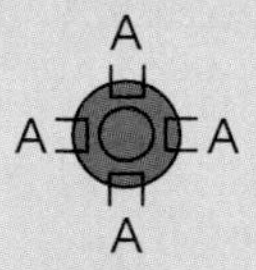 A⊏⊙⊐A (with A above and below)	Anti B	A, O
B	 B B ⊙ B B	Anti A	B, O
AB	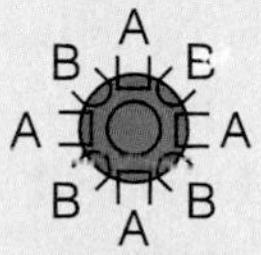 B A B A⊏⊙⊐A B A B	None	A, B, AB, O
O	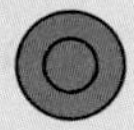 ⊙	Anti A Anti B	O

Figure 4–18 *Each blood group is characterized by the protein on the red blood cells and the clumping chemical in the plasma. What protein does group AB blood have?*

Several years after the discovery of the ABO blood group, Landsteiner and the American scientist Alexander Wiener discovered another group of about 18 proteins on the surface of human red blood cells. Because Landsteiner and Wiener first found this group of proteins in the rhesus monkey, they named the proteins the Rh blood group. You may be surprised to know that if a person has any one of the 18 Rh proteins, they are said to be Rh positive, or Rh^+. Those who do not have any of the Rh proteins in their blood are Rh negative, or Rh^-.

4–3 Section Review

1. List the four main components of whole blood.
2. What is plasma?
3. What is hemoglobin? What is its function?
4. Name, describe, and give the function of each of the three types of blood particles.

Critical Thinking—*Relating Facts*
5. Why do you think group O blood was once called the universal donor?

4–4 Cardiovascular Diseases

Today, people are living longer than they have at any time in the past. But as people's life expectancies have increased, so have the numbers of people who suffer from chronic disorders. Chronic disorders, which are lingering (lasting) illnesses, are a major health problem in the United States. Usually developing over a long time, chronic disorders also last a long time. In terms of numbers of people affected, **cardiovascular** (kahr-dee-oh-VAS-kyoo-ler) **diseases** are the most serious chronic disorders. **Cardiovascular diseases, such as atherosclerosis** (ath-er-oh-skluh-ROH-sihs) **and high blood pressure, affect the heart and the blood vessels.**

Atherosclerosis

One of the most common cardiovascular diseases in the United States today is **atherosclerosis.** Atherosclerosis is the thickening of the inner wall of an artery. For this reason, atherosclerosis is sometimes known as hardening of the arteries. This thickening occurs as certain fatlike substances in the blood, such as cholesterol, slowly collect on the artery wall. Gradually, the inside of the artery becomes narrower and narrower. As a result, the normal movement of the blood through the artery is reduced or, in some cases, totally blocked.

Figure 4–19 *A high-fat diet has caused fat droplets, which are the large yellow objects in this photograph, to become deposited on the inside wall of an artery. As more of these fat droplets accumulate inside the artery, it becomes narrower, causing the cardiovascular disease known as atherosclerosis.*

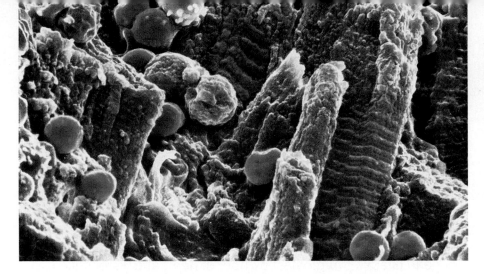

Figure 4–20 *A heart attack occurs when heart cells do not receive enough oxygen. Following a heart attack, dead muscle tissue replaces healthy muscle tissue. In this photograph, the dead muscle tissue appears brown, and the healthy muscle tissue appears red.*

If the flow of blood to a certain part of the body is reduced, the cells served by that blood may die. For example, if blood flow in the arteries of the heart is either partially or totally cut off, the heart cells will begin to die, and a heart attack may occur. If a blockage occurs in the arteries of the brain, a stroke may occur.

Atherosclerosis is often thought of as a chronic disorder affecting only older people. But it actually begins much earlier in life. By the age of 20, most people have some degree of atherosclerosis. For this reason, it is important to develop good eating habits and a proper exercise program to prevent atherosclerosis from becoming severe.

Many doctors suggest avoiding or limiting the intake of foods rich in fats and cholesterol. Such foods include red meats and dairy products. However, these foods are needed by the body in small amounts. So a person who wants to be sure that he or she gets these foods in their proper amounts should eat a sensibly balanced diet.

Even with proper diet and exercise, there is no guarantee that atherosclerosis and the problems associated with it can be avoided totally. Fortunately, more research and progress has occurred in the treatment of cardiovascular diseases than in any other area of medicine. For example, heart bypass operations have become commonplace. In this operation, a healthy blood vessel from the leg is removed and used to bypass damaged arteries serving the heart. In this way, blood flow to heart cells is increased.

FIND OUT BY
CALCULATING

Pumping Power

If the heart of an average person pumps about 9000 liters of blood daily, how much blood will be pumped in an hour? In a year?

Solving

Are Heart Attacks Influenced by the Time of Day?

Whenever blood flow to the arteries of the heart is partially or totally cut off, the heart cells begin to die and a heart attack may occur. Does the time of day have an effect on the frequency of heart attacks? To help answer this question, researchers have interviewed people who have had heart attacks. Some of the data from these interviews are contained in the accompanying graph.

Analyzing Graphs

1. Why do you think the graph was drawn in this particular shape?

2. Approximately how many heart attack patients are represented in this study?

3. At which hour(s) of the day did the greatest number of heart attacks occur? The least number of heart attacks?

4. Did heart attacks tend to occur more often in the morning, afternoon, or evening?

■ Based on the data, do you think there is a relationship between time of day and frequency of heart attacks? Explain your answer.

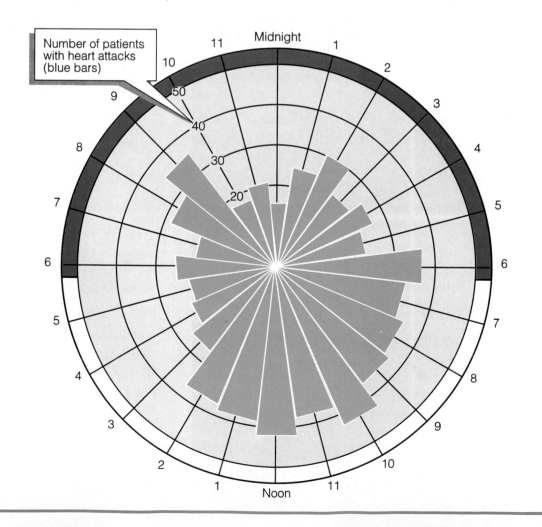

Unfortunately, even after having a bypass operation, some people may still have heart attacks. Until recently, doctors did not completely understand why this happened. Now a group of doctors have proposed an explanation for these mysterious heart attacks. The doctors think that the heart arteries have a memory. That is, the arteries themselves try to recreate the type of blood flow that they were used to when they were clogged. Not all doctors are convinced that this theory is correct. However, they do believe that the arteries-with-a-memory theory may shed some light on what is happening.

Hypertension

If you have ever used a garden hose, you know that you can increase the water pressure inside the hose in two ways. The first way is to turn up the flow of water at the faucet. Because there is more water, the water flows out of the hose with more force. The second way is to decrease the size of the opening of the nozzle. In this case, the water pressure in the hose is a result of both the force of the water rushing through the hose and the resistance of the walls of the hose to the flow of water.

You can compare the flow of water in the garden hose to the flow of blood in the blood vessels. Just as the force of the water through the hose is controlled by how much you turn up the faucet, the force of the blood through the blood vessels is controlled by the pumping action of the heart. And because blood vessel walls are similar to the walls of a hose, any change in the diameter of the blood vessel walls causes a change in blood pressure. As you can see, blood pressure is produced by the force of blood through the blood vessels and the resistance of the blood vessel walls to the flow of blood.

In order to measure a person's blood pressure, an instrument called a sphygmomanometer (sfihg-moh-muh-NAHM-uht-er) is used. This instrument actually records two readings—the first when the heart contracts and the second when the heart relaxes. Using these two measurements, the blood pressure measurement is expressed as a fraction—for example, 120/80, which is read as "120 over 80." The first number (120) is the measurement of the

CAREERS

Biomedical Engineer

A patient with a serious heart disease needs a heart transplant to survive. While waiting for a human donor to supply a heart, doctors might consider implanting a temporary artificial heart in the patient's body. The scientists who design and build body parts are **biomedical engineers.**

To learn more about biomedical engineering, write to the Biomedical Engineering Society, PO Box 2399, Culver City, CA 90231.

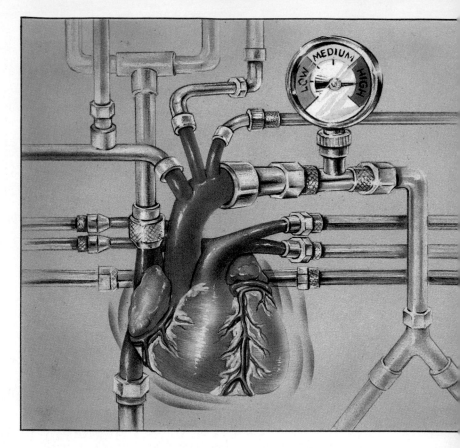

Figure 4–21 *Hypertension occurs when too much pressure builds up in the arteries. If this condition continues and goes untreated, damage to the walls of the arteries, to the heart, and to other organs may occur. What is another name for hypertension?*

blood pressure when the heart muscle contracts. The second number (80) is the measurement of the blood pressure when the heart muscle relaxes between beats. Why do you think the first number is larger than the second number?

Normally, blood pressure rises and falls from day to day and hour to hour. Sometimes, however, blood pressure goes up and remains above the normal level. This condition is called **hypertension,** or high blood pressure. The increased pressure makes the heart work harder and may cause leaks to develop in the blood vessels.

Because people with hypertension often have no obvious symptoms to warn them, hypertension is often called the "silent killer." This is why it is important for a person to have his or her blood pressure checked at least once a year. If a person does have hypertension, a doctor may suggest a few changes in the person's lifestyle. These changes may include watching one's weight, reducing the amount of salt in the diet, eating more sensibly, and exercising regularly. In some cases, medicines may also be taken to lower the blood pressure.

FIND OUT BY WRITING

Blood Pressure

Visit a library and look up information on what the two numbers of a blood pressure reading, such as 110/70, mean. In a written report, explain how a sphygmomanometer works. Explain what is meant by systole and diastole.

CONNECTIONS

It's All in a Heartbeat

When you think of *electric currents* (flows of electric charges), electrical appliances and wall outlets probably come to mind. So it may surprise you to learn that your body produces electric currents as well.

The heart, for example, produces electric currents in order to function properly. These electric currents are so powerful that they can be picked up by an instrument called an electrocardiograph. An electrocardiograph is one of a doctor's most important tools in helping to diagnose heart disorders. It translates the electric currents produced by the beating of the heart muscle into wavy lines on paper or a TV-type screen. This record of wavy lines is called an electrocardiogram, and it is often abbreviated as ECG or EKG.

An ECG is made by attaching electrodes (strips of metal that conduct electric currents) to the skin of a patient's chest, arms, and legs. The electrodes pick up the electric currents produced by the heartbeat and send them to an amplifier inside the electrocardiograph. An amplifier is a device that increases the strength of the electric currents. The amplified currents then flow through a fine wire that is suspended in a magnetic field. As the electric currents react with the magnetic field, they move the wire.

The wire's motion is eventually recorded on a moving paper chart in the form of an ECG. A normal heartbeat produces an ECG with a specific pattern of waves; heart disorders change the pattern. By examining the change in pattern, a doctor can identify the type of heart disorder.

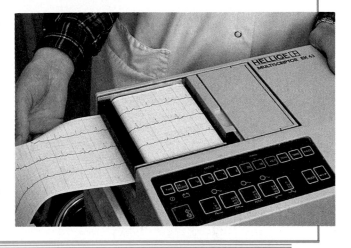

4–4 Section Review

1. What is a cardiovascular disease?
2. How do atherosclerosis and hypertension affect the circulatory system?

Connection—*Physical Education*

3. Predict two ways in which a regular exercise program could help a person with cardiovascular disease.

Laboratory Investigation

Measuring Your Pulse Rate

Problem

What are the effects of activity on pulse rate?

Materials *(per group)*

clock or watch with a sweep second
    hand
graph paper

Procedure

1. On a separate sheet of paper, construct a data table similar to the one shown here.
2. To locate your pulse, place the index and middle finger of one hand on your other wrist where it joins the base of your thumb. Move the two fingers slightly until you locate your pulse.
3. To determine your pulse rate, have one member of your group time you for 1 minute. During the 1 minute, count the number of beats in your pulse. Record this number in the data table.
4. Walk in place for 1 minute. Then take your pulse. Record the result.
5. Run in place for 1 minute. Again take your pulse. Record the result.
6. Sit down and rest for 1 minute. Take your pulse. Then take your pulse again after 3 minutes. Record the results in the data table.
7. Use the data to construct a bar graph that compares each activity and the pulse rate you determined.

Observations

1. What pulse rate did you record in step 3 of the Procedure? This is called your pulse rate at rest. How does your pulse rate at rest compare with those of the other members of your group? (Do not be alarmed if your pulse rate is somewhat different from those of other students. Individual pulse rates vary.)
2. What effect did walking have on your pulse rate? Running?
3. What effect did resting after running have on your pulse rate?

	Resting	Walking	Running	Resting After Exercise (1 min)	Resting After Exercise (3 min)
Pulse Rate					

Analysis and Conclusions

1. What conclusions can you draw from your data?
2. How is pulse rate related to heartbeat?
3. What happens to the blood supply to the muscles during exercise? How is this related to the change in pulse rate?

Study Guide

Summarizing Key Concepts

4–1 The Body's Transportation System

▲ The main task of the circulatory system is to transport materials through the body.

▲ Among the materials carried by the circulatory system are oxygen, carbon dioxide, food, wastes, disease-fighting cells, and chemical messengers.

4–2 Circulation in the Body

▲ Blood moves from the heart to the lungs and back to the heart. Then the blood travels to all the cells of the body and returns again to the heart.

▲ A wall of tissue called the septum divides the heart into a right and a left side.

▲ The two upper collecting chambers of the heart are called atria. The two lower pumping chambers of the heart are called ventricles. Valves between the atria and ventricles keep blood from flowing backward.

▲ Arteries carry blood away from the heart. Veins carry blood back to the heart. Capillaries connect the arteries and veins. Materials leave and enter the blood through the walls of the capillaries.

4–3 Blood—The River of Life

▲ The four main components of blood are plasma, red blood cells, white blood cells, and platelets.

▲ Plasma, which is mainly water, is the yellowish fluid portion of blood. Red blood cells, white blood cells, and platelets make up the solid portion of blood.

▲ Red blood cells contain hemoglobin, which binds to oxygen in the lungs and carries oxygen to body cells.

▲ White blood cells are part of the body's defense against invading bacteria, viruses, and other microscopic organisms.

▲ Platelets help form blood clots to stop the flow of blood when a blood vessel is cut.

▲ The two main blood group systems are the ABO blood group and the Rh blood group.

4–4 Cardiovascular Diseases

▲ The thickening of the inner lining of an artery is called atherosclerosis.

▲ Hypertension, or high blood pressure, makes the heart work harder and can cause damage to the blood vessels.

Reviewing Key Terms

Define each term in a complete sentence.

4–2 Circulation in the Body
atrium
ventricle
artery
capillary
vein

4–3 Blood—The River of Life
plasma
red blood cell
hemoglobin
white blood cell
platelet
fibrin

4–4 Cardiovascular Diseases
cardiovascular disease
atherosclerosis
hypertension

Chapter Review

Content Review

Multiple Choice

Choose the letter of the answer that best completes each statement.

1. The two upper heart chambers are called
   a. ventricles.   c. septa.
   b. atria.   d. valves.
2. Oxygen-rich blood from the lungs enters the heart through the
   a. left atrium.   c. left ventricle.
   b. right atrium.   d. right ventricle.
3. From the right atrium, blood is pumped to the
   a. brain.   c. right ventricle.
   b. lungs.   d. capillary network.
4. The heart chamber that works hardest is the
   a. right atrium.   c. left atrium.
   b. right ventricle.   d. left ventricle.
5. The blood vessels that carry blood back to the heart are the
   a. arteries.   c. capillaries.
   b. veins.   d. ventricles.
6. The cells that contain hemoglobin are the
   a. plasma.   c. white blood cells.
   b. platelets.   d. red blood cells.
7. Red blood cells are produced in the
   a. heart.   c. spleen.
   b. liver   d. bone marrow.
8. Platelets help the body to
   a. control bleeding. c. carry oxygen.
   b. fight infection.   d. do all of these.
9. People with group AB blood have
   a. both A and B proteins.
   b. neither A nor B proteins.
   c. both anti-A and anti-B clumping chemicals.
   d. none of these.
10. Cholesterol is a fatlike substance associated with
   a. hemoglobin.   c. atherosclerosis.
   b. fibrin.   d. salt.

True or False

If the statement is true, write "true." If it is false, change the underlined word or words to make the statement true.

1. The two lower heart chambers are called <u>ventricles.</u>
2. Oxygen-poor blood enters the heart through the <u>left</u> atrium.
3. The <u>capillaries</u> are the thinnest blood vessels.
4. <u>Veins</u> are blood vessels that contain valves.
5. An iron-containing protein in red blood cells is <u>hemoglobin.</u>
6. The type of blood cell that fights infection is the <u>white blood cell.</u>
7. When you cut yourself, a net of <u>hemoglobin</u> threads forms over the area to stop the blood flow.

Concept Mapping

Complete the following concept map for Section 4–1. Refer to pages H8–H9 to construct a concept map for the entire chapter.

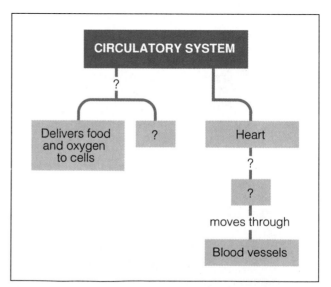

Concept Mastery

Discuss each of the following in a brief paragraph.

1. List and describe the four components of blood.
2. Explain why blood must be matched before a blood transfusion.
3. Explain why red blood cells are the most numerous of the blood cells.
4. What role do platelets have in the body?
5. Describe the path a single red blood cell would take through the heart.
6. Explain why oxygen-rich and oxygen-poor blood never mix in human beings.
7. Do all arteries carry oxygen-rich blood? Do all veins carry oxygen-poor blood? Explain your answer.

Critical Thinking and Problem Solving

Use the skills you have developed in the chapter to answer each of the following.

1. **Sequencing events** Starting at the right atrium, trace the path of the blood through the body.
2. **Relating facts** On a separate sheet of paper, add another column to Figure 4–18. Call it Can Donate Blood to Group(s). Fill in this column.
3. **Making predictions** Explain why chronic disorders are more of a problem today than they were 200 years ago. Predict how great a problem they will be in the future.
4. **Applying concepts** To determine whether a person has an infection, doctors often do blood tests in which they count white blood cells. Explain why such a count is useful.
5. **Making generalizations** To determine whether a person has abnormally high blood pressure, at least three blood-pressure measurements should be taken on three separate days at three different times. Explain why this is so.
6. **Relating cause and effect** How are the structures of an artery, a vein, and a capillary adapted to their functions?
7. **Making inferences** An artificial heart actually replaces only the ventricles of a human heart. Suggest a reason why replacing the atria is not necessary.
8. **Analyzing data** Suppose you are a doctor and have two patients who are in need of a transfusion. Patient 1 has group A blood and Patient 2 has group O blood. Which ABO blood group would you determine safe to give to each of your patients?
9. **Using the writing process** Develop an advertising campaign in favor of the reduction of animal fat in the diet. Make it a full media blitz!

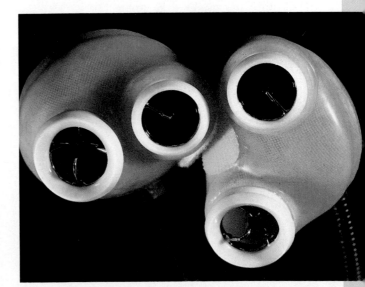

Respiratory and Excretory Systems

Guide for Reading

After you read the following sections, you will be able to

5–1 The Respiratory System

- Describe the structures of the respiratory system and give their functions.
- Explain how the lungs work.

5–2 The Excretory System

- Describe the structures of the excretory system and give their functions.

Watch a bicycle race on an autumn day and what do you see? You see cyclists pedaling hard and fast so that they can be the first to cross the finish line and win the race. What else do you notice about the cyclists? You probably see thin streams of sweat trickling down their faces and bodies. If you are close enough, you may see the quick, deep breaths that some cyclists take as they pedal. You may even see some cyclists drinking water from plastic bottles that are attached to their bicycles.

Why are the cyclists breathing so quickly and deeply? Where do the streams of sweat come from? What is the purpose of the water? In order to supply the cyclists with the energy they need to pedal their bicycles, the cells of their bodies must be provided with an enormous amount of oxygen. The oxygen must enter the cyclists' bodies, and an almost equal amount of wastes must be removed.

These vital functions are the tasks of two body systems: the respiratory system and the excretory system. Turn the page and begin to discover how these two systems perform their remarkable feats.

Journal *Activity*

You and Your World Have you ever had a sore throat or laryngitis? What did you do to make yourself feel better? Draw a sketch of yourself showing how you felt while you had either of these conditions.

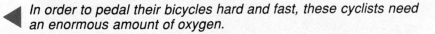

In order to pedal their bicycles hard and fast, these cyclists need an enormous amount of oxygen.

5–1 The Respiratory System

You cannot see, smell, or taste it. Yet it is as real as land or water. When it moves, you can feel it against your face. You can also see its effect in drifting clouds, quivering leaves, and pounding waves. It can turn windmills and blow sailboats across the sea. What is it?

If your answer is air, you are correct. Air is the mixture of gases that surrounds the Earth. The main gases that make up the air, or atmosphere, are nitrogen and oxygen. In fact, the atmosphere of the Earth is approximately 78 percent nitrogen and 21 percent oxygen. The remaining 1 percent is made of argon, carbon dioxide, water vapor (water in the form of an invisible gas), and trace gases—gases that are present in only very small amounts.

Humans, like all animals, need air to stay alive. You are breathing air right now. Every minute of the day you breathe in about 6 liters of air. Without this frequent intake of air, the cells in your body would soon die. Why? As you have just read, air contains the gas oxygen. It is oxygen that supports the energy-producing process that takes place in your cells. As a result of this process, your cells are able to perform all the various tasks that keep you alive. Try thinking of it this way. You know that a fire burns only if there is enough air—more specifically, enough oxygen in the air. Well, each body cell burns up the food it gets from the blood and releases the energy locked within the food only if it gets enough

Figure 5–1 *Like humans, plants, such as a heliconia, and animals, such as a barred leaf frog on the heliconia plant and a mountain gorilla, use the gases in the Earth's atmosphere to stay alive. What gases make up the Earth's atmosphere?*

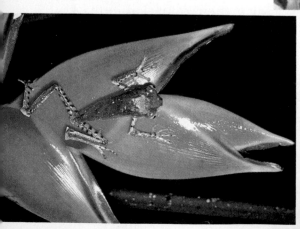

oxygen. The energy-releasing process that is fueled by oxygen is called **respiration.** In addition to energy, carbon dioxide and water are produced during respiration.

As you may recall from Chapter 3, the digestive system breaks down food into small particles so that the food can get inside body cells. And as you learned in Chapter 4, the circulatory system transports oxygen and food to body cells via the blood. Now you will discover how oxygen combines with food in the cells to produce the body's much-needed energy and the waste products carbon dioxide and water vapor. **The body system that is responsible for performing the task of getting oxygen into the body and removing carbon dioxide and water from the body is the respiratory system.** Figure 5–2 is a diagram of the respiratory system. You may wish to refer to it as you follow the passage of air from the time it enters the respiratory system to the time it leaves.

The Nose and Throat

Even the purest country air contains dust particles and bacteria; city air contains these materials as well as soot and exhaust fumes. But whether you breathe city air or country air, the air must travel through the nose, trachea (TRAY-kee-uh), and bronchi (BRAHNG-kee) in the few short seconds in which it moves from the environment to your lungs.

FIND OUT BY
DOING

What Is in Exhaled Air?

In the presence of carbon dioxide, a chemical called bromthymol blue solution turns green or yellow.

1. Fill two test tubes with 10 mL of water and a few drops of bromthymol blue solution.

2. Label the tubes A and B.

3. Using a straw, gently blow air into the liquid in test tube A.

4. Compare the test tubes. What happened in test tube A? In test tube B? Explain. What was the purpose of test tube B?

■ What characteristic of respiration is illustrated by this activity?

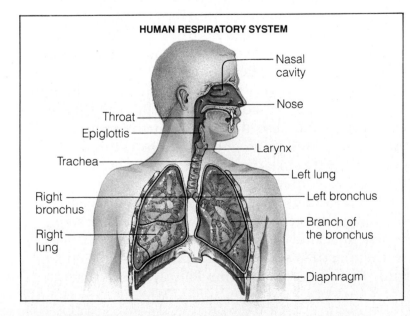

HUMAN RESPIRATORY SYSTEM

- Nasal cavity
- Nose
- Throat
- Epiglottis
- Larynx
- Trachea
- Left lung
- Right bronchus
- Left bronchus
- Branch of the bronchus
- Right lung
- Diaphragm

Figure 5–2 *The human respiratory system is composed of organs that work together to permit the exchange of oxygen and carbon dioxide with the environment. What is the name for the energy-releasing process that is fueled by oxygen?*

Figure 5–3 *When the spongy lungs are removed, the remaining parts of the respiratory system through which air passes resemble an upside-down tree.*

Figure 5–4 *A small piece of dirt that has invaded the body becomes trapped in the mucus and entangled in the cilia that line the bronchus.*

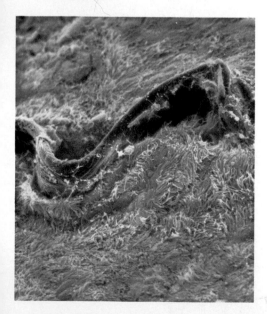

These structures are the channels through which air passes on its way to the lungs.

The air that you breathe usually enters the respiratory system through two openings in the **nose** called the nostrils. From there, the air flows into the nasal (pertaining to the nose) cavities, or two spaces in the nose. The cavities are separated by a wall of cartilage (flexible connective tissue) and bone. If the air is cold, as it may be in winter in certain locations, it is quickly heated by warm blood flowing through blood vessels in the lining of the nasal cavities. At the same time, slippery mucus in the nose moistens the air. This action keeps the delicate tissues of the respiratory system from drying out. In addition to moistening the air, the mucus traps unwanted dust particles and microscopic organisms such as bacteria and thereby cleanses the air.

It may surprise you to learn that the nose produces a fresh batch of mucus every 20 minutes or so. This amounts to about 0.9 liter of mucus per day. In order to get rid of the old mucus, billions of cilia (SIHL-ee-uh; singular: cilium), or tiny hairlike structures lining the nasal cavities, sweep the old mucus toward the esophagus and then into the stomach. The stomach, as you may recall from Chapter 3, gives off a digestive juice that contains hydrochloric acid. The hydrochloric acid destroys many of the bacteria that may have had the misfortune of becoming trapped in the mucus. Fortunately for you, some of the trapped particles never even make it past the nose. For one reason or another, they may begin to irritate the nasal cavities. Your body responds to this irritation by producing a little "explosion" to force the particles out. As you may already have guessed, this "explosion" is called a sneeze!

Because the nose warms, moistens, and filters the air coming into the body, it is healthier to take in air through the nose than through the mouth. However, if your nose is clogged because you have a cold, you have no other choice but to breathe through your mouth.

From the nose, the warmed, moistened, and filtered air moves into your throat, where it soon comes to a kind of fork in the road. One path leads to the digestive system. The other path leads deeper into the respiratory system. The structure that directs air down the respiratory path and food and water down the digestive path is the **epiglottis** (ehp-uh-GLAHT-ihs). As you may recall from Chapter 3, the epiglottis is a small flap of tissue that closes over the entrance to the rest of the respiratory system when you swallow. As a result, food and water are routed to the digestive system. When you breathe, the epiglottis opens, permitting air to enter the respiratory system.

The Trachea

Take a moment to gently run your finger up and down the front of your neck. Do you feel a bumpy tubelike structure? This tubelike structure is called the **trachea,** or windpipe. The bumps on the trachea are actually rings, or bands, of cartilage. The rings of cartilage make the trachea flexible enough so that you can bend your neck, yet rigid enough so that it keeps an open passageway for air. The rings of cartilage are held together by smooth muscle tissue. The smooth muscle tissue enables the diameter of the trachea to increase, thus allowing large amounts of air to move more easily along its path. Such action is especially helpful when you have to gulp down large amounts of air after doing some particularly strenuous work.

As the air moves down into the trachea, mucus along the inner lining traps dust particles and bacteria that have managed to get past the nose. These particles are swept out of the trachea and up to the mouth or nose by cilia that line the passageway.

Figure 5–5 *The larynx, which is located at the top of the trachea, contains the vocal cords (left). Notice that the vocal cords are made of two small folds of tissue that are stretched across the larynx (right). What is the function of the vocal cords?*

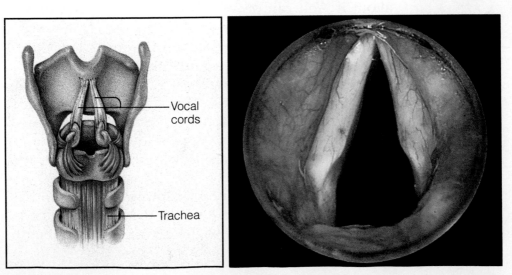

Vocal cords

Trachea

Sometimes, however, some of these particles may collect in the trachea, causing an irritation. This irritation triggers a response similar to a sneeze, or the tiny explosion that occurs in the nose. In the trachea, however, the explosion is called a cough. Air forced out of the trachea during a cough can sometimes reach speeds of up to 160 kilometers per hour!

Located at the top of the trachea is a box-shaped structure called the **larynx** (LAR-ihngks), or voice box. The larynx is made up of pieces of cartilage, one of which juts out from the neck rather noticeably. You know this piece of cartilage by the name Adam's apple. Everyone has an Adam's apple, although it tends to be more noticeable in males than in females. This is because the larynxes of males are generally larger, and also because males have less fat in their necks to hide the Adam's apple from view.

The structures in the larynx that are responsible for producing your voice are the **vocal cords.** The vocal cords are two small folds of tissue that are stretched across the larynx. These folds have a slit-like opening between them. When you talk, muscles in the larynx tighten, narrowing the opening. Then as air from your lungs rushes past the tightened vocal cords, it causes the vocal cords to vibrate. As they vibrate, they cause the air particles in the slit-like opening between them to vibrate. The result of this vibration is a sound: your voice.

The way that your vocal cords, muscles, and lungs work to produce sound is so well organized that you use them in combination without really thinking about it. You can prove this to yourself by trying the following activity. Speak in a high voice. Now speak in a low voice. Do you hear a difference? Do you know what you did to produce that difference? When you spoke in a high voice, you tightened your vocal cords, causing them to vibrate more rapidly and produce a higher sound. The reverse happened when you spoke in a low voice—you relaxed your vocal cords, causing them to vibrate more slowly and produce a lower sound.

The degree of highness or lowness of a sound is known as its pitch. The pitch of the human voice is determined by the size of the larynx and the length

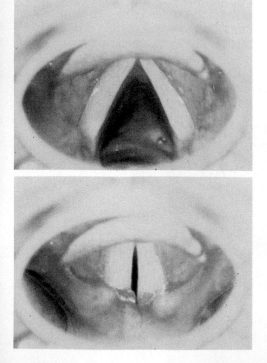

Figure 5–6 *These photographs show the vocal cords at work. When you breathe, the vocal cords move apart, allowing air to pass to and from the lungs (top). When you speak, the vocal cords move closer together (bottom).*

Figure 5–7 *In order to sing effortlessly, opera singers draw in a full breath by expanding the lower ribs and lowering the diaphragm. When babies cry, they use their diaphragms the way opera singers do. What is the diaphragm?*

of the vocal cords. Female voices are usually of a higher pitch than male voices because female vocal cords are shorter than male vocal cords. (The shorter the vocal cords, the more rapidly they vibrate and the higher the pitch of the sound they produce.) Actually, the vocal cords of males and females are about the same size until the teenage years. During that time, the larynxes of males begin to grow larger, causing their voices to become lower in pitch.

The vocal cords, muscles, and lungs are not alone in producing the sounds of your voice. They are helped by your lips, teeth, and tongue. In addition, vibrations of the walls in the nasal cavities give your voice its special quality. You may be more aware of the quality of your voice—or a change in the quality—when you have a cold and your nasal cavities are clogged. At such a time, your voice tends to sound different—a difference often described as nasal.

The Lungs

Having moved through the nose and the trachea, the incoming air is as clean, moist, and warm as it is going to get. Now the air reaches a place where the trachea branches into two tubes—the left and right **bronchi** (BRAHNG-kee; singular: bronchus). The left bronchus enters the left lung, and the right bronchus enters the right lung.

Once inside the **lungs,** which are the main organs of the respiratory system, the bronchi divide. They continue to divide again and again, becoming narrower each time, until they are tiny tubes the size of twigs. At the ends of these tiny tubes are hundreds of round sacs that resemble clusters of

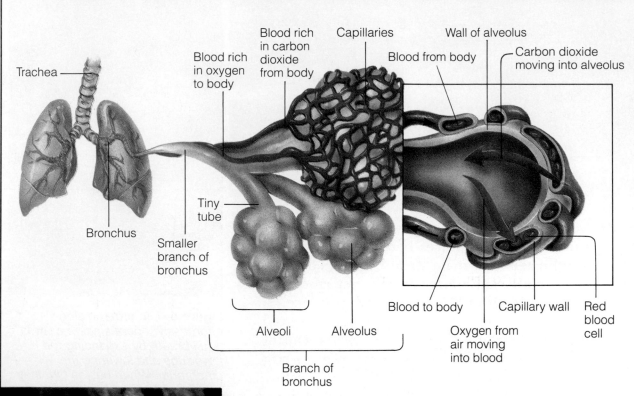

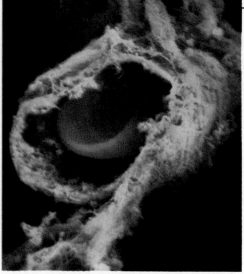

Figure 5–8 *Oxygen and carbon dioxide are exchanged between the blood in the capillaries and the air in the alveoli, or tiny air sacs. In the photograph, a single red blood cell squeezes through a capillary surrounding an alveolus that is less than 0.001 centimeter away.*

grapes. These round sacs are called **alveoli** (al-VEE-uh-ligh; singular: alveolus, al-VEE-uh-luhs). Alveoli are the gateways for oxygen into the body.

As you can see from Figure 5–8, each alveolus is surrounded by a network of tiny blood vessels called capillaries. It is here in the body's 600 million alveoli that the lungs perform their function—the exchange of oxygen and carbon dioxide in the blood. Let's take a closer look at this process.

When air enters the alveoli, oxygen in the air seeps through the thin walls of the tiny sacs into the surrounding capillaries. As blood slowly moves through the capillaries, it picks up the oxygen and carries it to cells throughout the body. When the oxygen-rich blood reaches the cells, it releases the oxygen. At the same time, the blood picks up the carbon dioxide produced by the cells during respiration and returns it to the alveoli.

Because air is rarely in the lungs for more than a few seconds, the exchange of gases (oxygen and carbon dioxide) must take place quickly. This is where the treelike structure of the respiratory system comes in. The branching structure enables more than 2400 kilometers of airways to fit into the small area called the chest cavity. (If these airways were placed end to end, they would extend from Los Angeles, California, to Minneapolis, Minnesota.) As a result, a great deal of oxygen can seep out of the lungs, and an equal amount of carbon dioxide can seep back in in a very short time.

How You Breathe

On the average, you breathe in and out about 1 liter of air every 10 seconds. This rate, however, increases when you are playing or working hard—just as the cyclists that you read about at the beginning of this chapter were doing. Their breathing rates probably jumped to triple the normal breathing rate of 12 to 14 times a minute. Their depth of breathing increased, too.

When you are about to inhale, or breathe in, muscles attached to your ribs contract and lift the rib cage up and outward. At the same time, a dome-shaped muscle called the **diaphragm** (DIGH-uh-fram) contracts and flattens out. The actions of these muscles make your chest expand. The expansion of your chest results in more room in the lungs for air. So the same amount of air now occupies a larger space. This causes the pressure (a force that acts over a certain area) of air to decrease. As a result, the air pressure in your lungs becomes lower than the air pressure outside your body. The difference in pressure causes air to rush into your lungs.

When you exhale, or breathe out, the diaphragm relaxes and returns to its normal dome-shaped position. This action causes the space inside the chest to decrease. As it does, the air pressure in the chest cavity increases. This increase in pressure causes the lungs to get smaller, forcing air out of the lungs. And so you exhale.

Because the diaphragm is a skeletal muscle, its ability to contract and relax is under your control. (You may recall from Chapter 2 that skeletal muscle is called voluntary muscle.) Sometimes, however, the diaphragm contracts involuntarily. This usually occurs because the nerves (bundles of fibers that carry messages throughout the body) that control the diaphragm become irritated by eating too fast or by some other condition. Then, as you inhale air,

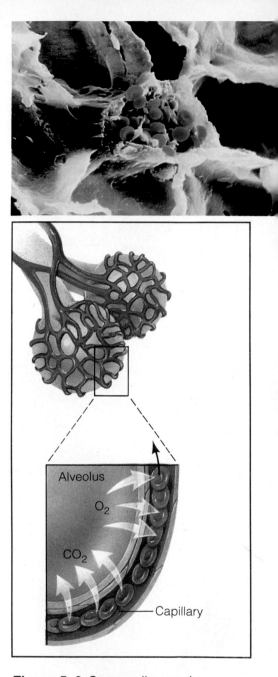

Figure 5–9 Surrounding each alveolus is a network of capillaries. As blood flows through the capillaries, oxygen moves out of the alveolus into the blood. Carbon dioxide moves in the opposite direction—out of the blood into the alveolus. The photograph shows a section of a lung in which you can see a capillary containing red blood cells surrounded by alveoli.

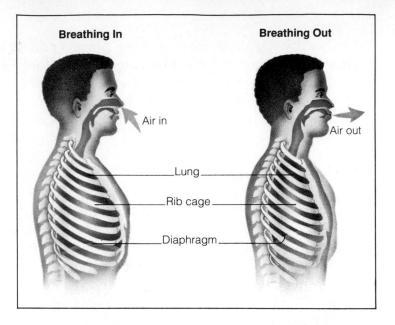

Figure 5–10 *When you breathe in, the muscles attached to your ribs contract and lift the rib cage up and outward, allowing more room in the lungs for air. When you breathe out, the muscles attached to your ribs relax and lower the rib cage, allowing less room in the lungs for air. What role does the diaphragm have in breathing?*

Breathing In   Breathing Out

Air in

Air out

Lung

Rib cage

Diaphragm

Figure 5–11 *A swimmer has to gulp for air so that his lungs can deliver oxygen to every cell in his body quickly and frequently. On Jupiter, which has an atmosphere consisting of about 85 percent hydrogen and 15 percent helium, he would not be able to survive.*

the space between the vocal cords snaps shut with a clicking sound. You know this clicking sound as a hiccup!

You have probably had lots of experience with hiccups. And you have probably tried almost every remedy to get rid of them—from drinking a glass of water without stopping for air to holding your breath until they cease. These methods may help somewhat because they reduce the oxygen supply and increase the carbon dioxide level of your body. This condition can cause the involuntary contractions of the diaphragm muscle to stop, thereby bringing your hiccups to a much-welcomed end.

5–1 Section Review

1. What is the function of the respiratory system?
2. What is respiration?
3. What are the structures of the respiratory system? What is the function of each?
4. Explain how the exchange of oxygen and carbon dioxide occurs in the lungs.
5. How do you breathe?

Connection—*You and Your World*

6. When you have laryngitis, or an inflammation of the larynx, you have a hoarse voice, or no voice at all. How might cheering too enthusiastically at a football game cause laryngitis?

CONNECTIONS

How a Lie Detector Gives Its Verdict

You have probably seen television courtroom dramas in which the defendant was found guilty solely on the basis of the results of a lie detector test. While being entertained by the television program, you probably never thought that its story line had anything to do with your study of life science. How wrong you were! A lie detector, or polygraph, is an instrument that works on the following idea: People who tell a lie become nervous. Their nervousness increases their blood pressure, pulse and breathing rates, and makes them sweat.

Actually, the lie detector is a combination of three different instruments. The results of each instrument are recorded by a pen that makes ink lines on moving graph paper.

One of the instruments is called the *cardiosphygmometer.* It detects changes in blood pressure (pressure of blood in the arteries) and pulse rate (beating of the arteries caused by the pumping action of the heart). This information is picked up by a cufflike device that is placed over the upper arm. This device is similar to the one your doctor uses when checking your blood pressure.

The second instrument, called the *galvanometer,* monitors the flow of a tiny electric current (flow of charged particles) through the skin. When the skin is moist, as it is with perspiration, it will conduct the electric current better. Small electrodes are taped to the hand to record this activity.

The third instrument is called the *pneumogram,* which records breathing patterns. It consists of a rubber tube that is strapped across the chest. Within the tube are instruments that measure changes in breathing patterns.

One drawback to the use of lie detectors is that some people get so nervous about taking the test that they may appear to lie even though they are telling the truth. And in rare instances, some people may be able to control their emotions so well that they can lie without affecting the results of the test. Although lie detectors are seen in television dramas, their results are generally not considered admissible in real-life courtrooms.

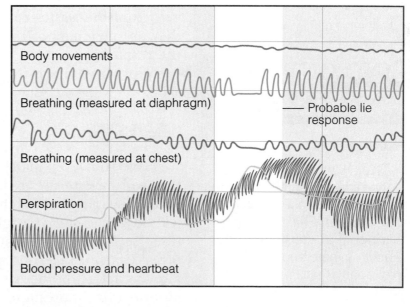

Body movements

Breathing (measured at diaphragm)

— Probable lie response

Breathing (measured at chest)

Perspiration

Blood pressure and heartbeat

5–2 The Excretory System

When the sixteenth-century English poet John Donne wrote that "No man is an island, entire of itself," he was actually talking about the human mind and spirit. However, this phrase can also be used to describe the human body: No human body can function without help from its surroundings. For example, your body must obtain food, water, and oxygen from its surroundings and get rid of wastes that may poison you. In order to do this, three body systems work together to provide a pathway for materials to enter and leave the body.

You have already learned about two of these systems: the digestive system and the respiratory system. The digestive system is the pathway for food and water to enter the body. The respiratory system enables oxygen to enter and carbon dioxide and water vapor to leave the body. The third system is the excretory (EHKS-kruh-tor-ee) system. **The excretory system provides a way for various wastes to be removed from the body.** These wastes include excess water and salts, carbon dioxide, and urea (a nitrogen waste). The process by which these wastes are removed from the body is called **excretion.**

You have just read about one of the organs of the excretory system: the lungs. Because the lungs get rid of the wastes carbon dioxide and water vapor, they are members of the excretory system as well as the respiratory system. The remaining organs of the excretory system are the kidneys, the liver, and the skin.

The Kidneys

Have your ever made spaghetti? If so, you know that you have to use a strainer to separate the cooked spaghetti from the cooking water or else you will be eating soggy spaghetti! The strainer acts as a filter, separating one material (spaghetti) from the other (water). Like the spaghetti strainer, the **kidneys** act as the body's filter. In doing so, the kidneys filter wastes and poisons from the blood.

The kidneys, which are the main organs of the excretory system, are reddish brown in color and

FIND OUT BY READING

Reading Poetry

The first line of John Donne's poem entitled "Meditation XVII" was quoted in this chapter. Find a copy of this poem in the library and read it. Is there another line in this poem that is familiar to you?

shaped like kidney beans. There is one kidney on each side of the spinal column just above the waist. Although each kidney is not much bigger than an extra-large bar of soap, together they receive and filter almost 1 liter of blood per minute, pumped into them from the aorta (the body's largest artery).

The actual filtering process takes place within the kidney's millions of microscopic chemical-filtering factories called **nephrons** (NEHF-rahnz). As you can see from Figure 5–12, each nephron is made up of a complex network of tubes enclosed in an even more complex network of capillaries.

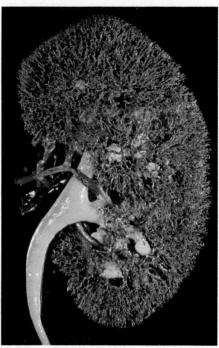

Figure 5–12 *The photograph shows the large number of blood vessels in a kidney. Some of the structures of a kidney as well as the structure of a microscopic nephron are shown in the illustrations.*

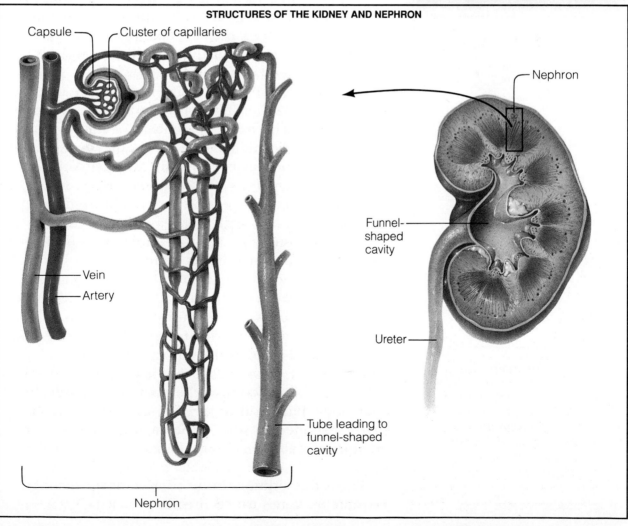

STRUCTURES OF THE KIDNEY AND NEPHRON

Capsule
Cluster of capillaries
Nephron
Vein
Artery
Funnel-shaped cavity
Ureter
Tube leading to funnel-shaped cavity
Nephron

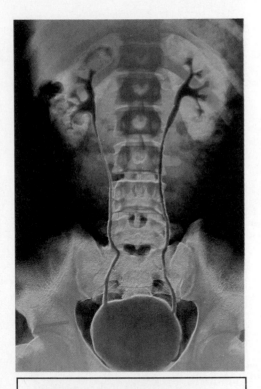

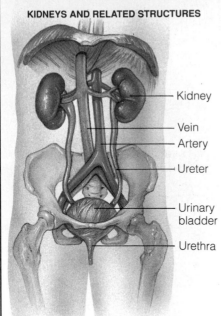

KIDNEYS AND RELATED STRUCTURES

Kidney

Vein
Artery

Ureter

Urinary
bladder

Urethra

Figure 5–13 *The main organs of the excretory system are the two kidneys, which are the green bean-shaped organs in this color-enhanced X-ray. Use the illustration to locate the other excretory organs in the X-ray. What is the function of the kidneys?*

As blood pours into the kidney through an artery, it travels through smaller and smaller arteries. Finally, it enters a bundle of capillaries. Here, materials such as water, salts, urea, and nutrients pass from the capillaries into a cup-shaped part of the nephron called the **capsule.** What remains in the capillaries are large particles such as proteins and blood cells. The capsule then carries the filtered material (water, salts, urea, and nutrients) to a tiny twisting tube. To picture this part of the nephron (the capsule and tiny tube), try the following: Clench one of your hands into a fist and then cup the other hand around your fist. Your clenched fist is the bundle of capillaries and your cupped hand is the capsule. The arm to which the cupped hand is attached is the tiny twisting tube.

As the filtered material moves through the tiny tube in the nephron, the nutrients, salts, and most of the water that passed through the capillaries are reabsorbed, or taken back, into the blood. If this reabsorption process did not take place, the body would soon lose most of the water, salts, and nutrients that it needs to survive.

The liquid that remains in the tiny tube after reabsorption has taken place is called urine. Urine is mostly water. The exact percentage of water in a person's urine varies depending on the person's health, what the person has been eating and drinking, and how much the person has been exercising. Generally, urine is about 96 percent water. The remaining 4 percent are wastes, such as urea and excess salts.

Suppose you drink a lot of liquid on a particular day. You will produce more urine than you normally would, and it will contain more water. If, on the other hand, you were to eat rather salty foods, you would produce less urine, and it would contain less water. So the amount of water or salts that you take into your body affects the amount of urine and the water content of the urine that is excreted. In this way, your kidneys control the amount of liquid in your body. Put another way, the amount of water that is excreted in your urine each day equals the amount of water that you take into your body each day.

From the kidneys, urine trickles down through two narrow tubes called **ureters** (yoo-REET-erz). The

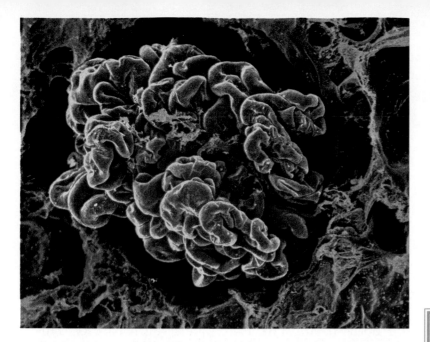

Figure 5–14 *The cluster, or bundle, of capillaries in the middle of this photograph carry waste-laden blood into the nephron. Here, wastes leave the blood through the walls of the capillaries and enter the nephron's cup-shaped capsule.*

ureters carry the urine to a muscular sac called the **urinary bladder.** The urinary bladder can store up to 470 milliliters of urine before releasing it from the body through a small tube called the **urethra** (yoo-REE-thruh).

Other Excretory Organs

In addition to the kidneys and the lungs, two other organs of the body play a major role in excretion. These organs are the liver and the skin.

THE LIVER You may recall from Chapter 3 that the **liver** plays a role in the digestion of foods. But did you also know that the liver helps to remove wastes from the body? The liver performs this function by filtering materials from the blood as the blood passes through the liver. One of the substances the liver removes from the blood is excess amino acids. You may recall from Chapter 3 that amino acids are the building blocks of protein. These amino acids are broken down in the liver to form urea, which, as you just learned, is a part of urine.

The liver also converts the hemoglobin from worn-out red blood cells into substances such as bile, which plays a role in the breakdown of fats. In addition, the liver cleanses the blood by removing and digesting most of the bacteria that enter from the large intestine.

CAREERS

Respiratory Therapy Technician

Because breathing is vital to life, any person who has difficulty breathing must be given help immediately. One group of trained professionals who help people with breathing difficulties are **respiratory therapy technicians.**

For more information about this exciting and challenging field, write to the American Association for Respiratory Care, 11030 Ables Lane, Dallas, TX 75229.

FIND OUT BY DOING

Close at Hand

1. Using a hand lens, examine the skin on your hand.

2. Identify the epidermis and pores on the ridges of the skin.

3. Place a plastic glove on your hand and remove it after 5 minutes. Look at your hand. Describe what happened to your hand. If you placed your hand against a chalkboard and then quickly removed it, what would you see?

■ How does this activity illustrate a function of the skin?

4. Now place the tip of your right forefinger (finger nearest the thumb) on an ink pad. Move your finger from left to right with a slight rolling motion.

5. Immediately remove your finger from the ink pad and place it on an index card using the same rolling motion. Compare your fingerprints with those of your classmates. Are they alike? How are they different? Do you notice any patterns that are similar in some of the fingerprints?

■ Are any two fingerprints ever exactly alike?

THE SKIN The remaining excretory organ is the **skin.** Are you surprised to learn that the skin is considered an organ? If so, you will be even more surprised to know that the skin is sometimes thought of as the largest organ of the human body. It covers an area of 1.5 to 2 square meters in an average person. This is about the size of a small area rug. It varies in thickness from under 0.5 millimeter on the eyelids to about 6 millimeters on the soles of the feet. The skin is made up of two main layers: the **epidermis** and the **dermis**. The word *-dermis* means skin. The prefix *epi-* indicates that the epidermis is on, or over, the dermis.

The top layer, or epidermis, contains mostly dead, flattened cells that are constantly shed from the body. If you have ever had a slight case of dandruff (flakes of skin from the scalp), then you have seen groups of these dead cells firsthand. If you are wondering why you still have skin even though its cells are constantly being shed from your body, wonder no more. The answer, you see, is that the innermost layer of the epidermis contains the living and active cells that produce more cells. As new cells are produced, they are pushed nearer the surface of the skin, where they become the outer layer of cells—soon to flatten and die.

Any experience you may have had accidentally jabbing your skin with a sharp object (such as a needle or a thorn) will tell you something else about the epidermis. Did you feel pain? Did you bleed? Probably not. The epidermis does not contain any nerves or blood vessels.

Unlike the epidermis, the dermis, or bottom layer of the skin, contains nerves and blood vessels. The dermis is also thicker than the epidermis. In addition, the upper part of the dermis contains small, fingerlike structures that are similar to the villi in the small intestine. Because the epidermis is built on top of these structures, it has an irregular outline that forms ridges. These ridges, in turn, form patterns on the fingertips, on the palms of the hands, and on the soles of the feet. On the fingertips, these patterns are more commonly known as fingerprints. Every human has a unique set of fingerprints. And although the fingerprints of identical twins are similar, no two fingertips are the same.

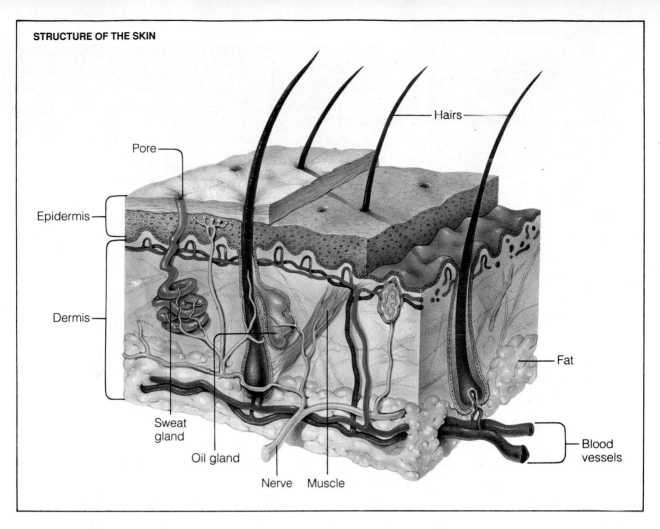

- Hairs
- Pore
- Epidermis
- Dermis
- Sweat gland
- Oil gland
- Nerve
- Muscle
- Fat
- Blood vessels

Thus fingerprints provide a foolproof way of identifying everyone, including those people who have lost their memories because of an injury or illness.

The skin also contains hair, nails, and sweat and oil glands. Hair and nails are formed from skin cells that first become filled with a tough, fiberlike protein

Figure 5–15 *The skin, which is the body's largest organ, is made of two main layers. The top layer is called the epidermis, and the bottom layer is called the dermis. In which layer of the skin would you find the blood vessels?*

Figure 5–16 *A close-up of a fingertip (right) shows the pattern of ridges that form a fingerprint. An even closer view shows the individual ridges (left).*

Figure 5–17 *Hair and nails are formed from skin cells that first become filled with a tough, fiberlike protein and then die. Nails grow at an average rate of 0.5 to 1.2 millimeters per day. Imagine how long it took for the man in the photograph to grow his nails!*

and then die. Sweat glands are coiled tubes that connect to pores, or openings, in the surface of the skin. Sweat glands help the body get rid of excess salts, urea, and about 0.5 liter of water every day. Together, these materials form a liquid called sweat, or perspiration.

Perspiration not only rids the body of wastes, it also helps to regulate body temperature. It does this by evaporating from body surfaces. Let's see how. When the temperature of your surroundings rises, or when you work really hard, you perspire more. As the sweat reaches the surface of the skin, it begins to evaporate, or change from a liquid to a gas. The process of evaporation requires heat. That heat comes from your body. Because the body loses heat, the evaporation of sweat is a cooling process—and your skin feels cool. During and after a strenuous activity, such as mowing the lawn or playing a game of soccer, you may sweat away up to 10 liters of liquid in a 24-hour period alone! However, as you may

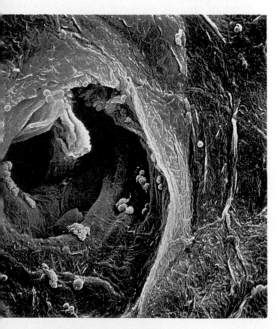

Figure 5–18 *One of the 3 million sweat glands contained in the skin of an adult is shown in this photograph. The tiny green round objects inside the sweat gland are bacteria. What is the function of the sweat glands?*

PROBLEM Solving

How Do I Explain This?

From what you have learned about the respiratory and excretory systems, try your hand at developing some explanations for the following situations.

Relating Concepts

1. A humidifier is a device that adds moisture to the surrounding air. A humidifier would be useful to have in a room or building during dry winter weather.

2. A dehumidifier removes moisture from the surrounding air. This device can make a person feel more comfortable during humid summer weather.

3. At higher altitudes, the air is less dense (packed closely together) than it is at lower altitudes. Mountain climbers and athletes who train at higher elevations often have difficulty breathing at these elevations.

remember from the story at the beginning of this chapter, sweating makes you thirsty. You drink lots of water and thereby replenish the water lost by sweating.

5–2 Section Review

1. What is the function of the excretory system? What structures enable it to perform this function?
2. What is urea? How is it formed?
3. Name and describe the two layers of the skin.
4. Why do you sweat?

Critical Thinking—*Applying Concepts*

5. Suppose that it is a very hot day and you drink a lot of water. Would your urine contain more or less water than it would on a cooler day? Explain your answer.

Laboratory Investigation

Measuring the Volume of Exhaled Air

Problem

What is the volume of exhaled air?

Materials *(per group)*

glass-marking pencil	paper towel
spirometer	graduated cylinder
red vegetable coloring	

Procedure ⚗

1. Obtain a spirometer. A spirometer is an instrument that is used to measure the volume of air that the lungs can hold.
2. Fill the plastic bottle four-fifths full of water. Add several drops of vegetable coloring to the water. With the glass-marking pencil, mark the level of the water.
3. Reattach the rubber tubing as shown in the diagram.
4. Cover the lower part of the shorter length of rubber tubing with the paper towel by wrapping the towel around it. This is the part of the rubber tubing that you will need to place your mouth against. **Note:** *Your mouth should not come in contact with the rubber tubing itself, only with the paper towel.*
5. After inhaling normally, exhale normally into the shorter length of rubber tubing.
6. The exhaled air will cause an equal volume of water to move through the other length of tubing into the graduated cylinder. Record the volume of this water in milliliters in a data table.
7. Pour the colored water from the cylinder back into the plastic bottle.
8. Repeat steps 3 through 7 two more times. Record the results in your data table. Calculate the average of the three readings.

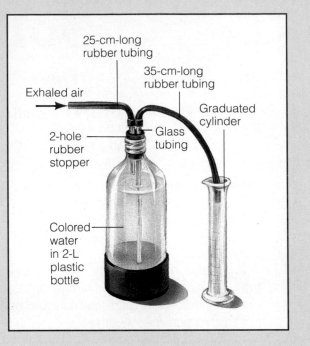

9. Run in place for 2 minutes and exhale into the rubber tubing. Record the volume of the water in the graduated cylinder.
10. Rest for a few minutes until your breathing returns to normal. Then repeat step 9 two more times and record the results. Calculate the average of the three readings.

Observations

How does your average volume of exhaled air before exercise compare to your average volume of exhaled air after exercise?

Analysis and Conclusions

1. Why is it important to measure the volume of exhaled air three times?
2. Explain how exercise affects the volume of exhaled air.
3. **On Your Own** Describe how you could determine the volume of air you exhale in a minute.

Summarizing Key Concepts

5–1 The Respiratory System

▲ Respiration is the combining of oxygen and food in the body to produce energy and the waste gases carbon dioxide and water vapor.

▲ The main task of the respiratory system is to get oxygen into the body and carbon dioxide out of the body.

▲ The respiratory system consists of the nose, throat, larynx, trachea, bronchi, and lungs. The bronchi divide into smaller tubes, which end inside the lungs in clusters of alveoli.

▲ The larynx, or voice box, contains the vocal cords. These structures are responsible for producing the human voice.

▲ The exchange of oxygen and carbon dioxide occurs in the alveoli, which are surrounded by a network of capillaries.

▲ Breathing consists of inhaling and exhaling. These motions are produced by movements of the diaphragm.

5–2 The Excretory System

▲ The excretory system is responsible for removing various wastes from the body.

▲ Excretion is the process by which wastes are removed.

▲ The principal organs of the excretory system are the kidneys.

▲ Each kidney contains millions of microscopic chemical filtration factories called nephrons.

▲ Within a nephron, substances such as nutrients, water, salt, and urea are filtered out of the blood. These substances pass into the cup-shaped part of the nephron called the capsule. Much of the water and nutrients is reabsorbed into the bloodstream. The liquid that remains in the tubes of the nephron is called urine.

▲ Urine travels from each kidney through a ureter to the urinary bladder. It then passes out of the body through the urethra.

▲ The liver removes excess amino acids from the blood and breaks them down into urea, which makes up urine. The liver also converts hemoglobin from worn-out red blood cells into bile.

▲ The skin has two main layers: the epidermis and the dermis. Sweat glands located in the dermis get rid of excess water, salt, and urea.

Reviewing Key Terms

Define each term in a complete sentence.

5–1 The Respiratory System
respiration
nose
epiglottis
trachea
larynx
vocal cord
bronchus
lung
alveolus
diaphragm

5–2 The Excretory System
excretion
kidney
nephron
capsule
ureter
urinary bladder
urethra
liver
skin
epidermis
dermis

Chapter Review

Content Review

Multiple Choice

Choose the letter of the answer that best completes each statement.

1. In the body cells, food and oxygen combine to produce energy during
   a. digestion.
   c. circulation.
   b. respiration.
   d. excretion.
2. The lungs, nose, and trachea are all part of the
   a. skeletal system.
   b. digestive system.
   c. respiratory system.
   d. circulatory system.
3. Air enters the body through the
   a. lungs.
   c. larynx.
   b. nose.
   d. trachea.
4. Another name for the windpipe is the
   a. alveolus.
   c. epiglottis.
   b. larynx.
   d. trachea.
5. The voice box is also known as the
   a. larynx.
   c. trachea.
   b. windpipe.
   d. alveolus.

6. The trachea divides into two tubes called
   a. alveoli.
   c. bronchi.
   b. air sacs.
   d. ureters.
7. The process by which wastes are removed from the body is called
   a. digestion.
   c. circulation.
   b. respiration.
   d. excretion.
8. The kidneys contain microscopic chemical filtration factories called
   a. alveoli.
   c. bronchi.
   b. nephrons.
   d. cilia.
9. Urine is stored in the
   a. urinary bladder.
   c. alveolus.
   b. urethra.
   d. kidneys.
10. The top layer of skin is the
    a. epidermis.
    c. alveolus.
    b. dermis.
    d. epiglottis.

True or False

If the statement is true, write "true." If it is false, change the underlined word or words to make the statement true.

1. The job of getting oxygen into the body and getting carbon dioxide out is the main task of the <u>respiratory</u> system.
2. Dust particles in the incoming air are filtered by <u>blood vessels</u> in the nose.
3. The flap of tissue that covers the trachea whenever food is swallowed is the <u>larynx</u>.
4. The clusters of air sacs in the lungs are called <u>alveoli</u>.
5. The organs that regulate the amount of liquid in the body are the <u>kidneys</u>.
6. The <u>ureter</u> is the tube through which urine leaves the body.
7. The <u>liver</u> converts hemoglobin into bile.
8. The <u>lungs</u> are excretory organs.

Concept Mapping

Complete the following concept map for Section 5–1. Refer to pages H8–H9 to construct a concept map for the entire chapter.

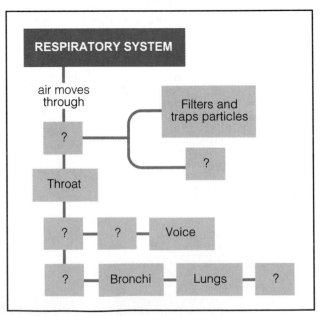

Concept Mastery

Discuss each of the following in a brief paragraph.

1. What is the difference between respiration and breathing?
2. How do the kidneys help to maintain homeostasis?
3. What role do the rib muscles and diaphragm play in breathing?
4. Why are the lungs considered to be both respiratory and excretory organs?
5. Explain the structure and function of a nephron.
6. Why is the skin classified as an excretory organ?
7. How is the kidney similar to a filter?
8. Why is the liver considered to be part of the digestive system as well as part of the excretory system?
9. What changes occur in the lungs when you inhale? What changes occur in the lungs when you exhale?
10. Name and describe four organs of excretion.
11. Trace the path of excess water from the nephrons to the outside of the body.

Critical Thinking and Problem Solving

Use the skills you have developed in this chapter to answer each of the following.

1. **Making comparisons** How are respiration and the burning of fuel similar? How are they different?
2. **Relating concepts** Would urine contain more or less water on a hot day? Explain.
3. **Relating concepts** How do respiration and excretion relate to the process of homeostasis?
4. **Designing an experiment** Design an experiment to show that the lungs excrete water.
5. **Interpreting data** Use your knowledge of the respiratory system to interpret the data table. What are the differences between inhaled air and exhaled air? How do you account for these differences?

	Inhaled Air	Exhaled Air
Nitrogen	79%	79%
Oxygen	21%	16%
Carbon Dioxide	0.04%	4.00%

6. **Applying concepts** What do you think is the advantage of having two kidneys?
7. **Making comparisons** How are the substances in the capsule of the nephron different from those in the urine that leaves the kidneys?
8. **Relating cause and effect** Emphysema is a disease in which the alveoli are damaged. How would this affect a person's ability to breathe?
9. **Relating cause and effect** Explain what happens to your throat when you sleep with your mouth open, especially when your nose is clogged because of a cold.
10. **Using the writing process** A children's television studio wants to make a movie that explains the process of respiration to young students. You have been asked to write a script that describes the travels of oxygen and carbon dioxide through the human respiratory system. Write a brief outline of your script, including information about what happens in each part of the respiratory system.

Nervous and Endocrine Systems

Guide for Reading

After you read the following sections, you will be able to

6–1 The Nervous System

- Describe the functions of the nervous system.
- Identify the structures of a neuron.
- Describe a nerve impulse.

6–2 Divisions of the Nervous System

- List the structures of the central nervous system and give their functions.
- Describe the peripheral nervous system and its function.

6–3 The Senses

- Summarize the functions of five sense organs.

6–4 The Endocrine System

- List eight endocrine glands and give the function of each.
- Explain the negative-feedback mechanism.

It is one o'clock on a Sunday morning. Suddenly, you find yourself face to face with a horrible-looking creature. You let out a scream and wake yourself out of a deep sleep. As you become more awake, you realize that it was all just a dream. The creature was not real. But your reaction to confronting the creature certainly was! Your heart pounded thunderously in your chest. Your breathing rate almost doubled, and your body was covered with perspiration. Even though you now know it was only a dream, your whole body seemed ready to respond by running away from or fighting the terrible creature.

Unknown to you, your nervous system and endocrine system were at work. Together, they control your body's activities. Parts of your nervous system—the brain, nerves, and sense organs—obtain information from the outside world. In turn, they alert your endocrine system to flood your bloodstream with chemicals. The chemicals cannot tell whether or not the threat is real. But that really does not matter, because a day may come when, faced with real danger, you will be glad that these two systems are working automatically. To find out how the nervous and endocrine systems perform their jobs, in any kind of situation, turn the page.

Journal *Activity*

You and Your World Imagine that you have to do without one of your sense organs for a day. Which one would you choose to give up? In your journal, list five everyday tasks you would ordinarily do using this sense organ. Then describe how the absence of this sense organ would affect these tasks.

◀ *A young person having a scary dream*

6–1 The Nervous System

You look up at the clock and realize that you have been working on this one particular math problem for more than half an hour. "Why am I having such a hard time solving this problem?" you ask yourself. Soon your mind begins to wander. Your thoughts turn to the summertime when you will no longer worry about math problems. Suddenly, the solution comes to you! This example, which may sound familiar, shows one of the many remarkable and often mysterious ways in which your nervous system functions. **The nervous system receives and sends out information about activities within the body. It also monitors and responds to changes in the environment.**

The extraordinary amount of information that your body receives at any one time is flashed through your nervous system in the form of millions of messages. These messages bring news about what is happening inside and outside your body—about the itch on your nose, or the funny joke you heard, or the odor of sweet-potato pie. Almost immediately, your nervous system tells other parts of your body what to do—scratch the itch, laugh at the joke, eat the pie.

In the meantime, your nervous system monitors (checks on) your breathing, blood pressure, and body temperature—to name just a few of the processes it takes care of without your awareness. The simple act of noticing that the weather is getting cooler is an example of the way the nervous system

Figure 6–1 *The nervous system controls and monitors all body activities—from the most simple to the most complex.*

Figure 6–2 *A nervous system enables organisms to respond to stimuli, or changes in the environment. In humans, the stimulus could be rain falling during a football game. The response could be opening umbrellas and donning rain gear, leaving the game, or both. In bears, a stimulus could be the sight of a salmon. What could the response be?*

monitors what is happening around you. The way the nervous system responds to this change is to make you feel chilly so you put on warmer clothes.

By performing all its tasks, the nervous system keeps your body working properly despite the constant changes taking place around you. These changes, whether they happen all the time or once in a while, are called **stimuli** (singular: stimulus). To help you better understand what a stimulus is, imagine this situation. An insect zooms toward your eye. You quickly and automatically blink to avoid damage to your eye. In this case, the insect zooming toward you is the stimulus and the blinking of your eye is the response.

Although some responses to stimuli are involuntary (not under your control), such as blinking your eyes and sneezing, many responses of the nervous system are voluntary (under your control). For example, leaving a football game because it begins to rain (stimulus) is a voluntary reaction. It is a conscious choice that involves the feelings of the moment, the memory of what happened the last time you stayed out in the rain, and the ability to reason.

So you can see how important the nervous system is to you. From the instant you are born, the nervous system controls and interprets (makes sense of) all the activities going on within your body. Without your nervous system, you could not move, think, laugh, feel pain, or enjoy the taste of a wonderfully juicy taco.

FIND OUT BY

CALCULATING

A Speedy Message

Messages in the nervous system travel at a speed of 120 meters per second. How many seconds would it take a nerve message to travel 900 meters? 1440 meters?

The Neuron—A Message-Carrying Cell

The nervous system is constantly alive with activity. It buzzes with messages that run to and from all parts of the body. Every second, hundreds of these messages make their journey through the body. The messages are carried by strings of one-of-a-kind cells called **neurons,** or nerve cells. Neurons are the basic units of structure and function in the nervous system. Neurons are unique because, unlike most other cells in the body, they can never be replaced. You need not worry about this, however. The number of neurons that you are born with is so large that you will have more than enough to last your entire lifetime.

Although neurons come in all shapes and sizes, they share certain basic characteristics, or features. You can see the features of a typical neuron in Figure 6–3. Notice that the largest part of the neuron is the **cell body.** The cell body contains the nucleus (a large dark structure), which controls all the activities of the cell.

You can think of the cell body as the switchboard of the message-carrying neuron. Running into this switchboard are one or more tiny, branching, thread-like structures called **dendrites.** The dendrites carry messages to the cell body of a neuron. A long tail-like fiber called an **axon** carries messages away from the cell body. Each neuron has only one axon, but the axon can be anywhere from 1 millimeter to more than 1 meter in length!

Figure 6–3 *Use the diagram to identify the basic structures in these neurons from the spinal cord. What is the function of the cell body?*

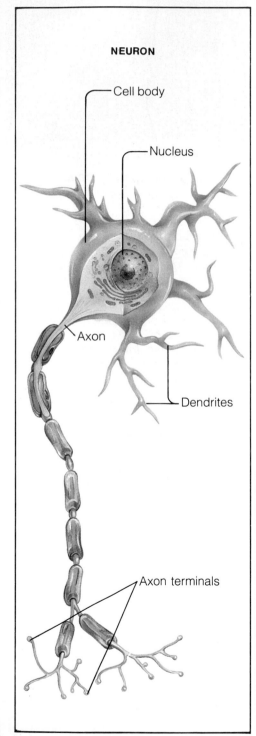

NEURON

- Cell body
- Nucleus
- Axon
- Dendrites
- Axon terminals

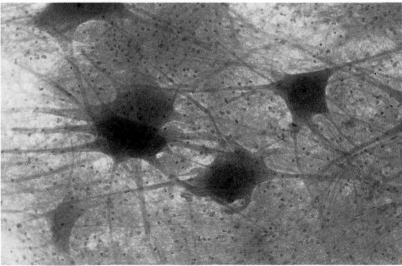

Notice in Figure 6–3 that the axon splits into many featherlike fibers at its far end. These fibers are called axon terminals (ends). Axon terminals pass on messages to the dendrites of other neurons. Axon terminals are usually found some distance from the cell body.

There are three types of neurons in your nervous system—sensory neurons, interneurons, and motor neurons. To find out the function of each neuron, try this activity: Press your finger against the edge of your desk. What happens? You feel the pressure of the desk pushing into your skin. You may even feel some discomfort or pain, if you press hard enough. Eventually, you remove your finger from this position.

How do neurons enable you to do all this? Special cells known as **receptors** receive information from your surroundings. In this activity the receptors are located in your finger. Messages travel from these receptors to your spinal cord and brain through **sensory neurons.** Your spinal cord and brain contain **interneurons.** Interneurons connect sensory neurons to **motor neurons.** It is through motor neurons that the messages from your brain and spinal cord are sent to a muscle cell or gland cell in your body. The muscle cell or gland cell that is stimulated by the motor neuron is called an **effector.**

Figure 6–4 *One of the body's billions of neurons can be seen in this photograph. The axon is the ropelike structure at the bottom of the photograph. What is the function of the axon?*

Figure 6–5 *There are three types of neurons in the nervous system: sensory neurons, interneurons, and motor neurons. What is an effector? A receptor?*

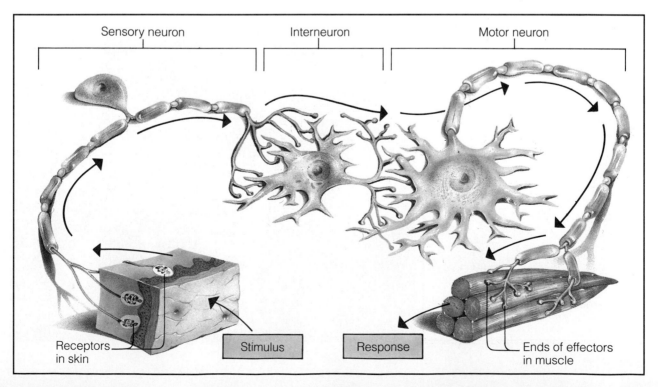

Sensory neuron | Interneuron | Motor neuron

Receptors in skin

Stimulus

Response

Ends of effectors in muscle

The Nerve Impulse

You have just read that the path of a message, which is more accurately known as a **nerve impulse,** is basically from sensory neuron to interneuron to motor neuron. But how exactly does a message travel along a neuron? And how does it get from one neuron to another neuron? **When a nerve impulse travels along a neuron or from one neuron to another neuron, it does so in the form of electrical and chemical signals.**

An electrical signal, which in simple terms is thought of as changing positive and negative charges, moves a nerve impulse along a neuron (or from one end of the neuron to the other). The nerve impulse enters the neuron through the dendrites and travels along the length of the axon. The speed at which a nerve impulse travels along a neuron can be as fast as 120 meters per second!

The way in which a nerve impulse travels from one neuron to another is a bit more complex. Do you know why? The reason is that the neurons do not touch one another. There is a tiny gap called a **synapse** (SIHN-aps) between the two neurons. Somehow, the nerve impulse must "jump" that gap. But how? Think of the synapse as a river that flows between a road on either bank. When a car gets to the

Figure 6–6 *The tiny gap between two neurons is called a synapse. The small reddish circles in the photograph are bubbles that contain chemicals which pour out of the axon terminal in one neuron, cross the synapse, and trigger a nerve impulse in the second neuron.*

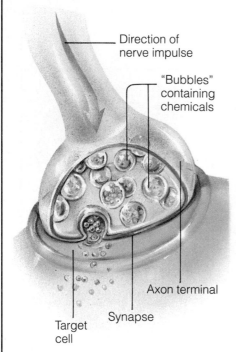

Direction of nerve impulse

"Bubbles" containing chemicals

Axon terminal

Synapse

Target cell

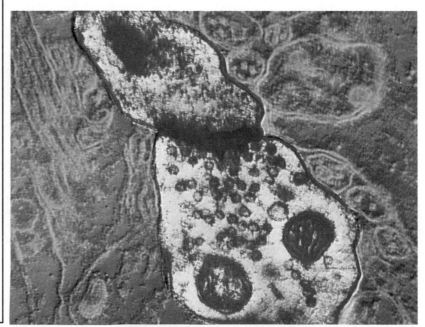

river, it crosses over by ferry. Then it drives right back onto the road and continues its journey.

Similarly, a nerve impulse is "ferried" across the synapse by a chemical signal. This chemical signal pours out of the ends of the neuron (axon terminals) as the nerve impulse nears the synapse. The electrical signal that brought the nerve impulse to this point shuts down, and the chemical signal takes the nerve impulse aboard, moving it across the synapse to the next neuron along its route. Then the chemical signal triggers the electrical signal again, and the whole process is repeated until the nerve impulse reaches its destination. You can appreciate how efficient this process is when you consider that for certain actions, this all happens in a matter of seconds!

6–1 Section Review

1. What are the functions of the nervous system?
2. What is a neuron? Describe its structure.
3. Identify the three types of neurons.
4. Describe a nerve impulse.

Critical Thinking—*Making Comparisons*
5. In the human nervous system, nerve impulses travel in only one direction along a neuron. How is this one-way traffic system better than a two-way traffic system along the same neuron?

6–2 Divisions of the Nervous System

In the previous section, you learned about the neuron as the basic unit of structure and function of the nervous system. You also gained some insight into the amazing job neurons do to keep you and your body in touch with the world inside and around you. Neurons, however, do not act alone. Instead, they are joined to form a complex communication network that makes up the human nervous

Guide for Reading

Focus on these questions as you read.

▶ *What are the two major parts of the human nervous system?*

▶ *What is the function and structure of each of the two major parts of the human nervous system?*

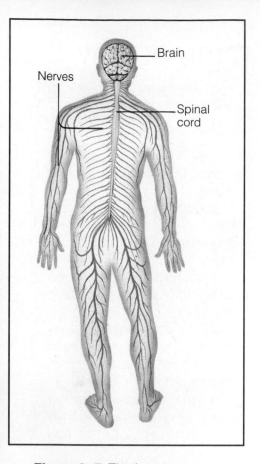

Figure 6–7 *The human nervous system is made up of the central nervous system and the peripheral nervous system. The central nervous system contains the brain and the spinal cord. The peripheral nervous system contains all the nerves that branch out from the central nervous system.*

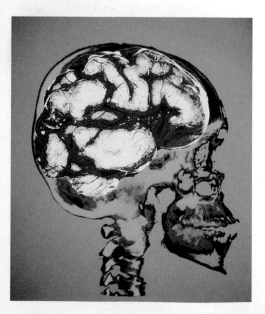

system. The human nervous system is divided into two parts: the central nervous system and the peripheral nervous system.

All information about what is happening in the world inside or outside your body is brought to the central nervous system. **The central nervous system, which contains the brain and the spinal cord, is the control center of the body.**

The other part of the human nervous system is the peripheral (puh-RIHF-uh-ruhl) nervous system. **The peripheral nervous system consists of a network of nerves that branch out from the central nervous system and connect it to the organs of the body.** Put another way, the peripheral nervous system is made up of all the nerves that are found outside the central nervous system. In fact, the word peripheral means outer part.

The Central Nervous System

If you were asked to write a list of your ten favorite rock stars and at the same time name all fifty states aloud, you would probably say you were being asked to do the impossible. And you would be quite correct. It is obvious that the nervous system is not able to control certain functions at the same time it is busy controlling other functions. What is less obvious, however, is just how many functions the brain can control at one time! For example, even an action as simple as sitting quietly in a movie theater requires several mental operations.

Many kinds of impulses travel between your central nervous system and other parts of your body as you watch a movie. Some nerve impulses control the focus of your eyes and the amount of light that enters them. Other nerve impulses control your understanding of what you see and hear. At the same time, still other nerve impulses regulate a variety of body activities such as breathing and blood circulation. And all these impulses may be related to one another. For example, if you are frightened by a scene in the movie, your breathing and heart rates

Figure 6–8 *This photograph is actually a combination of two photographs. One is an X-ray of a human skull. The other is of a human brain that has been properly positioned over the X-ray. What is the function of the skull?*

will likely increase. If, on the other hand, you are bored, these rates may decrease. In fact, you might even fall asleep!

The activities that occur within the central nervous system are very complex. Interpreting the information that pours in from all parts of your body and issuing the appropriate commands to these very same parts are the responsibility of the two parts of the central nervous system: the **brain** and the **spinal cord.** The brain is the main control center of the central nervous system. It transmits and receives messages through the spinal cord. The spinal cord provides the link between the brain and the rest of the body.

THE BRAIN If you are a fan of the English author Agatha Christie, you may remember the words uttered by her fictional detective Hercule Poirot as he attempted to solve a mystery: "These little gray cells! It is up to them." Indeed, much of the human brain does appear to be gray as a result of the presence of the cell bodies of billions of neurons. Underneath the gray material is white material, which is made of bundles of axons.

Despite the presence of billions of neurons, the mass of the brain is only about 1.4 kilograms. As you might expect of such an important organ, the brain is very well protected. A bony covering called the skull encases the brain. (You may recall from Chapter 2 that the skull is part of the skeletal system.) The brain is also wrapped by three layers of connective tissue, which nourish and protect it. The inner layer clings to the surface of the brain and follows its many folds. Between the inner layer and the middle layer is a watery fluid. The brain is bathed in this fluid and is thus cushioned against sudden impact, such as when you bump heads with another person while playing soccer or when you take a nasty fall. The outer layer, which makes contact with the inside of the bony skull, is thicker and tougher than the other two layers.

Looking like an oversized walnut without a shell, the **cerebrum** (SER-uh-bruhm) is the largest and most noticeable part of the brain. As you can see from Figure 6–11 on page 140, the cerebrum is lined with deep, wrinkled grooves. These grooves greatly increase the surface area of the cerebrum, thus allowing more

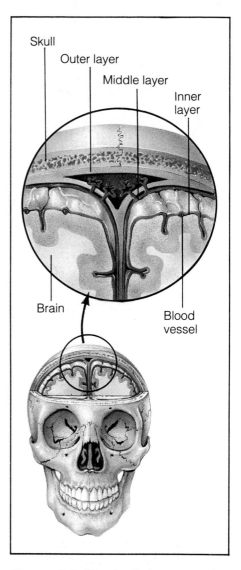

Figure 6–9 *The brain is wrapped by three layers of connective tissue, which nourish and protect it. Covering the brain and its three layers of connective tissue is a bony skull.*

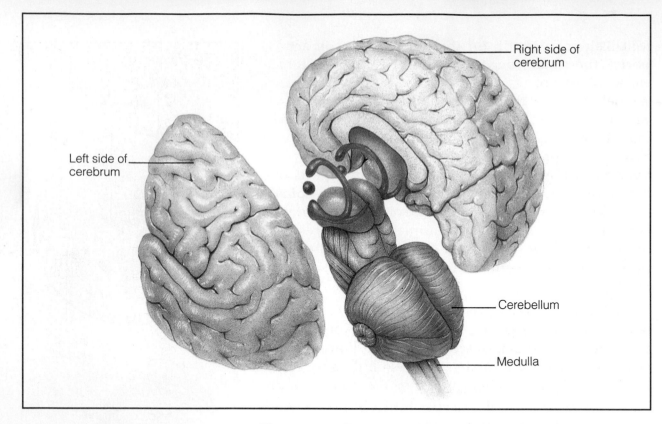

Figure 6–10 *The human brain consists of the cerebrum, cerebellum, and medulla. What is the function of each part?*

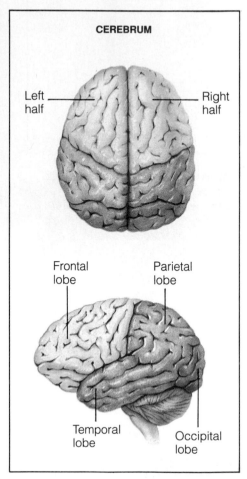

Figure 6–11 *The cerebrum is divided into two halves. Each half contains four lobes, or sections. What are the names of these lobes?*

activities to occur there. You can appreciate how important this feature is when you consider that the cerebrum is the area where learning, intelligence, and judgment occur. Increased surface area means increased thinking ability. But this is not all the cerebrum does. It also controls all the voluntary (under your control) activities of the body. In addition, it shapes your attitudes, your emotions, and even your personality.

Another interesting feature of the cerebrum (which you may have noticed in Figure 6–11) is that it is divided into halves: a right half and a left half. Each half controls different kinds of mental activity. For example, the right half is associated with artistic ability and the left half is associated with mathematical ability. And each half controls the movement of and sends sensations to the side of the body opposite it. In other words, the right side of the brain controls the left side of the body; the left side of the brain controls the right side of the body.

Below and to the rear of the cerebrum is the **cerebellum** (ser-uh-BEHL-uhm), the second largest part of the brain. The cerebellum's job is to coordinate the actions of the muscles and to maintain balance. As a result, your body is able to move smoothly and skillfully.

Below the cerebellum is the **medulla** (mih-DUHL-uh), which connects the brain to the spinal cord. The medulla controls involuntary actions, such as heartbeat, breathing, and blood pressure. Can you name some other types of involuntary actions?

SPINAL CORD If you bend forward slightly and run your thumb down the center of your back, you can feel the vertebrae that make up your spinal column. As you may recall from Chapter 2, the vertebrae are a series of bones that protect the spinal cord. The spinal cord runs the entire length of the neck and back. It connects the brain with the rest of the nervous system through a series of 31 pairs of

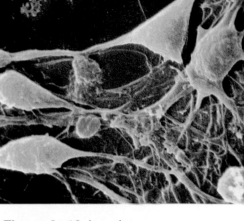

Figure 6–12 *Impulses are constantly traveling across neurons such as these located in the brain. To what part of the human nervous system does the brain belong?*

Figure 6–13 *The brain directs and coordinates all the body's activities. What is the function of the cerebellum?*

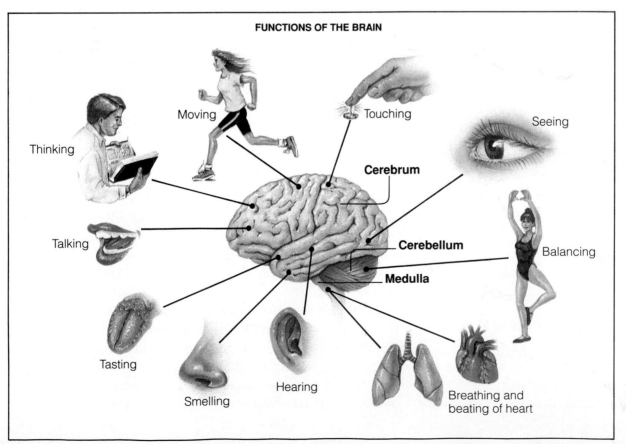

FUNCTIONS OF THE BRAIN

Thinking

Moving

Touching

Seeing

Cerebrum

Talking

Cerebellum

Balancing

Medulla

Tasting

Smelling

Hearing

Breathing and beating of heart

Figure 6–14 *The spinal cord, which provides the link between the brain and the rest of the body, is about 43 centimeters long and as flexible as a rubber hose. As the diagram shows, the spinal cord is protected by a series of bones called vertebrae that make up the vertebral column.*

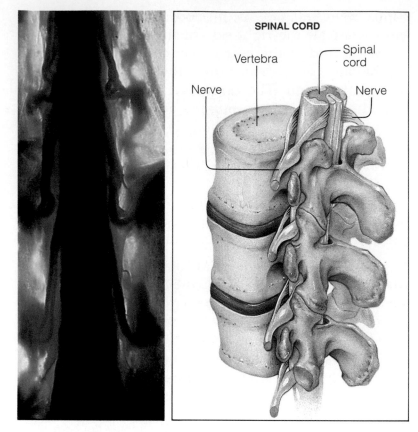

SPINAL CORD

Vertebra — Spinal cord

Nerve — Nerve

nerves. These nerves carry nerve impulses to and from the spinal cord.

Quite possibly, you are so interested in reading this chapter that you do not notice a fly circling in the air above your head. But if the fly happens to come close to your eyes, your eyes will automatically blink shut. Why?

A simple response to a stimulus (fly coming near your eyes) is called a **reflex.** In this example, the reflex begins as soon as the fly approaches your eyes. The fly's action sends a nerve impulse through the sensory neurons to the spinal cord. In the spinal cord, the nerve impulse is relayed to interneurons, which send the nerve impulse to motor neurons. The motor neurons stimulate the muscles (effectors) of the eyes, causing them to contract and so you blink.

Reflexes are not only lightning-fast reactions, they are also automatic. Their speed and automatic nature are possible because the nerve impulses travel only to the spinal cord, bypassing the brain. The brain does become aware of the event, however, but only after it has happened. So the instant after you

Figure 6–15 *If you touch a thumbtack, you will pull your finger away from it quickly. This reaction is an example of a reflex.*

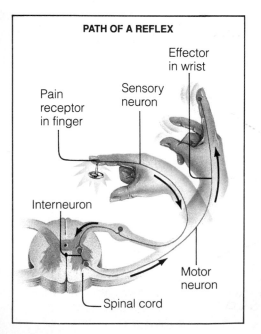

PATH OF A REFLEX

Effector in wrist

Sensory neuron

Pain receptor in finger

Interneuron

Motor neuron

Spinal cord

blink, your brain knows that you blinked and why you blinked.

The Peripheral Nervous System

The peripheral nervous system is the link between the central nervous system (brain and spinal cord) and the rest of the body. The peripheral nervous system consists of pairs of nerves (43 to be exact) that arise from the brain and spinal cord and lead to organs throughout your body. Many of the nerves in the peripheral nervous system are under the direct control of your conscious mind. For example, when you "tell" your leg to move, a message travels from your brain to your spinal cord and through a peripheral nerve to your leg. There is one part of the peripheral nervous system, however, that is not under the direct control of your conscious mind. This part, called the autonomic (awt-uh-NAHM-ihk) nervous system, controls body activities that are involuntary—that is, body activities that happen automatically without your thinking about them. For example, contractions of the heart muscle and movement of smooth muscles surrounding the blood vessels and the organs of the digestive system are activities under the control of the autonomic nervous system.

The nerves of the autonomic nervous system can be divided into two groups that have opposite effects on the organs they control. One group of nerves triggers an action by an organ while the other group of nerves slows down or stops the action. Thus, the nerves of the autonomic nervous system work against each other to keep body activities in perfect balance.

FIND OUT BY DOING

Fight or Flight?

1. Working with a partner, determine your pulse rate (heartbeats per minute) and breathing rate (breaths per minute) while you are at rest. Record your data.

2. Now do ten jumping jacks. **CAUTION:** *If you have any respiratory illnesses, do not perform steps 2 and 3.*

3. After exercising, measure your pulse rate and breathing rate. Your partner can measure your pulse while you are counting your breaths. Record this "after exercise" data.

Describe any changes in pulse rate and breathing rate after exercising.

■ How do these changes compare with those that occur when you are faced with an emergency situation? What other body changes occur when you react to an emergency?

Part of Body Affected	Autonomic Nervous System Nerve Group That Triggers Action	Autonomic Nervous System Nerve Group That Slows Down Action
Pupil of eye	Widened	Narrowed
Liver	Sugar released	None
Urinary bladder muscle	Relaxed	Shortened
Muscle of heart	Increased rate and force	Slowed rate
Bronchi of lungs	Widened	Narrowed

Figure 6–16 *The nerves of the autonomic nervous system can be divided into two groups that have opposite effects on the organs they control.*

For example, when you are frightened, nerves leading to organs such as the lungs and the heart are activated. This action causes your breathing rate and heartbeat to increase. Such an increase may be necessary if extra energy and strength are needed to deal with the frightening situation. But when the frightening situation is over, the other group of autonomic nerves bring your breathing rate and heartbeat back to normal.

6–2 Section Review

1. What are the two major parts of the human nervous system? What is the function of each?
2. Identify the three main parts of the brain and give their functions.
3. What is the function of the spinal cord?
4. Describe a reflex.

Critical Thinking—*Applying Concepts*
5. If a person's cerebellum is injured in an automobile accident, how might the person be affected?

Guide for Reading

Focus on these questions as you read.
▶ *What are the five sense organs?*
▶ *What are the functions of the five sense organs?*

6–3 The Senses

You know what is going on inside your body and in the world around you because of neurons known as receptors (neurons that respond to stimuli). Many of these receptors are found in your sense organs. Sense organs are structures that carry messages about your surroundings to the central nervous system. **Sense organs respond to light, sound, heat, pressure, and chemicals and also detect changes in the position of your body.** The eyes, ears, nose, tongue, and skin are examples of sense organs.

Most sense organs respond to stimuli from your body's external environment. Others keep track of the environment inside your body. Although you are not aware of it, your sense organs send messages to the central nervous system about almost everything—from body temperature to carbon dioxide and oxygen levels in your blood to the amount of light entering your eyes.

Vision

Your eyes are one of your most wonderful possessions. They enable you to watch a beautiful sunset, pass a thread through the eye of a needle, and learn about a variety of topics by reading the printed word. They can focus on a speck of dust a few centimeters away or on a distant star many light-years away. Your eyes are your windows on the world.

Your eyes are designed to focus light rays (a form of energy you can see) to produce images of objects. But your eyes are useless without a brain to receive and interpret the messages that correspond to these images. What the brain does is receive the messages coming in through the eyes. These messages are then interpreted by the brain's visual center, located at the back of the brain. You will learn more about the brain's role in vision a little later in this section.

The eye is more correctly known as an eyeball—which is an appropriate name, as it is shaped like a ball. You may wish to refer to Figure 6–18 on page 146 as you read about the structures of the eyeball. The eyeball is slightly longer than it is wide. The eye is composed of three layers of tissue. The outer, protective layer is called the sclera (SKLEER-uh). The sclera is more commonly known as the "white" of the eye. In the center of the front of the eyeball, the sclera becomes transparent and colorless. This area of the sclera is called the **cornea.** The cornea is the part of the eye through which light enters. For this reason, the cornea is sometimes called "the window of the eye."

CAREERS

Optometric Assistant

When you go to have your eyes examined, you are greeted first by the **optometric assistant,** who records your case history and prepares you for your eye exam. During the visit, the optometric assistant may perform certain eye tests, such as those for color vision, depth perception, and nearsightedness and farsightedness.

For further information about a career as an optometric assistant, write to the Opticians Association of America, 10341 Democracy Lane, PO Box 10110, Fairfax, VA 22030.

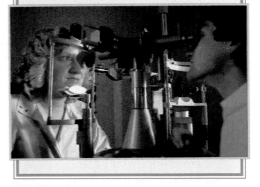

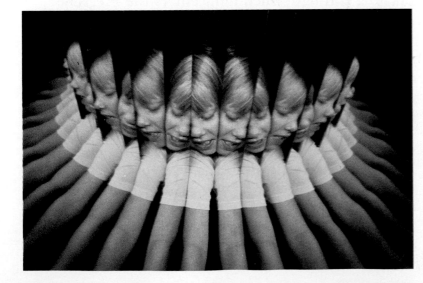

Figure 6–17 *Most sense organs respond to stimuli in the environment. But every now and then, sense organs can be fooled into sensing something that is not really as it should be. The optical illusion shown here, which is produced by mirrors, tricks the eyes into seeing many images of this young person.*

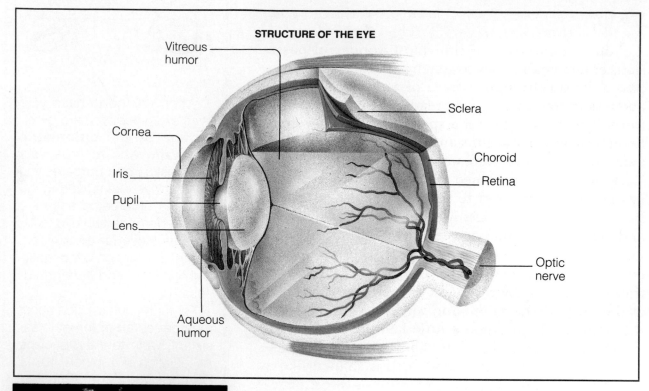

STRUCTURE OF THE EYE

Vitreous humor

Cornea

Iris

Pupil

Lens

Aqueous humor

Sclera

Choroid

Retina

Optic nerve

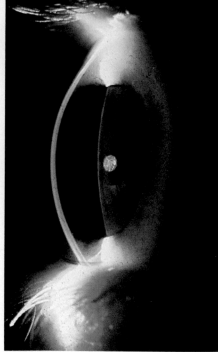

Figure 6–18 *What structures of the eye can you identify?*

Just inside the cornea is a small chamber filled with a fluid called aqueous (AY-kwee-uhs) humor. At the back of this chamber is the circular colored portion of the eye called the **iris.** The iris is the part of the eye people refer to when they say a person's eyes are blue, brown, black, or hazel. The iris is part of the choroid (KOR-oid), or middle layer of the eye. Unlike the sclera and the cornea, the choroid contains blood vessels.

In the middle of the iris is a small opening called the **pupil.** The pupil is not a structure but an actual opening through which light enters the eye. The amount of light entering the pupil is controlled by the size of the opening. And the size of the opening is controlled by tiny muscles in the iris, which relax or contract to make the pupil larger or smaller. By observing the pupils of your eyes in a mirror as you vary the amount of light in the room, you can actually see the opening change size. Your pupils get larger in dim light and smaller in bright light. Why? Pupils get smaller in bright light to prevent light damage to the inside of the eye. They get larger in dim light to let in more light.

Just behind the iris is the **lens.** The lens focuses the light rays coming into the eye. Small muscles attached to the lens cause its shape to change constantly, depending on whether objects are close by or far away. When the muscles relax, the lens flattens out, enabling you to see distant objects more clearly. When the muscles contract (shorten), the lens returns to its normal shape, enabling you to see objects that are close by more clearly. Behind the lens is a large chamber that contains a transparent, jellylike fluid called vitreous (VIH-tree-uhs) humor. This fluid gives the eyeball its roundish shape.

The light that passes through the lens is focused on the back surface of the eye, which is known as the **retina** (REHT-'n-uh). The retina is the eye's inner layer of tissue. It contains more than 130 million light-sensitive receptors called rods and cones. Rods react to dim light but not to colors. Cones are responsible for color vision, but they stop working in dim light. This is the reason why colors seem to disappear at night, when you are seeing with only your rods.

Both rods and cones produce nerve impulses that travel from the retina along the optic nerve to the visual center of the brain. There the nerve impulses are interpreted by the brain. Because of the way the lens bends light rays as they enter the eye, the image that appears on the retina is upside down. The brain must automatically turn the image right side up—and do so quickly! The brain must also combine the two slightly different images provided by each eye into one three-dimensional image. This is a complex task, indeed, but your brain does it quickly and automatically almost every second of your waking day. Just imagine what it would be like living in a world in which everything was upside down!

Figure 6–19 *This image of a cat was produced by a silicon chip developed to imitate the light-sensitive cells in the retina. What are these light-sensitive cells called?*

Figure 6–20 *The retina, which is the eye's inner layer of tissue, contains the light-sensitive cells called the rods and cones (right). The lens of the eye focuses light onto the retina. The upside-down image that you see in the photograph (left) was taken with a special camera that looked through the pupil of the eye.*

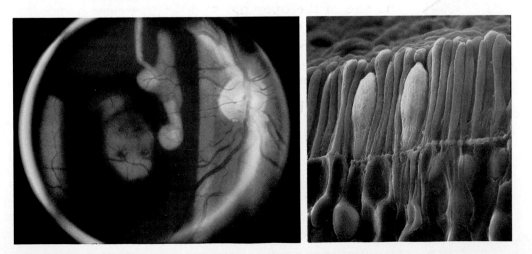

PROBLEM Solving

I Can See Clearly Now

Look around at the students in your classroom. You will notice that some of them are wearing eyeglasses. Why do some people need glasses whereas others do not? The answer to this question has to do with the structure of the eyeball. Look at the diagrams of the eyeball shown here. Notice that when the eyeball looks at an object, the light rays from that object enter the eyeball and come to a focus point on the retina.

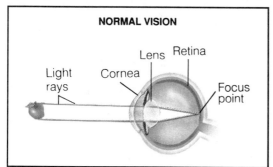

Sometimes, however, the light rays do not come to a focus point on the retina. When the eyeball is too long from front to back, the light rays come together at a point in front of the retina. The result is a blurred image of distant objects. This disorder is called nearsightedness. When the eyeball is too short from front to back, the light rays come together at a point behind the retina. The result is a blurred image of nearby objects. This disorder is called farsightedness.

To fix these disorders, eyeglasses containing corrective lenses are worn. Examine the path of the light rays through each of the two lenses below—a biconcave (sunken in at both surfaces) lens and a biconvex (arched at both surfaces) lens.

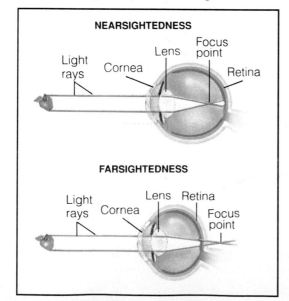

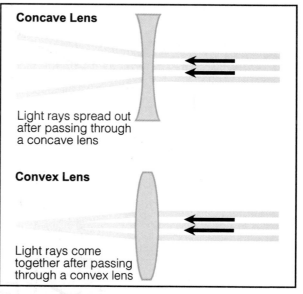

Interpreting Diagrams

1. Which type of lens corrects nearsightedness?

2. Which type of lens corrects farsightedness?

3. Why is nearsightedness an appropriate name for this disorder?

4. Why is farsightedness an appropriate name for this disorder?

5. What are bifocals?

Hearing and Balance

When someone laughs or the telephone rings, the air around the source of the sound vibrates. These vibrations move through the air in waves. Hearing actually begins when some of the sound waves enter the external ear. If you look at Figure 6–21, you will see the external ear. This is the part of the ear with which you are probably most familiar. It is made mostly of cartilage covered with skin. You may recall from Chapter 2 that cartilage is strong enough to support weight, yet flexible enough to be bent and twisted. You can prove this to yourself by bending your external ear.

The funnellike shape of the external ear enables it to gather sound waves. These waves pass through the tubelike ear canal to the **eardrum.** The eardrum is a tightly stretched membrane that separates the ear canal from the middle ear. As sound waves

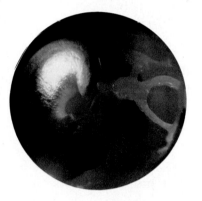

Figure 6–21 *Sound waves enter the ear and are changed into nerve impulses that are carried to the brain. The photograph of the middle ear shows the eardrum, which is colored yellow, and the three tiny bones known as the hammer, the anvil, and the stirrup.*

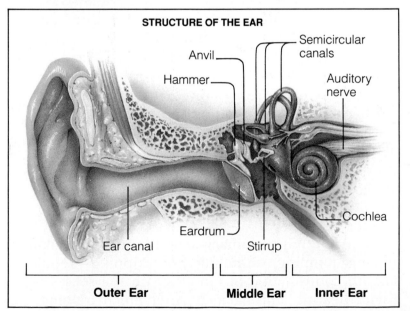

STRUCTURE OF THE EAR

Anvil

Hammer

Semicircular canals

Auditory nerve

Cochlea

Eardrum

Stirrup

Ear canal

Outer Ear   **Middle Ear**   **Inner Ear**

FIND OUT BY DOING

Reaction Time

1. Have a partner hold a ruler vertically above a table.

2. Without touching the ruler, position the zero mark between your thumb and forefinger.

3. Your partner should drop the ruler whenever he or she chooses. Moving only your thumb and forefinger, but not your hand, try to catch the ruler as soon as it falls.

4. Record the distance, in centimeters, that the ruler falls.

5. Repeat steps 1 through 4 four more times.

6. To obtain an average distance, add the five distances together and divide this sum by five. Record the average distance.

Why does measuring the distance that the ruler falls give a relative measure of reaction time, which is the length of time that passes between your seeing a change in your environment and your reacting to that change? Compare the reaction times of all your classmates. What can you conclude?

■ Design an experiment in which you determine the effect fatigue has on your reaction time.

strike the eardrum, it vibrates in much the same way that the surface of a drum vibrates when it is struck.

Vibrations from the eardrum enter the middle ear, which is composed of the three smallest bones in the body—the hammer, anvil, and stirrup. The hammer, the first of these bones, picks up the vibrations from the eardrum and passes them along to the anvil and then to the stirrup. The stirrup vibrates against a thin membrane covering the opening into the fluid-filled inner ear.

Vibrations in the inner ear pass through the fluid and are channeled into a snail-shaped tube called the **cochlea** (KAHK-lee-uh). The cochlea contains nerves that are stimulated by the vibrations from a wide variety of sounds and range of loudness. The stimulated nerves produce nerve impulses that are carried from the cochlea to the brain by the auditory nerve. Once in the brain, these nerve impulses are interpreted, and you hear.

The ear not only enables you to hear, it also enables you to be aware of changes in movement and to keep your balance. The structures in the ear that are responsible for your sense of balance are the **semicircular canals** and the two tiny sacs behind them. The semicircular canals are three tiny canals located within your inner ear just above the cochlea. They are called semicircular because, as you can see from Figure 6–22, each makes a half circle (the prefix *semi-* means half).

The semicircular canals and the tiny sacs near them are filled with fluid and lined with tiny hairlike cells. These cells are embedded in a jellylike substance that contains tiny grains called hearing stones. When your head moves, the hearing stones roll back and forth, bending the hairlike cells. The hairlike cells respond by sending nerve impulses to the cerebellum of your brain. If your brain interprets these impulses to mean that your body is losing its balance, it will automatically signal some muscles to contract and others to relax until your balance is restored.

Even the most ordinary actions—such as walking, jogging, jumping, swimming, and skipping—require smooth coordination of muscles with the senses of vision, hearing, and balance. After much training

Figure 6–22 *The semicircular canals are arranged at right angles to one another so that they can respond to up-and-down, side-to-side, and bending motions (top). Tiny grains commonly called hearing stones also play a part in maintaining balance (bottom). In what part of the ear are the semicircular canals located?*

Figure 6–23 *The role of the ears in maintaining balance makes all sorts of activities possible.*

and practice, your brain can learn to quickly coordinate balance with eye and hand movements so that you can walk a tightrope as easily as you can lift a spoon to your mouth!

Smell and Taste

Unlike the senses of vision and hearing, the senses of smell and taste do not respond to physical stimuli such as light and sound vibrations. To what stimuli, then, do these senses respond? The following story—perhaps similar to an experience in your own kitchen—may provide the answer.

You are standing near the oven. Suddenly you smell the wonderful aroma of a chocolate cake. You cannot see a cake, so what tells you that there is one baking in the oven? Your sense of smell tells you, of course. Sense receptors in your nose react to invisible stimuli carried by the air from the oven to your nose. The invisible stimuli are chemicals that affect the smell receptors in your nose. So your sense of smell is a chemical sense. In turn, the smell receptors produce nerve impulses that are carried to the brain, where they are interpreted. As a result, you are not only able to smell a cake, but you are able to identify the smell as a chocolate cake!

Your sense of taste is also a chemical sense. In the case of taste, the chemicals are not carried through the air but in liquids in your mouth (solid foods mix with saliva to form liquids). The receptors for taste are located in the taste buds on your tongue. Although there are only four basic kinds of tastes—sweet, sour, bitter, and salty—there are at least 80 basic odors. Taken together, tastes and odors produce flavors. Thus your sense of smell must work

Figure 6–24 *You have no trouble in identifying the wonderful aroma of a chocolate cake thanks to the sense receptors in the nose.*

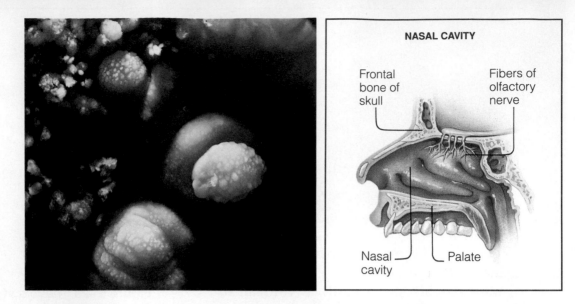

NASAL CAVITY

Frontal bone of skull

Fibers of olfactory nerve

Nasal cavity

Palate

Figure 6–25 *Smell receptors in your nose (right) and taste receptors on your tongue (left) are responsible for identifying the flavors of foods. What are taste receptors called?*

Figure 6–26 *The sense of touch, unlike the other senses, is not found in one particular place. All regions of the skin are sensitive to touch. For this reason, the sense of touch is one of the most important senses on which sightless people rely.*

with your sense of taste in order for you to detect the flavors of foods. Perhaps you are already aware of this fact. Think back to the last time you had a stuffy nose due to a cold or an allergy. Were you able to taste the flavor of food? Probably not. Because the smell receptors in your nose were covered by extra mucus, only your sense of taste was working—not your sense of smell. Without a combined effort, the food you ate had little, if any, flavor.

Touch

The sense of touch is not found in any one place. The sense of touch is found in all areas of the skin. For this reason, you can think of the skin as your largest sense organ!

Near the surface of the skin are touch receptors that allow you to feel the textures of objects. You do not need much force to produce nerve impulses in these receptors. Prove this to yourself by gently running your fingertips across a piece of wood so that you can feel the grain. You have stimulated these touch receptors. Located deeper within the skin are the receptors that sense pressure. The sense of pressure differs as much from the sense of touch as pressing your hand firmly against a piece of wood differs from feeling it with your fingertips.

Notice in Figure 6–27 that there are other types of sense receptors. These receptors respond to heat, cold, and pain. The receptors that respond to heat and cold are scattered directly below the surface of

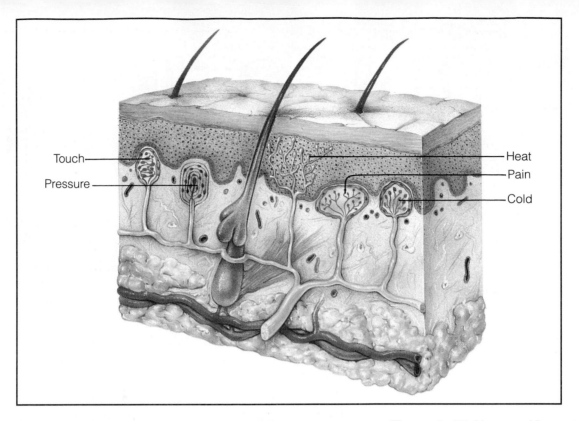

Figure 6–27 *Human skin contains five types of sense receptors: pressure, touch, pain, heat, and cold.*

the skin. Pain receptors are found all over the skin. It should not surprise you to learn that pain receptors are important to the survival of your body, no matter how uncomfortable they may seem at times. Pain, you see, often alerts your body to the fact that it might be in some type of danger.

6–3 Section Review

1. What are the five basic senses? What organs are responsible for these senses?
2. Describe the structure of the eye. Identify the functions of the major structures.
3. Trace the path of sound from the external ear to the auditory nerve.
4. Explain the role of the ear in maintaining balance.
5. What are the four basic tastes?

Connection—*You and Your World*
6. Design an experiment to show that your sense of smell is important in determining the flavor of food.

With or Without Pepperoni?

Do not be too surprised if sometime soon you walk into a pizzeria and discover that the pizza you ordered is being whipped together by a voice-activated robot. As you may already know, robots are mechanical devices that do routine tasks. However, PizzaBot, as the pizza-making robot is called, is equipped with a little something extra—*artificial intelligence*. Artificial intelligence is a branch of *computer science* concerned with designing computer systems that perform tasks which seem to require intelligence. These tasks include reasoning, adapting to new situations, and learning new skills. When you recognize a face, learn a new language, or figure out the best way to arrive at a destination, you are performing such tasks.

Until recently, computers have only been able to follow instructions (a computer program). Now, however, scientists have developed computers that "think," or are able to perform complex

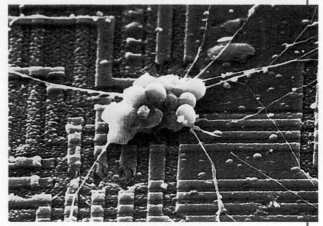

tasks such as diagnosing disease, locating minerals in the soil, and even making pizza! In order to "think," these computers need vast amounts of information. To make a pizza, a computer needs to recognize the sounds of a human voice as a pizza is ordered, to "decide" what possible pizza size and toppings it has just "heard," to repeat the order to confirm it (both aloud and on a screen), and then to follow the program for that pizza. The computer then processes these data one step at a time but extremely fast. (In contrast, your brain, with its billions of neurons, processes information along many pathways at the same time.)

As you can see, some of the applications of artificial intelligence are quite exciting, especially those in the field of *robotics*, or the study of robots. Just imagine the effects "thinking" robots such as PizzaBot could have on your life. The possibilities seem almost endless. In the not-too-distant future, you might even own a minirobot that would monitor your room, darting out every now and then to pick up the crumbs from your last snack! Seems impossible now, but who knows what will happen in the next few years. . . .

6–4 The Endocrine System

It is late at night, and your room is dark. As you feel your way toward the light switch in the pitch-black room, something warm brushes against your leg. You let out a piercing shriek, or perhaps only a gasp. It is not until you realize it is the cat you have encountered that you breathe a sigh of relief. As your pounding heart begins to slow down and your stiffened muscles relax, you begin to feel calmer. Have you ever wondered what causes your body to react this way? As you read on, you will find the answer to this question.

Endocrine Glands

The reactions you have just read about are set in motion not only by your nervous system, but also by another system called the endocrine (EHN-doh-krihn) system. **The endocrine system is made of glands that produce chemical messengers called hormones. Hormones help to regulate certain body activities.** By turning on and turning off or speeding up and slowing down the activities of different organs and tissues, **hormones** (HOR-mohnz) do their job. Together, the nervous system and the endocrine system function to keep all the parts of the body running smoothly.

The rush of fear that you felt as you brushed against an unknown object in the dark is an example of how the nervous system and the endocrine system work together. Your senses reported all the necessary information about the event to your brain. Because your brain interpreted the information as a threat, it quickly sent nerve impulses through selected nerves. These nerves triggered certain glands of the endocrine system. The selected glands produced hormones, which traveled through the blood to their specific destinations.

In this particular example, the hormones that were produced caused an increase in your heartbeat, made your lungs work harder, and prepared your muscles for immediate action. In such a state, you were ready to fight or to flee. Put another way, you were ready to defend yourself or to run. Your body

Guide for Reading

Focus on these questions as you read.

▶ *What is the function of the endocrine system?*
▶ *How does the endocrine system keep the internal environment of the body stable?*

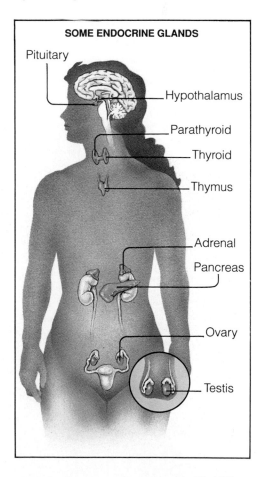

Figure 6–28 *The diagram shows some of the major glands of the endocrine system. What is the name of the chemicals produced by these glands?*

SOME ENDOCRINE GLANDS

Pituitary
Hypothalamus
Parathyroid
Thyroid
Thymus
Adrenal
Pancreas
Ovary
Testis

FIND OUT BY

WRITING

Bacterially Produced Hormones

Scientists have developed certain bacteria that produce large amounts of some human hormones. Using reference material in the library, find out more information about the bacterially produced hormones. Use the information in a written report. Be sure to provide answers for the following questions: Which hormones are produced by bacteria? What is the function of the hormone? How are these hormones produced? Include labeled diagrams that show how the bacteria are made to produce these hormones.

remained prepared for any further trouble until your brain stopped sending out danger signals. Then the endocrine glands responded in turn, and your body calmed down.

Endocrine glands are not the only type of glands found in your body. You have another set of glands called exocrine (EHKS-oh-krihn) glands. Exocrine glands give off their chemicals through ducts, or tubes, into nearby organs. Unlike endocrine glands, exocrine glands do not produce hormones. They produce tears, sweat, oil, and digestive juices to name a few examples. Common exocrine glands include the salivary glands in the mouth and sweat glands in the skin.

The hormones secreted (given off) by the endocrine glands are delivered to their destinations through the circulatory system. Thus, endocrine glands do not need to be near the organs they control. No matter where hormones enter the bloodstream, they always find their way through the nearly 100,000 kilometers of blood vessels (that's almost two and a half times around the Earth!) to their intended target area. How is this possible? Body tissues have the ability to "recognize" the hormones that are made for them. Tissue cells are programmed to accept certain hormones and reject others. Hormones not meant for a particular type of tissue or organ will pass on until they come to their target tissue or organ.

Each of your body's eight endocrine glands releases a different set of hormones and thus controls different body processes. In the next few pages, you will read about these glands, their hormones, and the body activities they control. This information is summarized in Figure 6–29. How many of these glands and hormones sound familiar to you?

HYPOTHALAMUS The **hypothalamus** (high-poh-THAL-uh-muhs) produces hormones that help turn on and turn off the seven other endocrine glands in your body. The hypothalamus, which is a tiny gland located at the base of the brain, is the major link between the nervous system and the endocrine system. In fact, the hypothalamus is as much a part of one system as it is of the other. That is why the hypothalamus can be thought of as the way in which the brain and body "talk" to each other.

SOME ENDOCRINE GLANDS

Gland	Location	Hormone Produced	Functions
Hypothalamus	Base of brain	Regulatory factors	Regulates activities of other endocrine glands
Pituitary Front portion	Base of brain	Human growth hormone (HGH)	Stimulates body skeleton growth
		Gonadotropic hormone	Stimulates development of male and female sex organs
		Lactogenic hormone	Stimulates production of milk
		Thyrotropic hormone	Aids functioning of thyroid
		Adrenocorticotrophic hormone (ACTH)	Aids functioning of adrenals
Back portion		Oxytocin	Regulates blood pressure and stimulates smooth muscles; stimulates the birth process
		Vasopressin	Increases rate of water reabsorption in the kidneys
Thymus	Behind breastbone	Thymosin	Regulates development and function of immune system
Thyroid	Neck	Thyroxine	Increases rate of metabolism
		Calcitonin	Maintains the level of calcium and phosphorus in the blood
Parathyroids	Behind thyroid lobes	Parathyroid hormone	Regulates the level of calcium and phosphorus
Adrenals Inner tissue	Above kidneys	Adrenaline	Increases heart rate; elevates blood pressure; raises blood sugar; increases breathing rate; decreases digestive activity
Outer tissue		Mineralocorticoids	Maintains balance of salt and water in the kidneys
		Glucocorticoids— cortisone	Breaks down stored proteins to amino acids; aids in breakdown of fat tissue; promotes increase in blood sugar
		Sex hormones	Supplements sex hormones produced by sex glands; promotes development of sexual characteristics
Pancreas Islets of Langerhans	Abdomen, near stomach	Insulin	Enables liver to store sugar; regulates sugar breakdown in tissues; decreases blood sugar level
		Glucagon	Increases blood sugar level
Ovaries	Pelvic area	Estrogen	Produces female secondary sex characteristics
		Progesterone	Promotes growth of lining of uterus
Testes	Scrotum	Testosterone	Produces male secondary sex characteristics

Figure 6–29 *The location of some endocrine glands, the hormones they produce, and the functions they perform are shown in the chart. Where is thymosin produced? What is its function?*

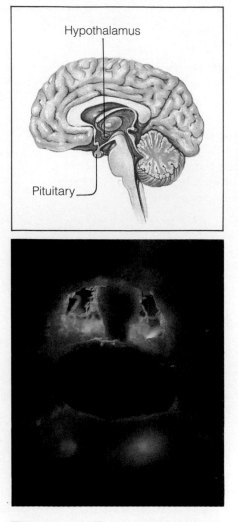

Figure 6–30 *The pituitary, which is found just under the hypothalamus, is located at the base of the brain in the center of the skull. The pea-shaped structure in the photograph is the pituitary, which is connected to the hypothalamus by a short stalk. What is the function of the pituitary?*

Messages that travel to and from the brain go through the hypothalamus. So the hypothalamus "knows about" sensations you are aware of—a lovely sunset, a painful bee sting, or a pleasant smell. It also controls things you are not aware of—the level of hormones in the blood, the amount of nutrients in the body, or the internal temperature of the body.

PITUITARY The hypothalamus depends on another endocrine gland for information about the body. This gland is the **pituitary** (pih-TOO-uh-tair-ee). The hypothalamus "talks to" the pituitary—sometimes by means of nerve impulses and sometimes by way of hormones. In response to these stimuli from the hypothalamus, the pituitary produces its own hormones.

The pituitary, which is no larger than a pea, is found in the center of the skull right behind the bridge of the nose. The pituitary controls blood pressure, growth, metabolism (all the chemical and physical activities that go on inside the body), sexual development, and reproduction. For many years, the pituitary was called the "master gland" of the body. This was because the hormones the pituitary produces control many of the activities of other endocrine glands. When it was discovered that the pituitary itself was controlled by its own master—the hypothalamus—the nickname "master gland" gradually dropped out of use.

THYMUS Just behind the breastbone is another endocrine gland—the **thymus** (THIGH-muhs). Large in infancy, the thymus begins to get smaller as you grow. By the time you reach adulthood, the thymus has shrunk to about the size of your thumb. The thymus is responsible for the development of the immune system, which you will learn in Chapter 8 is your main defense against disease-causing organisms. During infancy, the thymus produces white blood cells that protect the body's tissues, triggering an immune response against invaders. Later, other organs in the body take over the thymus's job of producing these white blood cells.

THYROID Before the mid-1800s, doctors actually thought that another endocrine gland, the **thyroid,** which is located in the neck, lubricated and protected the vocal cords. It was not until 1859 that the true function of the thyroid was discovered. That function is to control how quickly food is burned up in the body.

PARATHYROIDS Embedded in the thyroid are four tiny glands called the **parathyroids.** They release a hormone that controls the level of calcium in the blood. Calcium is a mineral that keeps your nerves and muscles working properly.

ADRENALS Of all the hormones in the body, adrenaline (uh-DREHN-uh-lihn) is perhaps one of the best understood by scientists. The effects of adrenaline are so dramatic and powerful that you can actually feel them as your heart rate increases and blood pulses through your blood vessels.

Adrenaline is part of the body's emergency action team. Whenever you are in a dangerous situation, such as the frightening dream you read about at the beginning of this section, your body reacts in a number of ways. Your first reaction is usually a nervous one—messages from your surroundings are sent to the brain, warning you of the danger. The brain shocks the body into action to avoid the threat. A rapid series of nerve impulses to the appropriate muscles makes you take whatever actions are necessary to ensure your safety. At the same time, the brain alerts the two **adrenals** to produce adrenaline. The word adrenal means above (*ad-*) the kidney (*-renal*). And that is exactly where each adrenal is located—atop each of the two kidneys.

PANCREAS Insulin, which is another hormone that scientists know a lot about, plays an important role in keeping the levels of sugar (glucose) in the bloodstream under control. It does this by helping body cells absorb the sugar and use it for energy. It also helps to change excess sugar into a substance called glycogen (GLIGH-kuh-juhn), which can be stored in the liver and the skeletal muscles until it is needed by the body. In this way, insulin prevents the level of sugar in the blood from rising too high. Without enough insulin, however, a person can develop diabetes mellitus (digh-uh-BEET-eez muh-LIGHT-uhs). Diabetes mellitus is a disorder in which the level of sugar in the blood is too high.

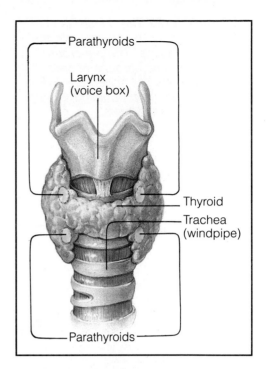

Figure 6–31 *The parathyroids are four tiny glands embedded in the thyroid, which is located in the neck. What hormone does the thyroid produce?*

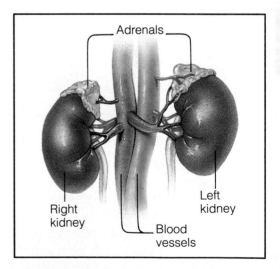

Figure 6–32 *Located atop each of the two kidneys is an adrenal gland. What is the function of the adrenal glands?*

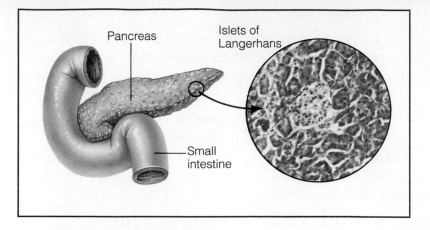

Figure 6–33 *The pancreas is located near the entrance to the small intestine. The pancreas contains small groups of cells called islets of Langerhans. What hormones are produced by the islets of Langerhans?*

Insulin is produced by a small group of cells called the **islets** (IGH-lihts) **of Langerhans** (LAHNG-er-hahns) within the pancreas. You may recall from Chapter 3 that the pancreas is also part of the digestive system, releasing enzymes into the small intestine. In addition to insulin, the islets of Langerhans produce another hormone called glucagon (GLOO-kuh-gahn). The effect of glucagon in the body is exactly opposite that of insulin. Glucagon increases the level of sugar in the blood by speeding up the conversion of glycogen to sugar in the liver.

Together, the effects of insulin and glucagon ensure that the level of sugar in the blood is always just right. If the level of sugar in the blood drops, the pancreas releases more glucagon to make up for the loss. If the level of sugar in the blood rises, the pancreas releases more insulin to get rid of the excess sugar.

OVARIES AND TESTES The **ovaries** (OH-vuh-reez) are the female reproductive glands, and the **testes** (tehs-teez; singular: testis, TEHS-tihs) are the male reproductive glands. The reproductive glands produce sex hormones that affect cells throughout the body. The ovaries and testes will be discussed in more detail in Chapter 7.

Negative-Feedback Mechanism

You can compare the way the endocrine system works to the way a thermostat in a heating and cooling system works. A thermostat is a device that controls the system in order to keep the temperature within certain limits. Suppose you set the thermostat in your classroom at 20°C. If the temperature of the room goes above 20°C, the thermostat turns on the

FIND OUT BY
CALCULATING

How Much Is Enough?

The body cells are very sensitive to hormones. As little as 0.000001 milligram of a hormone per milliliter of blood can cause body cells to respond. How much of a hormone is needed to cause a response in 5000 mL of blood? In 10,000 mL?

air conditioner. The cooling effect produced by the air conditioner brings the temperature of your classroom back down to 20°C. At this point, the thermostat turns the air conditioner off. If, on the other hand, the temperature of the room falls below 20°C, the thermostat turns on the heater rather than the air conditioner. The heater, which has a warming effect, stays on until the temperature again returns to 20°C. In this way, the thermostat controls the internal environment of your classroom. In a similar way, a **negative-feedback mechanism** automatically controls the levels of hormones in your body. **In a negative-feedback mechanism, the production of a hormone is controlled by the amount of another hormone in the blood, thereby keeping the body's internal environment stable.**

The actions of the pituitary and the thyroid are probably the best examples of the negative-feedback mechanism. The pituitary is very sensitive to the amount of thyroxine (thigh-RAHKS-een) in the blood. Thyroxine is the name of the hormone that is released by the thyroid. When the level of thyroxine in the blood drops too low, the pituitary releases its hormone, a hormone called thyroid-stimulating hormone, or TSH. This action causes the thyroid to make more thyroxine, thus restoring the level of thyroxine in the blood. When the amount of thyroxine in the blood is just right, the pituitary stops releasing TSH, and the thyroid stops producing thyroxine. In this way, the negative-feedback mechanism helps to keep the internal environment of the body stable.

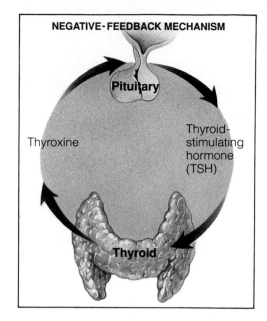

Figure 6–34 *The release of TSH into the bloodstream by the pituitary stimulates the production of thyroxine by the thyroid. When the level of thyroxine in the bloodstream increases, the pituitary reacts negatively by lowering the amount of TSH it releases. This is an example of a negative-feedback mechanism, which controls the levels of hormones in the blood.*

6–4 Section Review

1. What is the function of the endocrine system?
2. What is a hormone?
3. List eight endocrine glands in the body.
4. What is the negative-feedback mechanism?
5. Explain how the negative-feedback mechanism helps to maintain a state of balance within the body.

Critical Thinking—*Relating Facts*
6. If a person has diabetes mellitus, would his or her production of glucagon be increased or decreased? Explain your answer.

Laboratory Investigation

Locating Touch Receptors

Problem

Where are the touch receptors located on the body?

Materials *(per pair of students)*

scissors	9 straight pins
metric ruler	piece of card-
blindfold	board (6 cm x
	10 cm)

Procedure 🔪

1. Using the scissors, cut the piece of cardboard into five rectangles each measuring 6 cm x 2 cm.

2. Into one cardboard rectangle, insert two straight pins 5 mm apart. Into the second cardboard rectangle, insert two pins 1 cm apart. Insert two pins 2 cm apart into the third rectangle. Insert two pins 3 cm apart into the fourth rectangle. In the center of the remaining cardboard rectangle, insert one pin.

3. Construct a data table in which the pin positions on the cardboard appear across the top of the table.

4. Blindfold your partner.

5. Using the cardboard rectangle with the straight pins 5 mm apart, carefully touch the palm surface of your partner's fingertip, palm of the hand, back of the hand, back of the neck, and inside of the forearm. **CAUTION:** *Do not apply pressure when touching your partner's skin.* In the data table, list each of these body parts.

6. If your partner feels two points in any of the areas that you touch, place the number 2 in the appropriate place in the data table. If your partner feels only one point, place the number 1 in the data table.

7. Repeat steps 5 and 6 with the remaining cardboard rectangles.

8. Reverse roles with your partner and repeat the investigation.

Observations

On which part of the body did you feel the most sensation? The least?

Analysis and Conclusions

1. Which part of the body that you tested had the most touch receptors? The fewest? How do you know?

2. Rank the body parts in order from the most to the least sensitive.

3. What do the answers to questions 1 and 2 indicate about the distribution of touch receptors in the skin?

4. **On Your Own** Obtain a variety of objects. Blindfold your partner and hand one of the objects to your partner. Have your partner describe how the object feels. Your partner is not to name the object. Record the description along with the name of the object. Repeat the investigation for each object. Reverse roles and repeat the investigation. How well were you and your partner able to "observe" with the senses of touch?

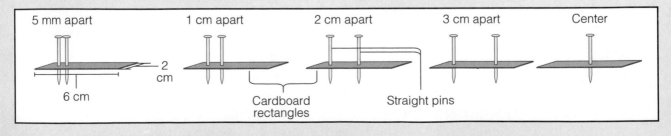

| 5 mm apart | 1 cm apart | 2 cm apart | 3 cm apart | Center |

2 cm

6 cm

Cardboard rectangles

Straight pins

Study Guide

Summarizing Key Concepts

6–1 The Nervous System

▲ The nervous system receives and sends out information about activities within the body and monitors and responds to changes in the environment.

▲ The basic unit of structure and function of the nervous system is the neuron, which is made up of the cell body, dendrites, an axon, and axon terminals.

▲ A nerve impulse sends messages in the form of electrical and chemical signals. The gap between neurons is called a synapse.

6–2 Divisions of the Nervous System

▲ The central nervous system is composed of the brain and the spinal cord. The brain is divided into three parts: the cerebrum, the cerebellum, and the medulla.

▲ The peripheral nervous system consists of all the nerves that connect to the central nervous system.

▲ The autonomic nervous system consists of two sets of nerves that have opposite effects on the organs they control.

6–3 The Senses

▲ Light entering the eye passes through the cornea, aqueous humor, lens, and vitreous humor to the retina. The optic nerve carries the impulses to the brain.

▲ Sound enters the ear as vibrations and strikes the eardrum, causing the hammer, anvil, and stirrup to vibrate. These vibrations finally reach the cochlea. The auditory nerve carries the impulses to the brain.

▲ Smell and taste are chemical senses.

▲ The skin contains receptors for touch, pressure, pain, heat, and cold.

6–4 The Endocrine System

▲ The endocrine system includes the hypothalamus, pituitary, thymus, thyroid, parathyroids, adrenals, pancreas, and ovaries or testes.

▲ In the feedback mechanism, the production of a hormone is controlled by the amount of another hormone in the blood, thereby keeping the body's internal environment stable.

Reviewing Key Terms

Define each term in a complete sentence.

6–1 The Nervous System
stimulus
neuron
cell body
dendrite
axon
receptor
sensory neuron
interneuron
motor neuron
effector
nerve impulse
synapse

6–2 Divisions of the Nervous System
brain
spinal cord
cerebrum
cerebellum
medulla
reflex

6–3 The Senses
cornea
iris
pupil
lens
retina
eardrum
cochlea
semicircular
  canal

6–4 The Endocrine System
hormone
hypothalamus
pituitary
thymus
thyroid
parathyroid
adrenal
islets of
  Langerhans
ovary
testis
negative-
  feedback
  mechanism

Chapter Review

Content Review

Multiple Choice

Choose the letter of the answer that best completes each statement.

1. A change in the environment is a(an)
   a. effector.   c. reflex.
   b. stimulus.   d. hormone.
2. The short fibers that carry messages from neurons toward the cell body are the
   a. dendrites.   c. synapses.
   b. axon terminals.   d. axons.
3. The gap between two neurons is called the
   a. dendrite.   c. synapse.
   b. cell body.   d. axon.
4. The part of the brain that controls balance is the
   a. spinal cord.   c. cerebellum.
   b. cerebrum.   d. medulla.
5. Which endocrine gland provides a link between the nervous system and the endocrine system?
   a. pituitary   c. parathryoid
   b. adrenal   d. hypothalamus

6. The largest part of the brain is the
   a. spinal cord.   c. cerebellum.
   b. cerebrum.   d. medulla.
7. Which of the following is part of the central nervous system?
   a. medulla
   b. semicircular canals
   c. retina
   d. auditory nerve
8. The pancreas produces the hormones insulin and
   a. thyroxine.
   b. glucagon.
   c. human growth hormone.
   d. adrenaline.
9. The layer of the eye onto which an image is focused is the
   a. retina.   c. choroid.
   b. sclera.   d. cornea.

True or False

If the statement is true, write "true." If it is false, change the underlined word or words to make the statement true.

1. The part of the neuron that contains the nucleus is the <u>axon</u>.
2. The <u>pituitary</u> produces adrenaline.
3. The brain and the spinal cord make up the <u>peripheral</u> nervous system.
4. The reproductive glands are the ovaries and the <u>testes</u>.
5. The <u>retina</u> is the watery fluid between the cornea and the lens of the eye.
6. The <u>auditory nerve</u> carries impulses from the ear to the brain.
7. The outer layer of the eye is the <u>choroid</u>.

Concept Mapping

Complete the following concept map for Section 6–1. Refer to pages H8–H9 to construct a concept map for the entire chapter.

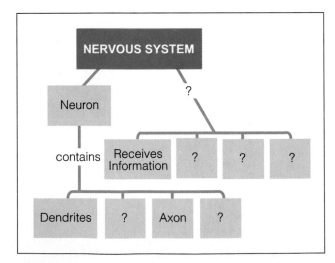

Concept Mastery

Discuss each of the following in a brief paragraph.

1. What is a stimulus? Give two examples.
2. What are the functions of the three types of neurons found in the nervous system?
3. Compare the functions of a receptor and an effector.
4. Explain how an impulse crosses a synapse.
5. Describe the role of the lens in vision.
6. Compare the effect of adrenaline and insulin on the body.
7. What is the function of the hypothalamus?
8. Explain what a negative-feedback mechanism is. Give an example.
9. Explain why it is an advantage to you that your reflexes respond quickly and automatically.
10. How does an endocrine gland differ from an exocrine gland?
11. How is the central nervous system protected?
12. Trace the path of light through the eye.
13. Trace the path of sound through the ear.

Critical Thinking and Problem Solving

Use the skills you have developed in this chapter to answer each of the following.

1. **Making comparisons** Compare the nervous system to a computer. How are they similar? Different?
2. **Applying concepts** Explain why many people become dizzy after spinning around for any length of time.
3. **Interpreting graphs** The accompanying graph shows the levels of sugar in the blood of two people during a five-hour period immediately after a typical meal. Which line represents an average person? Which line represents a person with diabetes mellitus? Explain your answers.

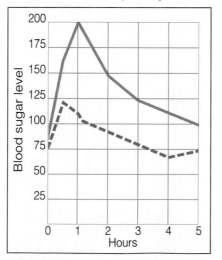

4. **Relating concepts** A routine examination by a doctor usually includes the knee-jerk test. What is the purpose of this test? What could the absence of a response indicate?
5. **Applying concepts** Explain why after entering a dark room, you are surprised to see how colorful the room is when the lights are turned on.
6. **Applying concepts** Sometimes as a result of a cold, the middle ear becomes filled with fluid. Why do you think this can cause a temporary loss of hearing?
7. **Making predictions** What might happen if the cornea becomes inflamed and as a result more fluid collects there?
8. **Using the writing process** Select a picture in a book or magazine. In a short essay, explain how what you see in the picture is influenced by your sense of touch, hearing, smell, or taste as well as your sense of vision.

Reproduction and Development

Guide for Reading

After you read the following sections, you will be able to

7–1 The Reproductive System

- Identify the function and importance of the reproductive system.
- Define fertilization.
- Compare the functions and structures of the male and female reproductive systems.

7–2 Stages of Development

- Describe the changes that occur between fertilization and birth.
- Describe the process of birth.
- List and describe the stages of development after birth.

Almost everyone loves babies—all kinds of babies: animal babies (bunnies, kittens, and puppies, to name just a few) and human babies. Babies can be one of the funniest and most appealing subjects of photography. Just look at the photograph on the opposite page!

One of the many common characteristics of all newborn human babies is their total helplessness. They cannot sit up, move from one place to another, feed themselves, or talk in a language understood by other people. Their basic means of communicating hunger, discomfort, unhappiness, or pain is by crying. With proper care and training, however, babies gradually learn to do some things for themselves. And they eventually become children, adolescents, and then adults.

At this point, you may be asking yourself this question: What changes take place as a baby develops and grows into a full-sized adult? As you read this chapter you will find the answer to this question as well as the answers to others. And you will also discover that human development is an exciting, ongoing process.

Journal *Activity*

You and Your World Place photographs of yourself as an infant, toddler, or young child in your journal. Below each photograph, describe what you were doing when the photograph was taken and what you remember about it. What physical and social changes have you undergone since the photographs were taken?

◄ *These human babies—products of reproduction—guarantee the survival of the human species.*

7–1 The Reproductive System

In the previous chapters of this textbook, you learned about the human body systems that are vital to the survival of the individual. Without the proper functioning of these systems, humans would no doubt be unable to live healthy, normal lives. The loss of the digestive system, nervous system, or circulatory system would be fatal (deadly) in humans. Can you explain why?

There is one body system, however, that is not essential to the survival of the individual. In fact, humans can survive quite well without the functioning of this system. What this system is important to is the survival of the human species—that is, the continuation on Earth of people just like you. Have you figured out what this system is?

The body system is the reproductive system, which contains special structures that enable reproduction to take place. Reproduction is the process through which living things produce new individuals of the same kind. Thus the reproductive system ensures the continuation of the species. Without it, a species will cease to exist. Do you know the scientific word that means a species no longer exists on Earth?

Figure 7–1 *The process of reproduction results in new individuals of the same kind. Without reproduction, humans, hippopotamuses, and, for that matter, all species of living things would cease to exist.*

In humans, the reproductive system produces, stores, nourishes, and releases specialized cells known as sex cells. From the union of these sex cells will come a new individual—the next generation. How does the reproductive system function? How does the extraordinary process of reproduction take place? And how do single cells become complete humans millions and millions of times every year?

Sexual Development

Does it surprise you to learn that you began life as one single cell? Well, that's just how you started. This single cell was produced by the joining of two other cells. These two other cells are specialized cells known as sex cells. Sex cells are unlike any other cells that make up your body. Biologists call the sex cells gametes (GAM-eets). There are two kinds of sex cells (or gametes)—a male sex cell and a female sex cell. The male sex cell is called the **sperm.** The female sex cell is called the **egg,** or ovum (OH-vuhm; plural: ova, OH-vuh). The joining of a sperm nucleus and an egg nucleus is called **fertilization.** Recall that the nucleus of a cell contains the genetic material. Fertilization is the process by which organisms produce more of their own kind. The result of fertilization is a fertilized egg—one single cell from which come all the trillions of cells in a human body!

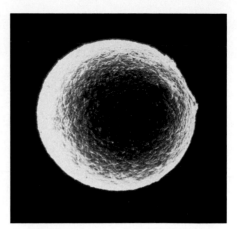

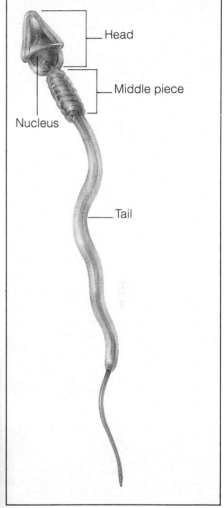

Head

Middle piece

Nucleus

Tail

Figure 7–2 *The tadpole-shaped sperm, which consists of a head, a middle piece, and a tail, is the male sex cell. The ball-shaped egg is the female sex cell. What is the name of the process in which the nuclei of these two sex cells join?*

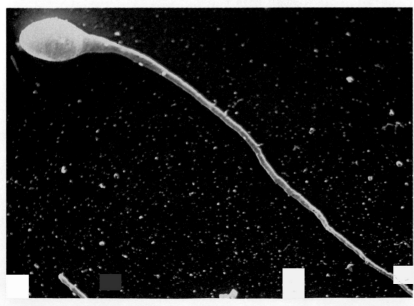

Figure 7–3 *Chromosomes are thick rodlike structures that are responsible for passing on inherited characteristics. The photograph shows the size, number, and pairs of chromosomes for a human body cell. How many chromosomes are in each human body cell?*

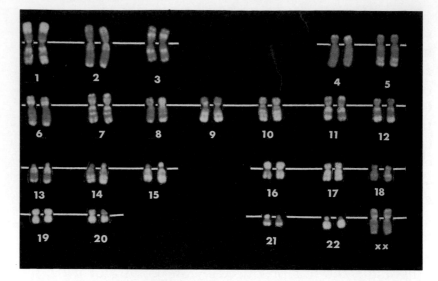

Both the sperm and the egg contain thick, rodlike structures called chromosomes (KROH-muh-sohmz). Chromosomes are responsible for passing on inherited characteristics such as skin, eye, and hair color from one generation of cells to the next. With the exception of the sex cells (sperm and egg), every cell in the human body contains 46 chromosomes. The sex cells contain only half this number, or 23 chromosomes. As a result of the joining of sperm (23 chromosomes) and egg (23 chromosomes) nuclei during fertilization, the nucleus of a fertilized egg contains 46 chromosomes—the normal number of chromosomes for all body cells. Within these 46 chromosomes is all the information needed to produce a complete new human—you!

If it surprised you to learn that humans begin life as a single cell, then the following fact will probably surprise you just as much, if not more. For the first 6 weeks after fertilization, male and female fertilized eggs (now called embryos) are identical in appearance. Then, during the seventh week of development, major changes occur. If the fertilized egg is a male, certain hormones are produced that cause the development of the male reproductive organs. If the fertilized egg is a female, certain other hormones are produced that cause the development of the female reproductive organs. (Hormones, you will recall from Chapter 6, are chemical messengers that regulate certain activities of the body.) Thus the male and female reproductive organs develop from exactly the same tissues in a fertilized egg.

After birth and for the next 10 to 15 years, the hormones specific to the male and those specific to the female continue to influence the development of their respective reproductive organs. Accompanying this development is the appearance of certain sex characteristics such as growth of facial hair in males and broadening of the hips in females. You will read more about this process in the next section. At the end of this process, the male and female reproductive organs are fully developed and functional.

The Male Reproductive System

The primary male reproductive organs are the **testes** (TEHS-teez; singular: testis, TEHS-tihs). The testes are oval-shaped organs found inside an external pouch (sac) of skin called the scrotum (SKROHT-uhm). The major role of the testes is to produce sperm. The fact that the testes remain in the scrotum outside the body is very important to the development of sperm. The external temperature is

Figure 7–4 *In the male reproductive system, sperm and the hormone testosterone are produced within two oval-shaped organs called the testes. Sperm travel from the testes through tubes to the urethra. What is the function of testosterone?*

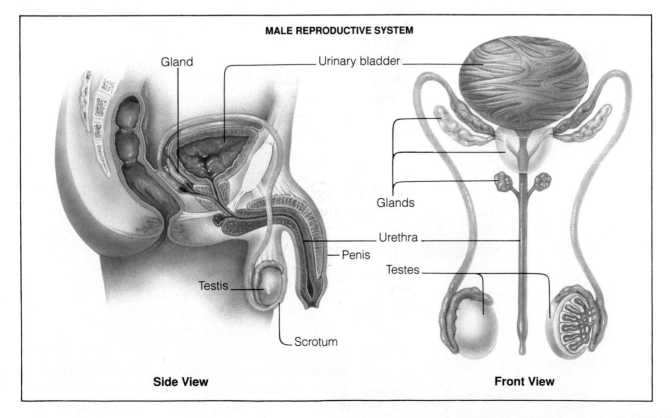

MALE REPRODUCTIVE SYSTEM

Gland
Urinary bladder
Glands
Urethra
Penis
Testes
Testis
Scrotum

Side View

Front View

about 1° to 3°C lower than the internal temperature of the body (37°C). Sperm development in the testes requires a lower temperature.

The testes are actually clusters of hundreds of tiny tightly coiled tubes. It is in these tubes that sperm are produced. Developed sperm travel from the tubes through several other structures to the urethra (yoo-REE-thruh). The urethra is a larger tube that leads to the outside of the body through the penis. During their passage to the urethra, sperm mix with a fluid produced by glands in the area. The combination of this fluid and sperm is known as semen (SEE-mehn). The number of sperm present in just a few drops of semen is astonishing. Between 100 and 200 million sperm are present in 1 milliliter of semen—about 5 million sperm per drop!

If you look at Figure 7–2 on page 169, you can see that a sperm cell consists of three parts: a head, a middle piece, and a tail. The head contains the nucleus, or control center of the cell. Energy-releasing cell structures pack the middle piece. And the tail propels the sperm cell forward.

In addition to producing sperm, the testes produce a hormone called testosterone (tehs-TAHS-ter-ohn). Testosterone is responsible for a number of male characteristics: the growth of facial and body hair, broadening of the chest and shoulders, and deepening of the voice.

The Female Reproductive System

Unlike the male reproductive system, all parts of the female reproductive system are within the female's body. The primary female reproductive organs are the **ovaries** (OH-vuh-reez). The ovaries are located at about hip level, one on each side of a female's body. The major role of the ovaries is to produce eggs, or ova. Located near each ovary, but not directly connected to it, is a **Fallopian** (fuh-LOH-pee-uhn) **tube**, or oviduct. From the ovary, an egg enters a Fallopian tube and travels slowly through it. At the opposite end of a Fallopian tube, an egg enters a hollow muscular organ called the **uterus** (YOOT-er-uhs), or womb. The uterus, which is shaped like an upside-down pear, is the organ in

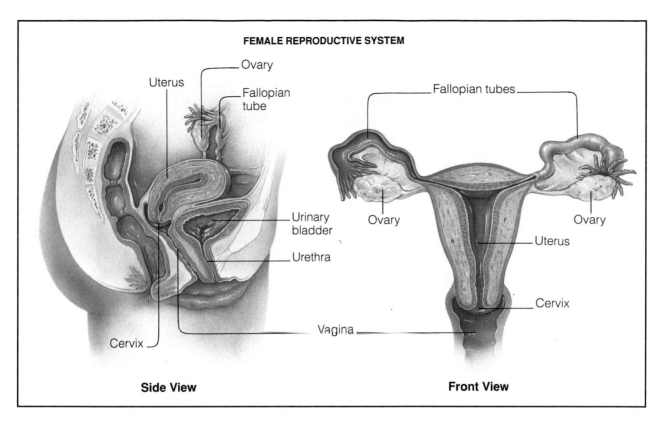

FEMALE REPRODUCTIVE SYSTEM

Side View

- Uterus
- Ovary
- Fallopian tube
- Urinary bladder
- Urethra
- Cervix

Front View

- Fallopian tubes
- Ovary
- Ovary
- Uterus
- Cervix
- Vagina

which a fertilized egg develops. The lower end of the uterus narrows into an area called the cervix (SER-vihks). The cervix opens into a wider channel called the vagina (vuh-JIGH-nuh), or birth canal. The vagina is the passageway through which a baby passes during the birth process.

Compared to a sperm cell, an egg cell is enormous. It is one of the largest cells in the body. It is so large, in fact, that it can be seen with the unaided eye. Its size is often compared to that of a grain of sand.

It is interesting to note that whereas a male continually produces sperm cells, a female is born with all the eggs she will ever have. A female will not produce any new eggs in her lifetime. The average number of undeveloped eggs a female has in her ovaries is about 400,000. Only about 500 of these, however, will actually leave the ovaries and journey to the uterus.

Like the testes, the ovaries produce hormones. One of these hormones is called estrogen (EHS-truh-juhn). Estrogen triggers the development of a number of female characteristics: broadening of the hips, enlargement of the breasts, and maturation (aging) of egg cells in the ovaries.

Figure 7–5 *In the female reproductive system, the ovaries produce eggs and hormones. From an ovary, an egg travels through a Fallopian tube to the uterus. What is another name for a Fallopian tube? For the uterus?*

The Menstrual Cycle

The monthly cycle of change that occurs in the female reproductive system is called the **menstrual** (MEHN-struhl) **cycle**. The menstrual cycle has an average length of about 28 days, or almost a month. In fact, the word menstrual comes from the Latin word *mensis,* meaning month. The menstrual cycle involves the interaction of the reproductive system and the endocrine system. It is controlled by hormones operating on a negative-feedback mechanism. Do you remember how such a mechanism works? If you do not, you may want to review Section 6–4 in the previous chapter.

Although the menstrual cycle affects the entire body of a female, it has two basic purposes: (1) the development and release of an egg for fertilization and (2) the preparation of the uterus to receive a fertilized egg. The menstrual cycle consists of a complex series of events that occur in a periodic fashion. It is not necessary for you to know about these events in detail. What you should understand and appreciate is the purpose of the menstrual cycle and some of its basic characteristics.

As you just learned, unlike male sex cells, female sex cells are formed in the ovaries at birth. Each sex cell, or egg, is held within a little pocket of cells called a follicle (FAHL-ih-kuhl). By the time a female

Figure 7–6 *During ovulation, an egg bursts from a follicle (right). The egg is then swept into the feathery tunnel-shaped opening of a Fallopian tube (left). What organ does an egg enter after it leaves a Fallopian tube?*

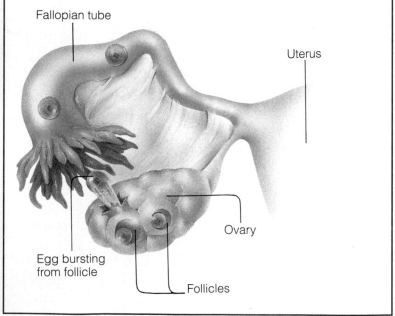

Fallopian tube

Uterus

Egg bursting from follicle

Ovary

Follicles

is ready to begin the menstrual cycle, there may be nearly half a million follicles in the ovaries. Only a few follicles, however, release ripened (mature) eggs.

If an egg does ripen, increased hormone levels cause the follicle to burst through the side of the ovary, releasing the egg. This process is called **ovulation** (ahv-yoo-LAY-shuhn). The egg is then swept into the feathery funnel-shaped opening of a Fallopian tube. Pushed along by microscopic cilia lining the walls, the egg is moved through the Fallopian tube toward the uterus.

If sperm are present in the Fallopian tube when the egg arrives, the egg can be fertilized. Although hundreds of millions of sperm are released by the male, only relatively few—perhaps 10,000 to 100,000 enter the proper Fallopian tube (the Fallopian tube containing the egg). Of these sperm, barely 1000 make it to the egg. Nevertheless, only 1 sperm is needed for fertilization.

The changes occurring in the ovary are not the only changes taking place during the menstrual cycle. In preparation for the arrival of a fertilized egg, the lining of the uterus is thickening, and the blood

Figure 7–7 *Although hundreds of millions of sperm are released by the male (top left), very few sperm enter the proper Fallopian tube (top right). The proper Fallopian tube is the one that contains the egg (bottom left). Of all the sperm that make it to the egg (bottom right), only one is needed to fertilize it.*

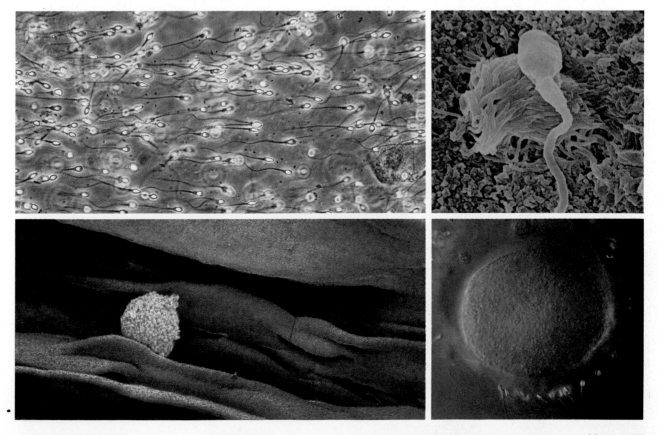

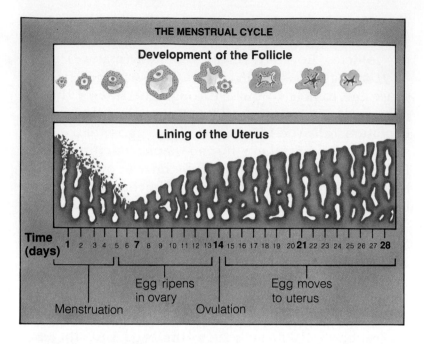

Figure 7–8 *The monthly cycle of change that occurs in the female reproductive system is called the menstrual cycle. It consists of a complex series of events that occur in a periodic fashion. What events take place during menstruation?*

THE MENSTRUAL CYCLE

Development of the Follicle

Lining of the Uterus

Time (days) 1 2 3 4 5 6 **7** 8 9 10 11 12 13 **14** 15 16 17 18 19 20 **21** 22 23 24 25 26 27 **28**

Menstruation

Egg ripens in ovary

Ovulation

Egg moves to uterus

supply to the tissues is increasing. If a fertilized egg reaches the lining, it implants (inserts) itself there, divides and grows, and eventually develops into a new human.

If the egg is not fertilized, it and the lining of the uterus will begin to break down. When this happens, the extra blood and tissue in the thickened lining of the uterus pass out of the body through the vagina. This process is called menstruation (mehn-STRAY-shuhn). On the average, menstruation lasts 5 days. At the same time menstruation is occurring, a new egg is maturing in its follicle in the ovary, and the changing levels of hormones are causing the cycle to begin anew.

7–1 Section Review

1. What are the structures and functions of the male and female reproductive systems?
2. What is fertilization?
3. Describe the menstrual cycle.

Critical Thinking—*Relating Facts*

4. A Fallopian tube is lined with mucus. How does this contribute to the function of the tube?

7–2 Stages of Development

Guide for Reading

Focus on these questions as you read.

▶ *What are the stages of human development that occur before birth?*

▶ *What are the stages of human development that occur after birth?*

You have just read that an egg can be fertilized only during ovulation and for several days after. Ovulation usually occurs about 14 days after the start of menstruation. If the egg is fertilized, the remarkable process of human development begins. In the course of this process, a single cell no larger than the period at the end of this sentence will undergo a series of divisions that will result in the formation of a new human. Approximately 9 months after fertilization, a baby will be born. As you well know, this is only the beginning of a lifetime of developmental changes.

Humans go through various stages of development before and after birth. **Before birth, a single human cell develops into an embryo and then a fetus. After birth, humans pass through the stages of infancy, childhood, adolescence, and adulthood.**

Development Before Birth

As the fertilized egg, now called a **zygote** (ZIGH-goht), begins its 4-day trip through the Fallopian tube to the uterus, it begins to divide. From one cell it becomes two, then four, then eight, and so on. At this point, the cells resemble a hollow ball. During this early stage of development, and for the next 8 weeks or so, the developing human is called an **embryo** (EHM-bree-oh).

Soon after the embryo enters the uterus, it attaches itself to the wall and begins to grow inward. As it does so, several membranes form around it. One of those membranes develops into a fluid-filled sac called the **amniotic** (am-nee-AHT-ihk) **sac**. The amniotic sac cushions and protects the developing baby. Another membrane forms the **placenta** (pluh-SEHN-tuh). The placenta is made partly from tissue that develops from the embryo and partly from tissue that makes up the wall of the uterus.

The placenta provides a connection between developing embryo and mother. The developing embryo needs a supply of oxygen and food. It also needs a way of getting rid of wastes. You may think that the embryo's needs could be met if the blood supply of mother and embryo were joined. But such

FIND OUT BY WRITING

The Developing Embryo

The first trimester, or 3 months, of a pregnancy is the most important in the development of a baby. Use reference materials in the library to find out about the changes that occur in the developing baby during the first trimester. On posterboard, construct a chart in which you describe these changes on a weekly basis for the first 12 weeks of a typical pregnancy.

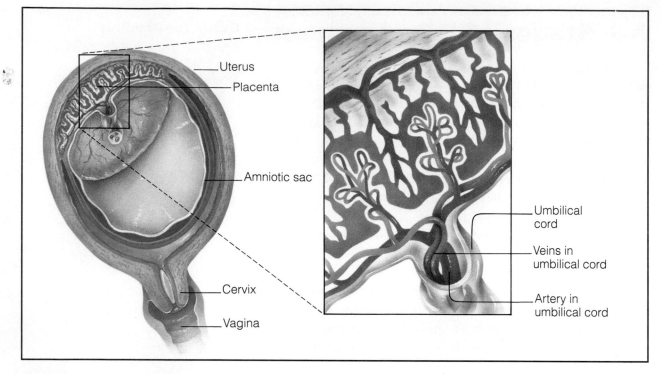

Uterus
Placenta
Amniotic sac
Cervix
Vagina
Umbilical cord
Veins in umbilical cord
Artery in umbilical cord

Figure 7–9 *The placenta provides a connection between the mother and the developing baby. Through blood vessels in the umbilical cord, food and oxygen from the mother and wastes from the developing baby are exchanged. What is the function of the amniotic sac?*

an arrangement would also allow diseases to spread from mother to embryo and would cause other problems related to the mixing of different blood types.

Actually, the blood of mother and embryo flow past each other, but they do not mix. They are separated by a thin membrane that acts as a barrier. Across this thin barrier, food, oxygen, and wastes are exchanged. Thus the placenta becomes the embryo's organ of nourishment, respiration, and excretion. The placenta also permits harmful substances such as alcohol, chemicals in tobacco smoke, and drugs to pass from the mother to the developing baby. For this reason, it is important that pregnant women not drink alcohol, smoke tobacco, or take any type of drug without a doctor's approval.

After eight weeks of development, the embryo is about the size of a walnut. Now called a **fetus** (FEET-uhs), it begins to take on a more babylike appearance. By the end of 3 months, it has the main internal organs, dark eye patches, and fingers and toes. During this time, a structure known as the **umbilical** (uhm-BIHL-ih-kuhl) **cord** forms. The umbilical cord, which contains two arteries and one vein, connects the fetus to the placenta. The large size of the fetus's head—about half the total size—indicates the rapid brain development that is taking place. At this point, the fetus is about 9 centimeters long and has a mass of about 15 grams.

During the fourth, fifth, and sixth months, the tissues of the fetus continue to become more specialized. A skeleton begins to form, a heartbeat can be heard with a stethoscope, and a layer of soft hair grows over the skin. The mass of the fetus is now about 700 grams.

The final 3 months prepare the fetus for a completely independent existence. The lungs and other organs undergo a series of changes that prepare them for life outside the mother. The mass of the fetus quadruples. A baby is about to be born. The entire time period between the fertilization of an egg and the birth of a baby is known as pregnancy. An average full-term pregnancy is about 9 months.

In recent years, medical technology has made it possible to detect, and in some cases treat, fetal disorders. Such advances have opened up a new frontier in medicine: diagnosing and treating babies before they are born! In one technique, a small amount of the amniotic fluid in which a fetus floats is removed through a hollow needle. The amniotic fluid, which contains cells from the fetus, is then studied to determine the health of the fetus. If there are problems that can be corrected, doctors are now able to inject medication through the hollow needle into the fetus. In a recent medical breakthrough, doctors have safely given blood transfusions to babies still in the uterus. This amazing feat was performed

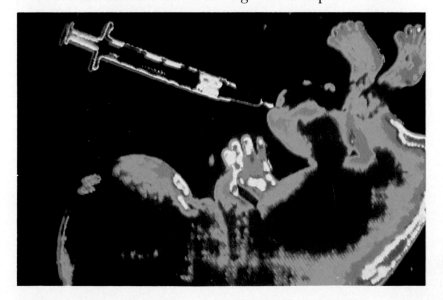

Figure 7–10 *In this photograph you can see a needle removing a small amount of fluid from the amniotic sac. This sac contains cells from the fetus that will be examined to determine the health of the fetus.*

Multiple Births

A multiple birth occurs when two or more children are born at one time to one mother. Using reference materials in the library, look up information on twins. In a written report, describe how twins develop. You might wish to use diagrams in your explanation.

■ What is the difference in origin and appearance between identical and fraternal twins?

■ How do identical triplets develop?

■ How do fraternal triplets develop?

with the help of sound waves, which produce an image on a television screen similar to the one shown in Figure 7–10 on page 179.

Birth

After about 9 months of development and growth inside the uterus, the fetus is ready to be born. Strong muscular contractions of the uterus begin to push the baby through the cervix into the vagina. These contractions are called labor. Labor is the first stage in the birth process. As labor progresses, the contractions of the uterus become stronger and occur more frequently. Finally, the baby—who is still connected to the placenta by the umbilical cord—is pushed out of the mother (usually head first). This stage, known as delivery, is the second stage in the birth process. Delivery usually takes less time than labor does. For example, labor may last anywhere from 2 to 20 hours or more; delivery may take from several minutes to a few hours. Within a few seconds of delivery, a baby may begin to cough or cry. This action helps to rid its lungs of fluid with which they have been filled, as well as to expand and fill its lungs with air.

Shortly after delivery, the third stage in the birth process begins. The umbilical cord, which is still attached to the placenta, is tied and then cut about 5 centimeters from the baby's abdomen. This procedure does not cause the baby any pain. A few minutes later, another set of contractions pushes the placenta and other membranes from the uterus. This is appropriately called afterbirth. Within 7 to 10

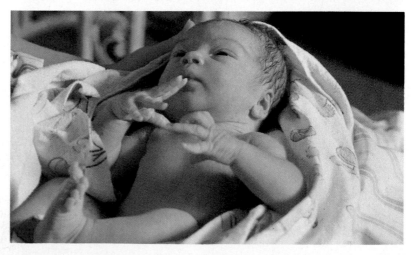

Figure 7–11 *After about 9 months of growth and development inside the uterus, a baby is born. This baby is only minutes old. What are the names of the three stages in the birth process?*

days, the remaining part of the umbilical cord dries up and falls off the baby's abdomen, leaving a scar. This scar is known as the navel. Do you know a more common name for the navel?

Development After Birth

The human body does not grow at a constant rate. The most rapid growth occurs before birth, when in the space of 9 months the fetus increases its mass about 2.4 billion times! After birth, there are two growth spurts (sudden increases in height and mass). These growth spurts occur in the first 2 years of life and again at the beginning of adolescence.

You may be surprised to learn that as you grow from infancy to adulthood, the number of bones in your body decreases. The 350 or so bones you were born with gradually fuse (come together) into the approximately 206 bones you will have in your skeleton as an adult. (Some simple arithmetic should tell you that is about 144 fewer bones.) The actual number of bones in a person's body varies because some people may have an extra pair of ribs or they may have fewer vertebrae in their spine.

INFANCY Have you ever watched a 6-month-old baby for a few minutes? Its actions, or responses, are simple. It can suck its thumb, grasp objects, yawn, stretch, blink, and sneeze. When lying in bed, the infant often curls up in a position much like the one it had in the uterus.

One of the most obvious changes during **infancy**, which extends from 1 month to about 2 years of age, is a rapid increase in size. The head of a young

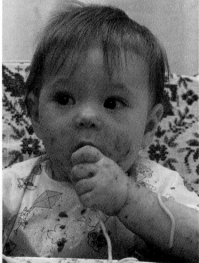

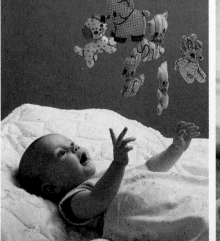 

Figure 7–12 *During infancy, which extends from about 1 month to 2 years, mental and muscular skills begin to develop. What skills are illustrated by the 5-month-old (left), the 1-year-old (top), and the 1½-year-old (right)?*

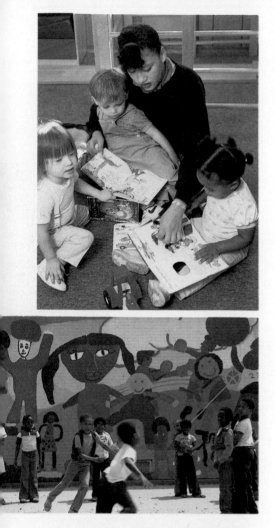

Figure 7–13 *Childhood begins around the age of 2 years and continues until the age of 13 years. In addition to understanding and speaking a language, children can be taught to read before they attend school (top). Children also learn to interact socially with others, as these 8- to 11-year-olds are doing (bottom).*

baby is rather large compared to the rest of its body. Actually, a baby's head makes up about one fourth of its body length. As an infant gets older, the head grows more slowly—and the body, legs, and arms begin to catch up.

Mental and muscular skills begin to develop in a fairly predictable order. The exact ages at which they occur, however, vary from baby to baby. A newborn infant cannot lift its head. But after about 3 months, it can hold its head up and can also reach for objects. Within the next 2 months, the infant can grasp objects. At about 7 months, most infants are able to move around by crawling. Somewhere between 10 and 14 months, most infants begin to walk by themselves.

CHILDHOOD   Infancy ends and **childhood** begins around the age of 2 years. Childhood continues until the age of 13 years. During childhood, mental abilities increase and memory is strengthened. Muscular skills develop. With practice, a small child becomes better at walking, holding a knife and fork, writing with a pencil, and playing sports. Over a period of several years, baby teeth are lost and replaced by permanent teeth.

During childhood, young children develop language skills. As you probably already know, all babies make babbling sounds. However, as a child becomes aware of itself and others, these sounds are shaped into language. Language skills come from observing and imitating others. At first, a child uses only one word at a time. For example, the child might say "ball." Soon after that, the child uses an action word and produces a two-word sentence, perhaps "Hit ball." By the age of 4 or 5, the child is able to speak in adultlike conversation.

In addition to understanding and speaking a language, children can be taught to read and solve problems even before they attend school. During childhood, children learn a great deal about their environment. They also learn to behave in socially appropriate ways.

ADOLESCENCE   In many cultures, **adolescence** is thought of as a passage from childhood to adulthood. The word adolescence comes from a Latin word meaning to grow up. Adolescence begins

Figure 7–14 *In many cultures, adolescence is seen as a passage from childhood to adulthood. In this ceremony, a 14-year-old Apache girl is sprinkled with cattail pollen by members of her tribe to signify this passage. In Austin, Texas, teenagers socialize at a dance.*

at **puberty** (PYOO-bcr-tee) and continues through the teenage years to the age of 20. During puberty, the sex organs develop rapidly. Menstruation begins in females and the production of sperm begins in males. In addition, a growth spurt occurs. In females, this rapid growth occurs between the ages of 10 and 16. During these years, females may grow about 15 centimeters in height and gain about 16 kilograms or more in mass. In males, the growth spurt occurs between the ages of 11 and 17. During this time, males may grow about 20 centimeters in height and gain about 20 kilograms in mass.

ADULTHOOD At about the age of 20, **adulthood** begins. All body systems, including the reproductive system, have become fully matured, and a person's full height has been reached. As a human passes from infancy through adulthood, fat beneath the skin keeps moving farther and farther away from the surface. The round, padded, button-nosed face of a baby is slowly replaced by the leaner, more defined face of an adult. The nose and the ears continue to grow and take on more individual shapes.

After about 30 years, a process known as aging begins. This process becomes more noticeable between the ages of 40 and 65. During this time, the skin loses some of its elasticity (capacity to return to its original shape), the eyes lose their ability to focus on close objects, the hair sometimes loses its coloring, and muscle strength decreases. During this period, females go through a physical change known as

Figure 7–15 *By the time people reach adulthood, all their body systems have become fully matured.*

menopause, in which menstruation stops and ovulation no longer occurs. Males do not go through similar changes in their reproductive processes. In fact, males continue to produce sperm throughout their lives. However, the number of sperm they produce decreases as they age.

After age 65, the aging process continues, often leading to less efficient heart and lung action. But the effects of aging can be slowed down or somewhat reversed if people follow sensible diets and good exercise plans throughout their lives.

FIND OUT BY

WRITING

You Only Look as Old as You Feel

Use reference materials in the library to find out about gerontology, or the study of aging. You may wish to interview a doctor who specializes in geriatrics, or the branch of medicine involving diseases of old age. Here are some questions that you should ask: What are the most common diseases of old age? What can a person do to lessen the chances of getting these diseases?

7–2 Section Review

1. What stages of development does a human go through before birth?
2. What stages of development does a human go through after birth?
3. What is a developing baby called during the first 8 weeks of development? After the first 8 weeks?
4. What is the function of the amniotic sac? The placenta?
5. What is puberty?

Connection—*Medicine*

6. Why is it important for pregnant women to have good health practices?

Electronic Reproduction

Have you ever wondered what it would be like to have several exact copies of yourself? One could go to class and do homework. One could do chores at home. One could spend the day playing—or perhaps you would let the real you do that. Well, dream on. By now, you know how complex the process of human reproduction really is and that there is only one "you" in the world. There will never be another.

Fortunately, the same is not true for photographs, illustrations, or the printed word. For today, modern photocopying machines can print out exact copies at the rate of hundreds per minute. Hundreds of copies per minute—now that's reproduction!

sheet of paper you want to copy on the machine, light shines onto it. The blank parts of the paper reflect the light and the light strikes the circular drum. Wherever the light strikes, the charge on the drum is removed. The dark parts of the paper (either words or visuals) do not reflect the light onto the drum. So the drum has parts that are charged and parts that have had the charge removed. When, in the next step, a liquid known as toner is introduced onto the drum, the toner is attracted to the charged parts only. The parts of the drum that are not charged do not attract toner. In seconds, the toner is laid down and an image is created on the photocopying machine paper.

You might be surprised to learn that photocopying machines do not use ink. They rely instead on *electricity,* or the flow of charged particles called electrons. Inside the photocopy machine is a circular drum. The drum is charged with static electricity and is coated with a material that conducts electricity when exposed to light.

Let's say you want to make a copy of a page of this textbook. When you place the

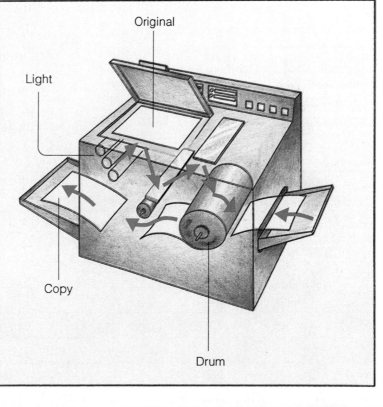

Original

Light

Copy

Drum

Laboratory Investigation

How Many Offspring?

Problem

How do the length of gestation, number of offspring per birth, age of puberty, and life span of various mammals compare?

Materials *(per group)*

graph paper
colored pencils

Procedure

1. Study the chart, which shows the length of gestation (pregnancy), the average number of offspring per birth, the average age of puberty, and the average life span of certain mammals.

2. Construct a bar graph that shows the length of gestation for each mammal.

3. Construct another bar graph that shows the average number of offspring of each mammal.

4. Construct a third bar graph that shows the life span of each mammal. Color the portion of the bar that shows the length of childhood, or time from birth to puberty.

Observations

1. Which of the mammals has the longest gestation period?

2. Which mammal has the largest number of offspring per birth?

3. Which of the mammals has the shortest life span?

4. Which mammal takes longer to reach puberty than Rhesus monkeys?

Analysis and Conclusions

1. What general conclusions can you draw after studying the graphs you have made?

2. If a mouse produces five litters per year, how many mice does the average female mouse produce in a lifetime?

3. Of all the mammals listed, which care for their young for the longest period of time after birth? Why do you think this is the case?

4. **On Your Own** Gather the same kinds of data for five additional mammals. Add these data to your existing graphs. How do the five new mammals compare with those provided in this investigation?

Mammal	Gestation Period (days)	Number of Offspring per Birth	Age at Puberty	Life Span (years)
Opossum	12	13	8 months	2
House mouse	20	6	2 months	3
Rabbit	30	4	4 months	5
Dog	61	7	7 months	15
Lion	108	3	2 years	23
Rhesus monkey	175	1	3 years	20
Human	280	1	13 years	74
Horse	330	1	1.5 years	25

Study Guide

Summarizing Key Concepts

7–1 The Reproductive System

▲ The joining of a sperm, or male sex cell, and an egg, or female sex cell, is known as fertilization.

▲ Each sperm and egg contains 23 chromosomes, which pass on inherited characteristics from one generation of cells to the next.

▲ The male reproductive system includes two testes, which produce sperm and a hormone called testosterone. The female reproductive system includes two ovaries, which produce eggs and hormones.

▲ Located near each ovary is a Fallopian tube that leads to a hollow, muscular uterus. At the lower end of the uterus is a narrow cervix, which opens into the vagina, or birth canal.

▲ The monthly cycle of change that occurs in the female reproductive system is called the menstrual cycle.

▲ During the menstrual cycle, ovulation, or the release of an egg from an ovary, occurs. The lining of the uterus also thickens in preparation for the attachment of a fertilized egg. If fertilization does not take place, the egg and thickened lining of the uterus break down and pass out of the body. This process is called menstruation. If sperm are present in the

Fallopian tube at the time of ovulation, an egg may become fertilized.

7–2 Stages of Development

▲ A fertilized egg is called a zygote. A zygote undergoes a series of divisions, forming a ball-shaped structure of many cells.

▲ During the first 8 weeks of its development, the developing human is called an embryo. It is surrounded and protected by several membranes. One of these membranes, called the placenta, provides the embryo with food and oxygen and eliminates its wastes. Another membrane forms around the fluid-filled amniotic sac, which cushions and protects the embryo.

▲ The umbilical cord, which contains blood vessels, connects the embryo to the placenta.

▲ During the birth process, the fetus and placenta pass out of the uterus through the cervix into the vagina.

▲ Humans pass through various stages of development during their lives. These stages are infancy, childhood, adolescence, and adulthood. Adolescence begins at puberty, when the sex organs develop rapidly.

Reviewing Key Terms

Define each term in a complete sentence.

7–1 The Reproductive System
sperm
egg
fertilization
testis
ovary
Fallopian tube
uterus

menstrual cycle
ovulation

7–2 Stages of Development
zygote
embryo
amniotic sac
placenta

fetus
umbilical cord
infancy
childhood
adolescence
puberty
adulthood

Chapter Review

Content Review

Multiple Choice

Choose the letter of the answer that best completes each statement.

1. What is the female sex cell called?
   - a. testis
   - c. egg
   - b. sperm
   - d. ovary
2. Sperm are produced in male sex organs called
   - a. testes.
   - c. scrotums.
   - b. ovaries.
   - d. urethras.
3. Sperm leave the male's body through the
   - a. testes.
   - c. vagina.
   - b. scrotum.
   - d. penis.
4. Eggs are produced in the
   - a. scrotum.
   - c. cervix.
   - b. ovaries.
   - d. Fallopian tubes.
5. A structure made up of tissues from both the embryo and the uterus is the
   - a. ovum.
   - c. cervix.
   - b. placenta.
   - d. fetus.
6. Another name for the womb is the
   - a. Fallopian tube.
   - c. vagina.
   - b. uterus.
   - d. scrotum.
7. The release of an egg from the ovary is known as
   - a. ovulation.
   - c. menstruation.
   - b. fertilization.
   - d. urination.
8. The structure in which a fertilized egg first divides is the
   - a. ovary.
   - c. uterus.
   - b. Fallopian tube.
   - d. vagina.
9. Sex organs develop rapidly during
   - a. infancy.
   - c. puberty.
   - b. childhood.
   - d. adulthood.
10. Adulthood begins at about the age of
    - a. 13 years.
    - c. 20 years.
    - b. 1 year.
    - d. 30 years.

True or False

If the statement is true, write "true." If it is false, change the underlined word or words to make the statement true.

1. The joining of a sperm and an egg is called <u>fertilization</u>.
2. The testes are found inside a sac called the <u>scrotum</u>.
3. To reach the uterus, an egg travels through the <u>cervix</u>.
4. An egg can be fertilized only while it is in a <u>Fallopian tube</u>.
5. If an egg is not fertilized, the lining of the uterus leaves the body through the <u>urethra</u>.
6. The structure that connects the embryo to the placenta is the <u>uterus</u>.
7. At 2 years of age, a person is considered to be an <u>infant</u>.

Concept Mapping

Complete the following concept map for Section 7–1. Refer to pages H8–H9 to construct a concept map for the entire chapter.

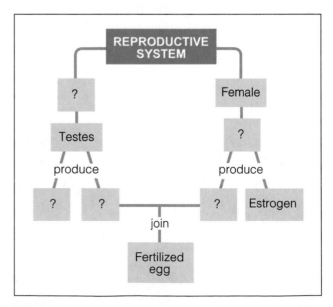

Concept Mastery

Discuss each of the following in a brief paragraph.

1. What changes occur in the female reproductive system during the menstrual cycle?
2. Describe how a fetus receives food and oxygen and how it gets rid of wastes.
3. How does a zygote form?
4. Describe the birth process.
5. Describe one method that is used by doctors to study babies while they are in the uterus.
6. Summarize the four stages of human development after birth.
7. Why is the process of reproduction so important?

Critical Thinking and Problem Solving

Use the skills you have developed in this chapter to answer each of the following.

1. **Making comparisons** In what way is development during adolescence similar to development before birth?
2. **Relating cause and effect** Why is it dangerous for pregnant women to smoke, drink, or use drugs not prescribed by a doctor?
3. **Relating facts** Why do you think the first stage in the birth process is called labor?
4. **Making inferences** The word adolescence means to grow up. Why is adolescence a good name for the teenage years of life?
5. **Applying concepts** Explain why a proper diet and an adequate amount of exercise can lessen the effects of aging.
6. **Drawing conclusions** Why do broken bones heal more rapidly in young children than in elderly people?
7. **Making comparisons** In what way is amniotic fluid similar to the shock absorbers of a car?
8. **Making predictions** Explain how a child's environment can affect its development.
9. **Relating facts** Explain how the shape of a sperm helps it function.
10. **Relating concepts** Why do you think a 1- to 2-year-old child is called a toddler?
11. **Making graphs** Use the information in the table to construct a graph. What conclusions can you draw from the graph?

Age Group in Years	Average Height in Centimeters	
	Female	*Male*
At birth	50	51
2	87	88
4	103	104
6	117	118
8	128	128
10	139	139
12	152	149
14	160	162
16	163	172
18	163	174

12. **Using the writing process** Develop an advertising campaign highlighting the dangers of alcohol and drug use during pregnancy.

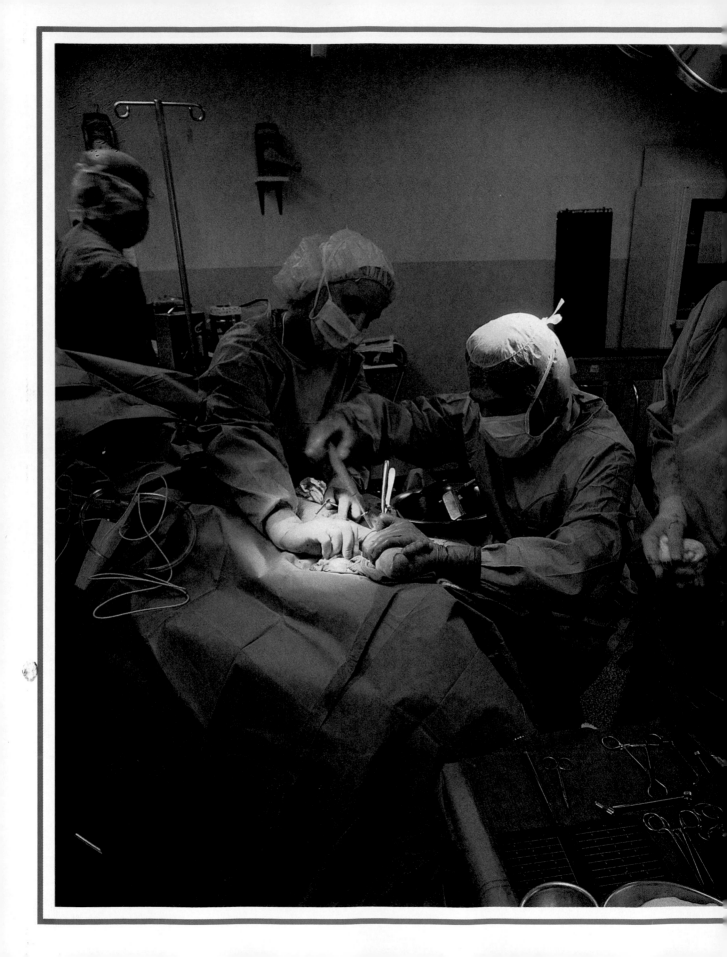

Immune System

Guide for Reading

After you read the following sections, you will be able to

8–1 Body Defenses

- Describe the function of the immune system.
- Describe the body's three lines of defense against invading organisms.
- Define antibody and antigen.

8–2 Immunity

- Define immunity.
- Compare active and passive immunity.
- Describe how vaccines work.

8–3 Diseases

- Define disease.
- Describe how diseases spread.
- List some examples of infectious and noninfectious diseases.

The scene: a dimly lit room. Occupying the middle of the room is a rectangular table covered with large soiled cloths. A patient ready for surgery lies on the table. The operation is about to begin.

But wait! Why is the patient lying on dirty cloths? Why are the surgeons wiping their hands (and on soiled cloths!) instead of washing them? Is this a scene from a horror movie?

What you are reading about actually occurred in hospital operating rooms before the middle of the 1800s. Fortunately, such scenes no longer take place. And we have the work of the English surgeon Joseph Lister to thank for that! In 1865, Lister demonstrated that microorganisms were the cause of many deaths after surgery. Thus Lister reasoned that if the microorganisms could be kept away from surgical wounds many more patients would survive surgery.

Today, surgeons wash thoroughly before an operation and wear surgical gowns, masks, and gloves. And operating rooms are kept spotlessly clean and free of germs. As you read the pages that follow, you will learn some interesting things about microorganisms and disease. And you may even make a discovery as important as Lister's!

Journal *Activity*

You and Your World Have you ever had a sore throat? How about an upset stomach? A fever? How did you feel? What did you do? In your journal, explore your thoughts and feelings during these times.

Today, operations are performed in spotlessly clean operating rooms by surgical teams wearing gowns, gloves, and masks.

Focus on these questions as you read.

▶ What is the function of the immune system?

▶ What are the body's three lines of defense against invading organisms?

8–1 Body Defenses

Considering the number of entries that invaders can successfully make into the body, it is amazing that a disease rarely occurs. Amazing, but no accident. Almost every human has a body system that works 24 hours a day all over the body to ensure its health. This body system is the immune system. **The immune system is the body's defense against disease-causing organisms.** The immune system not only repels disease-causing organisms, it also "keeps house" inside the body. It does this by removing dead or damaged cells and by looking for and destroying cells that do not function as they should.

The immune system has the remarkable ability to distinguish friend from foe. It identifies and destroys invaders and, at the same time, recognizes the body's own tissues. How does the immune system do all this? If you continue reading, you will find the answer.

The Body's First Line of Defense

Your body has certain important structures that help the immune system, although they are not actually part of it. Most invaders must first encounter these structures. These structures make up your body's first line of defense, forming a barrier between the body and its surroundings. The skin and the substances it produces, as well as protective reflexes such as sneezing and coughing, make up the first line of defense.

Figure 8–1 *Every minute of every day fierce battles are fought within your body. The invaders in these battles—such as influenza viruses (left) and the flatworm that causes the disease known as schistosomiasis (right)—are incredibly tiny. What body system defends against disease-causing organisms?*

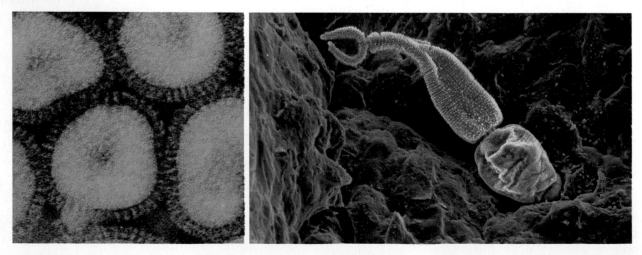

As you may recall from Chapter 5, the skin forms a protective covering over most of the body. This extraordinary organ has the ability to produce new cells and repair itself. Despite its daily dose of ripping, scratching, burning, and exposure to harsh chemicals and weather, the skin still performs admirably. It continues to produce new cells in its outer layer (epidermis) and repair tears in its inner layer (dermis). When cuts occur in the skin, however, they provide a means of entry for disease-causing organisms. What results is an infection, or a successful invasion into the body by disease-causing organisms.

Not all disease-causing organisms enter the body through the skin, however. Some are inhaled from the air. In much the same way as the skin defends the entire body against invaders, mucus (MYOO-kuhs) and cilia (SIHL-ee-uh) defend the respiratory system against airborne organisms. Mucus is a sticky substance that coats the membranes of the nose, trachea, and bronchi (parts of the respiratory system). As organisms enter these structures along with incoming air, they are trapped by the mucus and are thus prevented from traveling any farther into the body. In addition to mucus, the membranes are lined with tiny hairlike structures called cilia. The cilia, acting like brooms, sweep bacteria, dirt, and excess mucus out of the air passages at an amazing rate—about 2.5 centimeters a minute! These unwanted materials are carried to the throat, where they can be coughed out or swallowed.

Sometimes disease-causing organisms enter the body through the mouth, rather than through the skin or the nose. Here they mix with saliva, which is loaded with invader-killing chemicals. Most invaders do not survive the action of these chemicals. Those that do soon find themselves encountering a powerful acid in the stomach. This acid is so strong that it destroys the invaders. The dead invaders are eliminated from the body along with the body's other wastes.

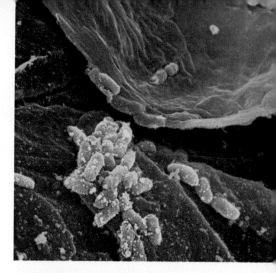

Figure 8–2 *The green objects in this photograph of the surface of the skin are bacteria. The skin is one of the body's first lines of defense against invading organisms.*

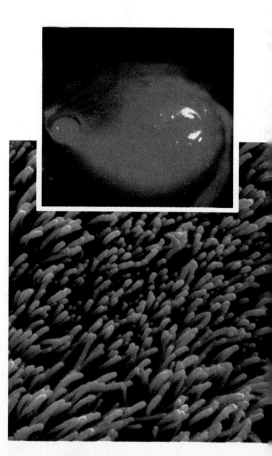

Figure 8–3 *As disease-causing organisms invade the body through the respiratory system, they are trapped by excess mucus that coats the membranes of the bronchus (top). The membranes are also lined with hairlike cilia that sweep the organisms out of the respiratory system (bottom).*

FIND OUT BY WRITING

Antiseptics and Disinfectants

Find out the following information about antiseptics and disinfectants by using reference materials in the library. What is the function of these substances? How do they help to control disease? What are three examples of each substance? Arrange this information in the form of a written report. Include the work of Joseph Lister and any other scientists who contributed to the discovery of these substances.

The Body's Second Line of Defense

If the first line of defense fails and disease-causing organisms enter the body, the second line of defense goes into action. When disease-causing organisms such as bacteria enter through a cut in the skin, they immediately try to attack body cells. The body, however, is quick to respond by increasing the blood supply to the affected area. This action causes white blood cells, which constantly patrol the blood and defend the body against disease-causing organisms, to leave the blood vessels and move into nearby tissues. Once inside, some of the white blood cells—the tiny ones—attack the invading organisms and then gobble them up.

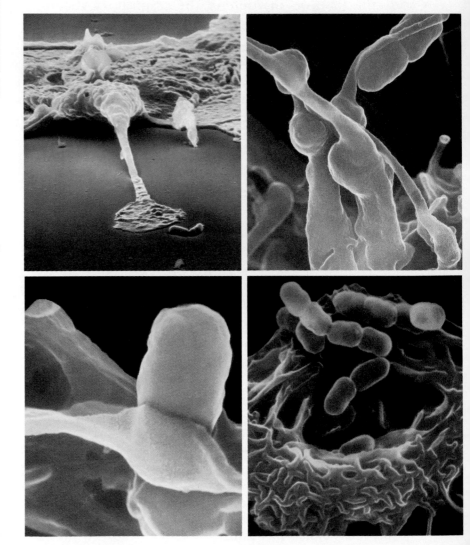

Figure 8–4 *White blood cells make up the body's second line of defense. This sequence of photographs shows what happens when a white blood cell encounters bacteria. The white blood cell first reaches out toward two bacterial cells (top left). Extensions from the white blood cell trap the bacteria (top right). Chemicals produced by the white blood cells begin to digest one of the bacterial cells (bottom left). Eventually, the bacteria will be digested and the material of which they are made will be absorbed by the white blood cells (bottom right).*

Soon after, the tiny white blood cells are joined by reinforcements—larger white blood cells. The larger white blood cells, which are similar to the heavy artillery used by an attacking army, destroy almost all bacteria they attack. In time, the area resembles a battlefield. Dead bacteria and the dead and wounded white blood cells are everywhere. Taken together, these events form the body's second line of defense—the **inflammatory** (ihn-FLAM-uh-tor-ee) **response.** Sometimes an infection (a successful invasion into the body by disease-causing organisms) causes a red, swollen area to develop just below the skin's surface. If you were to touch the infected area, you would discover that it is hotter than the surrounding skin area. For this reason, the area is said to be inflamed, which actually means "on fire."

In addition to the inflammatory response, the body has another second line of defense called **interferon.** Interferon is a substance produced by body cells when they are attacked by viruses. Interferon "interferes" with the reproduction of new viruses. As a result, the rate at which body cells are infected is slowed down. Other lines of defense have the time to move in and destroy the viruses.

Figure 8–5 *Although having a fever is no fun, there is a good reason for it. A fever, if mild and short-lived, helps the body fight disease-causing organisms.*

The Third Line of Defense

Although most disease-causing invaders are stopped by the body's first and second lines of defense, a few invaders are able to make it past them. If this happens, it is time for the body's third line of defense—the **antibodies**—to go to work. Antibodies are proteins produced by the immune system. Some antibodies are attached to certain kinds of white blood cells. Others are found floating freely in the blood. But regardless of their type, all antibodies are responsible for destroying harmful invaders.

Unlike the body's first two lines of defense, which you just read about, antibodies are very specific— they attack only a particular kind of invader. Thus, they can be thought of as the body's guided missiles, zeroing in on and destroying a particular target. The invading organism or substance that triggers the action of an antibody is called an **antigen**. The word antigen is derived from the term *anti*body *gen*erator, which means producer of antibodies.

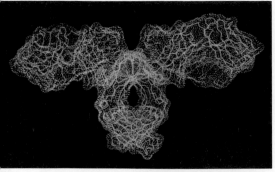

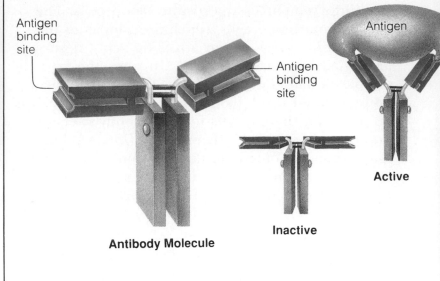

Antigen binding site

Antigen binding site

Antigen

Active

Inactive

Antibody Molecule

Figure 8–6 *Antibodies, such as the one in the computer-generated photograph, are proteins produced by the immune system. As the diagram illustrates, an antibody particle has two identical antigen-binding sites. What happens to the shape of an antibody particle when it encounters its specific antigen?*

What does an antibody look like? If you look at Figure 8–6, you can get a pretty good idea. Notice that the shape of an antibody is much like the letter T. When an antibody encounters its specific antigen, it changes shape—converting from a T shape to a Y shape. This action activates the antibody so that the two arms of the Y attach and bind to the antigen. In this way, an antibody prevents invaders such as viruses from attaching to cells.

When antibodies attach to surfaces of antigens such as bacteria, fungi, and protozoans, they slow down these organisms so that they can be gobbled up by white blood cells. Some antibodies may even destroy invaders by blasting a hole in the outer covering of the invaders' cells.

How does the immune system produce specific antibodies? How do the antibodies bind to antigens? The answers involve special white blood cells called T-cells and B-cells. (The T in T-cells stands for thymus, which is where T-cells originate; the B in B-cells refers to the bone marrow, which is where B-cells mature.) The function of T-cells is to alert B-cells to produce antibodies. If this is the first time the body is invaded by a particular antigen, it may take the B-cells a longer time to produce antibodies. During

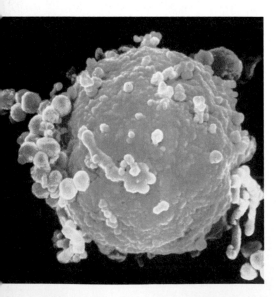

Figure 8–7 *This photograph shows a B-cell covered with bacteria. B-cells produce antibodies that attack particular kinds of invaders. What are these invaders called?*

this time, the person is experiencing the symptoms, or physical signs, of the disease. In other words, the person feels sick. Eventually, the B-cells begin to produce antibodies. The antibodies then join with the invading antigens much as the pieces of a jigsaw puzzle join together. Once joined to the invaders, the antibodies are able to destroy them. It is important to note that an antibody is specific for a certain antigen, and thus is not effective against any other antigens.

8–1 Section Review

1. What is the function of the immune system?
2. What are the body's three lines of defense against invading organisms?
3. What roles do B-cells and T-cells play in the immune system?

Critical Thinking—*Relating Concepts*
4. Explain why it is an advantage that the immune system produces antibodies specific for certain antigens rather than antibodies that work against any and all antigens.

8–2 Immunity

As you have just read, it takes time for your immune system to produce antibodies the first time a particular antigen enters your body. While your body is waiting for the immune system to make antibodies, you will, unfortunately, become ill. However, the next time the same antigen invades your body, your immune system will be ready for it. Your B-cells and T-cells, which are now familiar with the antigen, will be ready and waiting. In fact, they will produce antibodies so quickly that the disease will never even get a chance to develop. And what is more important, you will now have an **immunity** (ihm-MYOON-ih-tee) to that antigen. **Immunity is the resistance to a disease-causing organism or a harmful substance. There are two basic types of immunity: active immunity and passive immunity.**

Guide for Reading

Focus on these questions as you read.

▶ *What is immunity, and what is the difference between the two types of immunity?*

▶ *How do vaccines work?*

Figure 8–8 *There are two types of immunity: active and passive. This young boy is receiving a vaccine. Vaccines are made from disease-causing organisms that have been killed or weakened in a laboratory. Which type of immunity do you develop as a result of having a disease or receiving a vaccine?*

Active Immunity

Suppose you come into contact with an antigen. Your immune system responds by producing antibodies against the invader. Because your own immune system is responding to the presence of an antigen, this type of immunity is called **active immunity**. The word active means you are doing the action. In this case, you are making the antibodies.

In order to gain active immunity, one of two things must occur—either you come down with the disease or you receive a **vaccination** (vak-sih-NAY-shuhn) for the disease. A vaccination is the process by which antigens are deliberately introduced into a person's body to stimulate the immune system. The antigens are usually developed from disease-causing organisms that have been killed or weakened in a laboratory. Now called a vaccine (vak-SEEN), the antigens alert the body's white blood cells to produce antibodies. Most vaccines are introduced into the body by an injection through the skin. You probably experienced this firsthand when you received your measles vaccination. Some other vaccines, such as the Sabin polio vaccine, are taken into the body through the mouth. In general, vaccines will not usually cause the symptoms of a disease to occur.

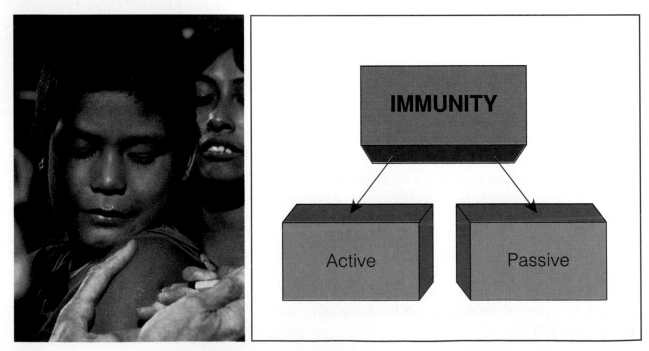

How long does active immunity last? There is no set answer to this question because the length of immunity to a disease (actually to the antigen that causes the disease) varies with the type of antigen. For example, an immunity to the common cold lasts only a few weeks, whereas an immunity to the chicken pox lasts for a person's lifetime. Even after receiving a vaccination, the body sometimes has to be reminded how to produce antibodies. In such a case, a booster shot has to be given. A booster shot, as its name implies, boosts (increases) the production of antibodies in the body. Diseases that require the use of booster shots include measles, German measles, poliomyelitis, mumps, whooping cough, diphtheria, and tetanus.

Passive Immunity

The way in which you receive **passive immunity**, the second type of immunity, is to get the antibodies from a source other than yourself. In other words, you are not actually producing the antibodies that protect you—another organism is. (You are not active; you are passive.) For example, passive immunity can be acquired by the transfer of antibodies from a mother to her unborn baby across the placenta. Following the baby's birth, the antibodies give protection to the baby during its first few months. Eventually, however, the mother's antibodies become ineffective, and the baby must rely on its own immune system to protect itself from disease.

A person can receive passive immunity in another way. If an animal such as a horse is vaccinated, its immune system will respond by producing antibodies. The antibodies can be removed from the animal and injected into a person's bloodstream. Unfortunately, this method gives the body only temporary immunity. Soon after these antibodies do their job (which is only about a few weeks), they are eliminated from the body.

Immune Disorders

As you have just read, the function of the immune system is to defend the body against invaders. Sometimes, however, the immune system

FIND OUT BY DOING

How Antibodies Work

1. On a sheet of white paper, trace two adjacent pieces of a jigsaw puzzle.

2. With scissors, cut out the drawings. **CAUTION:** *Be careful when using scissors.*

3. Repeat steps 1 and 2 using two other sets of adjacent pieces of the puzzle.

4. Mix up the six puzzle pieces. Place them on a flat surface. Label three pieces Antibody A, Antibody B, and Antibody C. Label the remaining puzzle pieces Antigen A, Antigen B, and Antigen C.

5. Now try to fit the matching pieces of the puzzle together.

Prepare a chart that shows which antibody fits together with which antigen. How are antibodies and antigens like the pieces of a puzzle?

■ Why do you think it is important that each antibody attaches to a specific antigen?

Figure 8–9 *Allergies result when the immune system is overly sensitive to certain substances called allergens. Examples of allergens are dust, which contains dust mites (top left); feathers (top right); pet hairs (bottom left); and pollen (bottom right).*

becomes overly sensitive to foreign substances or overdoes it by attacking its own tissues. In some instances, the immune system may be fooled by invaders that hide within its cells. Whatever the cause of the malfunction, the outcome is usually serious, as you will now discover.

ALLERGIES   Achoo! Achoo! And so it begins. Another attack of hay fever. As you may already know, hay fever is neither a fever nor is it caused by hay. Hay fever is an **allergy** that is caused by ragweed pollen. An allergy results when the immune system is overly sensitive to certain substances called allergens (AL-er-jehnz). Allergens may be in the form of dust, feathers, animal hairs, pollens, or foods.

When an allergen such as pollen enters the body, the immune system reacts by producing antibodies. Unlike the antibodies that help to fight infection,

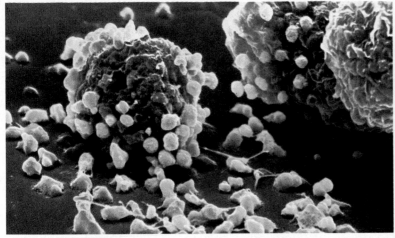

the antibodies that are produced by allergens release histamines (HIHS-tuh-meenz). Histamines are chemicals that are responsible for the symptoms of the allergy—that is, the itchy, watery eyes; the runny nose; the tickly throat; and the sneezing.

Although no complete cure for an allergy exists, people may be able to avoid allergy attacks by avoiding the allergen that causes them. This may involve removing from their diet the foods that contain the allergen or finding a new home for their pet. But if parting with a favorite food or a beloved pet is simply out of the question, then some relief may be obtained from antihistamines. As the name implies, antihistamines work against the effects of histamines.

Figure 8–10 *The large round objects in this photograph are white blood cells that are found in the lining of the nose, eyes, and throat. When allergens attach themselves to white blood cells, the white blood cells explode, releasing tiny structures that contain histamines. For those who suffer from hayfever, a bubble helmet with hose and filter may be the last resort.*

AIDS *Acquired Immune Deficiency Syndrome*, or **AIDS,** is a very serious disease caused by a virus that hides out in healthy body cells. The virus, first discovered in 1984, is named *human immunodeficiency virus,* or HIV. When HIV enters the body, it attacks helper T-cells. This action prevents helper T-cells from carrying out their regular job—to activate the immune system when a threat arises. Once inside a helper T-cell, HIV reproduces and thereby destroys the T-cell. Although the body produces antibodies against HIV, the virus evades them by growing within the cells that make up the immune system. HIV slowly destroys most of the helper T-cells.

The destruction of helper T-cells leaves the body practically undefended. As a result, disease-causing invaders that would normally be destroyed by a healthy immune system grow and multiply. It is the

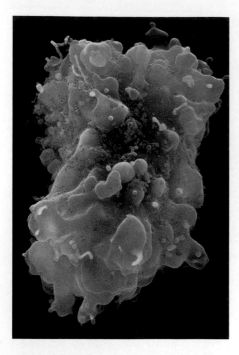

Figure 8–11 *The virus that causes AIDS— seen as tiny blue dots in this photograph—has infected a T-cell. What is the function of a T-cell?*

repeated attacks of disease that weaken and eventually kill people with AIDS.

How is AIDS spread? Contrary to popular belief, AIDS can be spread only if there is direct contact with the blood and/or body secretions of an infected person. Because HIV has been found in semen and vaginal secretions, it can be spread through sexual contact. In fact, recent data point to an alarming increase in AIDS among sexually active teenagers. Contaminated blood can also spread HIV from one person to another. Prior to 1985, this made blood transfusions a possible source of HIV transmission. Since 1985, however, mandatory screening of all blood donations for HIV has been in effect. AIDS can also be spread by the sharing of needles among intravenous (directly into a vein) drug users. Even unborn babies can be victims of AIDS, as HIV can also travel across the placenta from mother to unborn child.

Is there a cure for AIDS? Unfortunately, there is none at this time. However, there are several drugs that appear effective in slowing down the growth of the virus, thereby allowing AIDS patients to live longer. It is hoped that a drug to cure this terrible disease will be developed soon. In the meantime, there is only one way to prevent AIDS—avoid exposure to HIV, or the virus that causes AIDS.

8–2 Section Review

1. What is immunity? Compare active immunity and passive immunity.
2. How do vaccines work?
3. What is an allergy? An allergen?
4. What is AIDS? What causes it? How does AIDS affect the immune system?

Critical Thinking—*You and Your World*
5. After receiving a vaccine, you may develop mild symptoms of the disease. Explain why this might happen.

Figure 8–12 *Pamphlets such as these inform people about AIDS: what it is and how it is spread. What is the name of the virus that causes AIDS?*

8–3 Diseases

You may not realize it, but few people go through life without getting some type of disease. Even the healthiest person has probably come down with the common cold at one time or another. Now that you have an understanding of how the body defends and protects itself, let's see just what it is up against. In the next few pages, you will read about the causes and symptoms of several diseases.

Infectious Disease

Many diseases are caused by tiny living things such as bacteria, viruses, protozoans, and fungi that invade the body. These living things are commonly called germs. Scientists, however, call them microorganisms. **Diseases that are transmitted among people by disease-causing microorganisms are called infectious** (ihn-FEHK-shuhs) **diseases.** There are three ways by which an **infectious disease** can be transmitted, or spread. They are by people, by animals, and by nonliving things. Sometimes, an infectious disease becomes very contagious (catching) and sweeps through an area. This condition is called an epidemic.

Many common infectious diseases are spread as a result of close contact with a sick person. Such contact often takes place through coughing or sneezing. A cough or a sneeze expels droplets of moisture that may contain disease-causing microorganisms. You

Guide for Reading

Focus on these questions as you read.

▶ *What are some examples of infectious diseases, and how are they spread?*

▶ *What are some examples of noninfectious diseases?*

Figure 8–13 *Bacterial diseases can be caused by certain round bacteria called cocci (right) and by certain rod-shaped bacteria called bacilli (left).*

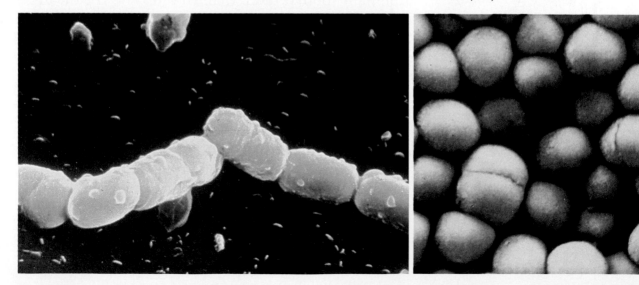

Figure 8–14 *Many infectious diseases are spread by the cough of a sick person (left), by infected animals such as mosquitoes (center), and by contaminated water (right).*

may be surprised to learn that a sneeze may contain as many as 5000 droplets and that these droplets may travel as far as 3.7 meters (almost the entire length of a small room)! If you are standing near a person who coughs or sneezes, you will probably breathe in these droplets—and the disease-causing microorganisms along with them. Diseases that are spread mainly through coughing and sneezing include colds, flu, measles, mumps, and tuberculosis.

Some infectious diseases are transmitted when a healthy person comes into direct contact with a person who has the disease. Such is the case for gonorrhea and syphilis, which are examples of sexually transmitted diseases, or STDs.

Animals can spread infectious diseases, too. Ticks, which are cousins of the spider, are responsible for spreading Lyme disease (named after the town in Connecticut where it was first observed) and Rocky Mountain spotted fever (named after the region in the United States where it was first discovered). Some other types of animals that are responsible for spreading disease are mammals and birds. Rabies, a serious disease that affects the nervous system, is transmitted by the bite of an infected mammal such as a raccoon or a squirrel.

Living things are not the only transmitters of disease. Contaminated (dirty) food or water can also spread infectious diseases. Food contaminated with certain bacteria, for example, can cause food poisoning. And in areas that have poor sanitation, diseases such as hepatitis, cholera (KAHL-er-uh), and typhoid (TIGH-foid) fever are fairly common.

Figure 8–15 *Animals are also responsible for the spread of disease. The female deer tick can carry the microorganism that causes Lyme disease. What is another disease that is spread by the bite of a tick?*

DISEASES CAUSED BY VIRUSES Your head aches, your nose is runny, and your eyes are watery. You also have a slight cough. But do not be alarmed. More than likely, you are suffering from the common cold.

The common cold is caused by perhaps one of the smallest disease-causing organisms—a virus. A virus is a tiny particle that can invade living cells. When a virus invades the body, it quickly enters a body cell. Once inside the cell, the virus takes control of all the activities of the cell. Not only does the virus use up the cell's food supply, it also uses the cell's reproductive machinery to make more viruses. In time, the cell—now full of viruses—bursts open, releasing more viruses that are free to invade more body cells. Viruses cause many infectious diseases, including measles, chicken pox, influenza, and mononucleosis.

DISEASES CAUSED BY BACTERIA If you are like most people, you probably think that all bacteria (one-celled microscopic organisms) are harmful and cause disease in humans. Then perhaps this fact will surprise you: Most bacteria are harmless to humans! Those bacteria that do produce diseases do so in a variety of ways. Some bacteria infect the tissues of the body directly. For example, the bacterium that causes tuberculosis grows in the tissues of the lungs. As the bacterium multiplies, it kills surrounding cells, causing difficulty and pain in breathing.

Other bacteria cause disease by producing toxins, or poisons. One such bacterium causes tetanus. The tetanus bacterium lives in dust and dirt and enters the body through breaks in the skin. Once inside the body, the tetanus bacterium begins to produce a toxin that affects muscles far from the wound. Because the toxin causes violent contractions of the jaw muscles, which make it hard for an infected person to open his or her mouth, tetanus is commonly called lockjaw.

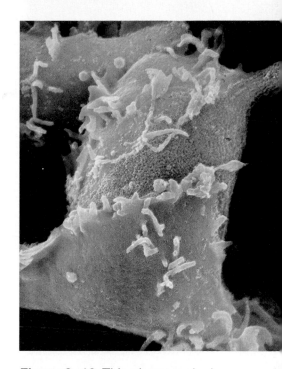

Figure 8–16 *This photograph shows how viruses—seen as tiny blue dots—are released by an infected human cell when it ruptures.*

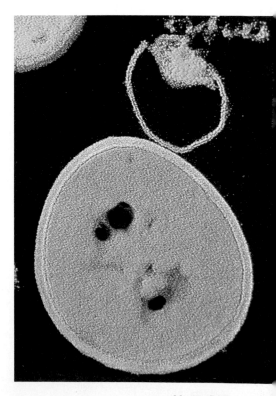

Figure 8–17 *The round objects in this photograph are bacterial cells. The bacterial cell at the top of the photograph has burst because of the addition of an antibiotic. An antibiotic is a substance produced by living organisms such as fungi that weakens or kills bacteria.*

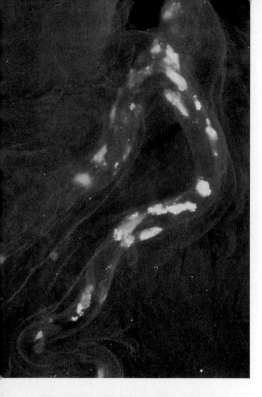

Figure 8–18 *The yellow-colored material in these arteries of the heart is a buildup of fatty substances. Such substances block the flow of blood to the heart muscle. What are the diseases that affect the heart and blood vessels called?*

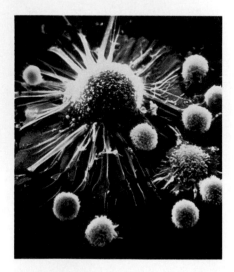

Figure 8–19 *Notice the crablike growth of the large cancer cell. The round objects are T-cells that have surrounded the cancer cell and are preparing to attack and destroy it.*

Noninfectious Diseases

Diseases that are not caused by microorganisms are called noninfectious diseases. There are many causes of **noninfectious diseases**. Some noninfectious diseases are caused by substances that harm or irritate the body. Others come from not eating a balanced diet. Still others are produced when the immune system fails to function properly. Worry and tension can also cause illness.

Because modern medicine has found more and more ways to combat many infectious diseases through the use of drugs and vaccines, people have begun to live longer. And as people's life spans have increased, so have the number of people who suffer from noninfectious diseases.

Some of the more serious noninfectious diseases are cancer, diabetes mellitus (digh-uh-BEET-eez muh-LIGHT-uhs), and cardiovascular diseases. You will now read about two noninfectious diseases—cancer and diabetes mellitus. Cardiovascular diseases, or diseases that affect the heart and blood vessels, were discussed in Chapter 4.

CANCER The noninfectious disease that is second only to cardiovascular diseases in causing death is **cancer**. Cancer is a disease in which cells multiply uncontrollably, destroying healthy tissue. Cancer is a unique disease because the cells that cause it are not foreign to the body. Rather, they are the body's own cells. This fact has made cancer difficult to understand and treat.

Cancer develops when something goes wrong with the controls that regulate cell growth. A single cell or a group of cells begin to grow and divide uncontrollably, often resulting in the formation of a tumor. A tumor is a mass of tissue. Some tumors are benign (bih-NIGHN), or not cancerous. A benign tumor does not spread to surrounding healthy tissue or to other parts of the body. Cancerous tumors, on the other hand, are malignant (muh-LIHG-nehnt). Malignant tumors invade and eventually destroy surrounding tissue. In some cases, cells from a malignant tumor break away and are carried by the blood to other parts of the body.

Although the basic cause of cancer is not known, scientists believe that it develops because of repeated and prolonged contact with carcinogens (kahr-SIHN-uh-juhnz), or cancer-causing substances. In a few cases, scientists have found certain cancer-causing hereditary material (genes) in viruses. The hereditary material in the viruses transforms normal, healthy cells into cancer cells. Scientists also suspect that people may inherit a tendency to develop certain types of cancer. This does not mean, however, that such people will get cancer.

The most important weapon in the fight against cancer is early detection. If a cancer is detected early on, the chances of successfully treating it are quite good. Doctors mainly use three methods to treat cancer: surgery, radiation therapy, and drug therapy. These methods may be used alone or in combination with one another.

Doctors tend to use surgery to remove malignant tumors that are localized, or are not capable of spreading. In radiation therapy, radiation (energy in the form of rays) is used to destroy cancer cells. Drug therapy, or chemotherapy, is the use of specific chemicals against cancer cells. Like radiation, these chemicals not only destroy cancer cells, but they also can injure normal cells. These injuries may account for undesirable side effects, such as nausea and high blood pressure, that often accompany such treatment.

Recently, scientists have been experimenting with drugs that can strengthen the body's immune system against cancer cells. These drugs, called monoclonal (mahn-oh-KLOH-nuhl) antibodies, are produced by joining cancer cells with antibody-producing white blood cells. Monoclonal antibodies have already

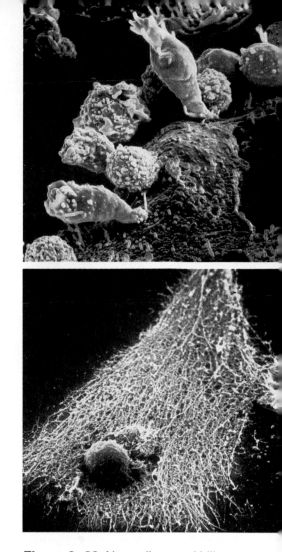

Figure 8–20 *Normally round killer T-cells become elongated when they are active, such as when they are destroying a cancer cell (top). All that remains of a cancer cell that has been attacked by a T-cell is its fibrous skeleton (bottom). What is cancer?*

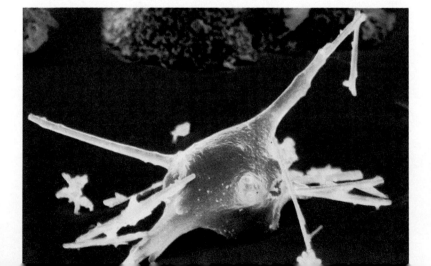

Figure 8–21 *Some chemicals, such as asbestos, are carcinogenic, or cancer-causing. The asbestos fibers visible in this photograph are being engulfed by a white blood cell.*

Figure 8–22 *With proper treatment and diet control, people who have diabetes can exercise and participate in sports. Wade Wilson of the Minnesota Vikings is a perfect example. What is diabetes mellitus?*

proven to be effective against certain types of flu virus and a type of hepatitis virus. It is hoped that monoclonal antibodies will play an important role in the fight against cancer.

DIABETES MELLITUS Loss of weight, excess urine production, weakness, and extreme hunger and thirst are all symptoms of a serious disease known as **diabetes mellitus.** Diabetes mellitus occurs because the body either secretes (releases) too little insulin or is not able to use the insulin that it does secrete.

As you may recall from Chapter 6, insulin is a hormone that is produced by the islets of Langerhans (clusters of cells in the pancreas). The job of insulin is to reduce the level of sugar (glucose) in the blood by helping the body cells absorb sugar and use it for energy. Without insulin, sugar cannot be absorbed into body cells and energy cannot be produced. This condition causes the body to look elsewhere for its energy. And, unfortunately, the body looks to its own tissues for "food." As a result, a person begins to show the symptoms of diabetes (weight loss, weakness, and extreme hunger).

There are two types of diabetes mellitus. Juvenile-onset diabetes, as its name implies, most commonly develops in people under the age of 25. In this type of diabetes, there is little or no secretion of insulin. The treatment for this type of diabetes includes daily insulin injections and strict diet control. Adult-onset diabetes, on the other hand, develops in people over the age of 25. Although most people with adult-onset diabetes produce normal amounts of insulin, for some unknown reason their body cells cannot use the insulin to absorb the much-needed sugar. Adult-onset diabetes can often be controlled by diet.

8–3 Section Review

1. What is an infectious disease? A noninfectious disease? Give two examples of each.
2. How are infectious diseases spread?

Critical Thinking—*Applying Facts*
3. It's a fact: There is no single cure for the common cold. Why do you think this is so?

CONNECTIONS

A Cure for Us or Yews?

Recently, doctors announced the discovery of a new cancer drug capable of melting away tumors that have resisted all other treatment. Unfortunately, very few people will receive this drug, which is known as taxol. Why? The answer lies in its source—the Pacific yew tree.

When it became clear that taxol has great potential in the fight against cancer, certain people became alarmed about what effect this would have on the Pacific yew trees. They started asking how many Pacific yews there were and what was going to happen to them. These people are concerned about *ecology*. Ecology is the study of the relationships and interactions of living things with one another and with their environment. As one ecology activist said of the Pacific yews, "Our concern is that there will not be any left the way we are approaching this."

In the past, Pacific yews were seen as commercially unimportant. So they were treated as weeds and were cut down and burned. As a result, the population of Pacific yews, which are found in forests in the Pacific Northwest, dwindled. Of the remaining Pacific yews, most are far too small to be used for making taxol. The height at which a Pacific yew is harvested for taxol is about 9 meters (or the distance needed to make a first down in football). It takes 100 years for a yew to grow that tall! In addition, it takes six 100-year-old Pacific yews to treat one cancer patient!

To further complicate the situation, Pacific yews are found in areas where logging is prohibited in order to protect the habitat of the spotted owl. The spotted owl is an endangered species. But if the yews continue to be harvested for taxol, they, too, may become an endangered species. So what can be done? Does a decision have to be made as to which is more important—cancer treatment or ecology? Most ecology activists believe that if people are careful, the yew can be preserved even as the maximum number of trees are harvested for taxol. What do you think?

Laboratory Investigation

Observing the Action of Alcohol on Microorganisms

Problem

What effect does alcohol have on the growth of organisms?

Materials (per group)

glass-marking pencil	alcohol
2 paper clips	100-mL beaker
2 thumbtacks	transparent tape
2 pennies	graduated cylinder
	forceps
2 petri dishes with sterile nutrient agar	

Procedure 🧪 📷

1. Obtain two petri dishes containing sterile nutrient agar.

2. Using a glass-marking pencil, label the lid of the first dish Soaked in Alcohol. Label the lid of the second dish Not Soaked in Alcohol. Write your name and today's date on each lid. **Note:** *Be sure to keep the dishes covered while labeling them.*

3. Using a graduated cylinder, carefully pour 50 mL of alcohol into a beaker.

4. Place a paper clip, a thumbtack, and a penny into the alcohol in the beaker. Keep these objects in the alcohol for 10 minutes.

5. Slightly raise the cover of the dish marked Not Soaked in Alcohol. **Note:** *Do not completely remove the cover from the dish.* Using clean forceps, place the other paper clip, thumbtack, and penny into the dish. Cover the dish immediately.

6. Again using clean forceps, remove the paper clip, thumbtack, and penny from the alcohol in the beaker. Slightly raise the cover of the dish marked Soaked in Alcohol and place these objects into it.

7. Tape both dishes closed and put them in a place where they will remain undisturbed for 1 week.

8. After 1 week, examine the dishes. Make a sketch of what you see.

9. Follow your teacher's instructions for the proper disposal of all materials.

Observations

What did you observe in each dish after 1 week?

Analysis and Conclusions

1. What effect did alcohol have on the growth of organisms?

2. Why did you use forceps, rather than your fingers, to place the objects in the dishes?

3. Why did you have to close the petri dishes immediately after adding the objects?

4. Explain why doctors soak their instruments in alcohol.

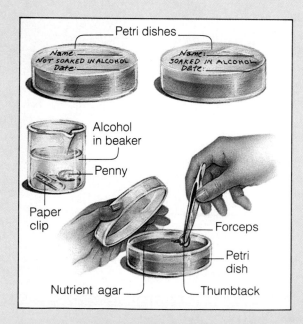

Study Guide

Summarizing Key Concepts

8-1 Body Defenses

▲ The immune system is the body's defense against disease-causing organisms.

▲ The body's first line of defense consists of the skin, mucus, and cilia.

▲ The body's second line of defense is the inflammatory response.

▲ The body's third line of defense consists of antibodies. Antibodies are produced by special white blood cells called B-cells. B-cells are alerted to produce antibodies by T-cells when there is an antigen in the body.

8-2 Immunity

▲ Immunity is the resistance to a disease-causing organism or a harmful substance. There are two types of immunity: active and passive.

▲ Active immunity results when a person's own immune system responds to an antigen by producing antibodies. To have active immunity, a person must get the disease or receive a vaccination. Passive immmunity results when antibodies are produced from a source other than oneself.

▲ An allergy occurs when the immune system is overly sensitive to certain substances called allergens.

▲ AIDS is a disease caused by a virus called HIV. HIV destroys helper T-cells, which ordinarily activate the immune system when a threat arises.

8-3 Diseases

▲ Diseases that are transmitted among people by disease-causing microorganisms are called infectious diseases. Some infectious diseases are caused by viruses and bacteria.

▲ Diseases that are not caused by microorganisms are called noninfectious diseases. Cancer, diabetes mellitus, and cardiovascular diseases are examples of noninfectious diseases.

▲ Cancer is a disease in which cells multiply uncontrollably, destroying healthy tissue.

▲ In diabetes mellitus, the body either secretes too little insulin or is not able to use the insulin that it does secrete.

Reviewing Key Terms

Define each term in a complete sentence.

8-1 Body Defenses
inflammatory response
interferon
antibody
antigen

8-2 Immunity
immunity
active immunity
vaccination

passive immunity
allergy
AIDS

8-3 Diseases
infectious disease
noninfectious disease
cancer
diabetes mellitus

Chapter Review

Content Review

Multiple Choice

Choose the letter of the answer that best completes each statement.

1. What is the body's second line of defense?
   a. skin   c. inflammatory response
   b. antibodies d. cilia
2. Proteins that are produced by the immune system in response to disease-causing invaders are called
   a. antibodies.   c. allergens.
   b. antigens.   d. vaccines.
3. The resistance to a disease-causing invader is called
   a. immunity.   c. interferon.
   b. vaccination. d. antigen.
4. A vaccination produces
   a. active immunity.
   b. passive immunity.
   c. no immunity.
   d. both active and passive immunity.
5. An example of an allergy is
   a. rabies.   c. tetanus.
   b. diabetes mellitus. d. hay fever.

6. Which disease is caused by HIV?
   a. rabies   c. hay fever
   b. cancer   d. AIDS
7. Which is an example of an infectious disease?
   a. cancer
   b. diabetes mellitus
   c. measles
   d. allergy
8. Tumors that are not cancerous are said to be
   a. benign.   c. malignant.
   b. infectious. d. contagious.
9. Another name for a cancer-causing substance is a(an)
   a. carcinogen. c. interferon.
   b. allergen.   d. vaccination.
10. Which disease results from the secretion of too little insulin?
   a. measles c. AIDS
   b. cancer   d. diabetes mellitus

True or False

If the statement is true, write "true." If it is false, change the underlined word or words to make the statement true.

1. The body's first line of defense against invaders is the <u>inflammatory response</u>.
2. An <u>allergen</u> is a substance that is produced by body cells when they are attacked by viruses.
3. Antibodies are produced to fight <u>antigens</u>.
4. <u>T-cells</u> produce antibodies.
5. A vaccine usually contains dead or weakened <u>antigens</u>.
6. <u>Cancer</u> is a disease in which cells multiply uncontrollably
7. Cancer and diebetes mellitus are examples of <u>noninfectious diseases</u>.

Concept Mapping

Complete the following concept map for Section 8–1. Refer to pages H8–H9 to construct a concept map for the entire chapter.

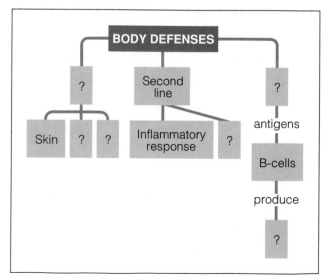

Concept Mastery

Discuss each of the following in a brief paragraph.

1. Explain how the skin functions as the body's first line of defense.
2. Explain how antibodies are produced.
3. Describe three methods by which infectious diseases are spread.
4. What is a benign tumor? A malignant tumor?
5. What are three methods that are used for treating cancer?
6. What are monoclonal antibodies? How are they produced?
7. Describe what happens in the body of a person who has an allergy to dust.
8. How do antibodies fight antigens in the body?
9. What effect does AIDS have on the body? How is AIDS prevented?

Critical Thinking and Problem Solving

Use the skills you have developed in this chapter to answer each of the following.

1. **Relating concepts** Why do you get mumps only once?
2. **Relating facts** Why should you clean and bandage all cuts?
3. **Applying concepts** Explain why you should not go to school with the flu.
4. **Interpreting diagrams** The chart shows the occurrence and survival rates of some cancers in the United States. Which type of cancer has the worst survival rate? The best? Why do you think the five-year survival rates increased between 1960 and 1963 and between 1977 and 1983?

5. **Applying concepts** Explain why it is important for you to know what vaccines you have been given and when they were given.
6. **Making predictions** Suppose your cilia were destroyed. How would this affect your body?
7. **Recognizing fact and opinion** Are colds caught by sitting in a draft? Explain your answer.
8. **Applying concepts** Suppose a person was born without a working immune system. What are some of the precautions that would have to be taken so that the person could survive?
9. **Relating concepts** The Black Death, or bubonic plague, swept through England in the seventeenth century killing thousands of people. This disease is spread by fleas infected with plague microorganisms. These fleas transmit the plague microorganisms to humans by biting them. Explain why the Black Death is not a problem today.
10. **Using the writing process** In the United States, the incidence of sexually transmitted diseases is on the rise. Prepare an advertising campaign in which you alert people to the serious medical problems of these diseases.

FIVE-YEAR SURVIVAL RATES		
Site of Cancer	**1960–63**	**1977–83**
Digestive tract		
Stomach	9.5%	16.0%
Colon and rectum	36.0%	46.0%
Respiratory tract		
Lung and bronchus	6.5%	12.0%
Urinary tract		
Kidney and other urinary structures	37.5%	51.0%
Reproductive system		
Breast	54.0%	68.0%
Ovary	32.0%	38.0%
Testis	63.0%	74.5%
Prostate gland	42.5%	63.0%
Skin	60.0%	79.0%

"Before I'll ride with a drunk, I'll drive myself." —Stevie Wonder

Driving after drinking, or riding with a driver who's been drinking, is a big mistake. Anyone can see that.

Alcohol, Tobacco, and Drugs

Guide for Reading

After you read the following sections, you will be able to

9–1 What Are Drugs?
- Define the word drug.
- Describe the effects of drug abuse.

9–2 Alcohol
- Describe the effects of alcohol abuse.

9–3 Tobacco
- Relate cigarette smoking to certain diseases.

9–4 Commonly Abused Drugs
- Describe the effects of smoking marijuana.
- Classify inhalants, depressants, stimulants, hallucinogens, and opiates.

Only one more kilometer to go and you will have reached your goal! You and your friends are running a marathon to raise money for SADD, or Students Against Drunk Driving. You are running to gain support for your battle against a dangerous combination—alcohol and driving. Alcohol-related accidents are the greatest health hazard facing teenagers today.

What effect does alcohol have on the body? Why do people use alcohol? Why do they abuse it? What are the long-term effects of heavy drinking? Is alcoholism a disease? Is there a cure for it? As you read the pages that follow you will find the answers to these questions. And you will learn that alcohol is not the only substance that threatens the health and safety of teenagers and adults. Tobacco and other drugs have profound effects on the body. Read on and get wise!

Journal *Activity*

You and Your World A friend of yours is thinking of smoking cigarettes. In your journal, write a letter to your friend explaining that tobacco use is harmful. Then, after you have completed the chapter, reread your letter.

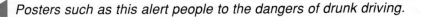

Posters such as this alert people to the dangers of drunk driving.

Guide for Reading

*Focus on these questions as
you read.*
▶ *What is a drug?*
▶ *What are some dangers of
drug misuse and abuse?*

9–1 What Are Drugs?

Drugs! You probably hear and see that word a lot today—on radio, television, billboards, and in newspaper articles and advertisements. What is a drug, and why are drugs drawing so much attention? **A drug is any substance that has an effect on the body.** Many substances fit this definition—even aspirin, which is used to reduce pain. Drugs that are used to treat medical conditions are called medicines. Aspirin is a medicine. There are two groups of medicines: prescription drugs and over-the-counter drugs.

Figure 9–1 *Drugs come in many shapes and sizes. Some are legal; some are not. What is a drug?*

Prescription drugs usually are strong drugs that are safe to use only under the supervision of a doctor. Prescription drugs are used to treat diseases or to control conditions such as high blood pressure and pneumonia. Over-the-counter drugs, on the other hand, do not need a doctor's prescription and may be purchased by anyone. Aspirin and cold tablets are examples of over-the-counter drugs.

Drug Misuse and Drug Abuse

When you use a prescription drug exactly as it is prescribed or take an over-the-counter drug according to its directions, you are engaging in drug use. Some people, however, use prescription or over-the-counter drugs incorrectly. Usually these people do so because they are misinformed. The improper use of drugs is called drug misuse.

Some people misuse drugs by taking more than the amount a doctor prescribes. They mistakenly believe that such action will speed their recovery from an illness. Other people take more of the drug because they have missed a dose. This action is particularly dangerous because it could cause an overdose. An overdose can cause a serious reaction to a drug, which can sometimes result in death.

When people deliberately misuse drugs for purposes other than medical ones, they are taking part in **drug abuse**. Some drugs prescribed by doctors are abused. Other drugs that are abused are illegal drugs. Drug abuse is extremely dangerous. Do you know why? As you have just read, drugs are substances that have an effect on the body. Drugs can produce powerful changes in your body.

Why do people use drugs? There are many answers to this question. Some seek to "escape" life's problems; others to intensify life's pleasures. Some take drugs because their friends do; others because their friends do not. Some people abuse drugs to feel grown up; others to feel young again. The list is as endless as the range of human emotions. Unfortunately, the desired effects are often followed by harmful and unpleasant side effects.

Figure 9–2 *This clay tablet contains the world's oldest known prescriptions, dating back to about 2000 BC. The prescriptions show the medicinal use of plants.*

Dangers of Drug Abuse

People of all ages abuse drugs. Some know that they are abusing drugs; others do not. And still others deny their abuse. The 18- to 25-year-old age group has the highest percentage of drug abuse.

Drug abuse is dangerous for a number of reasons. When you take a drug, for example, the internal functioning of your body changes immediately. Over time, your body also changes its response to the drug. These responses can produce some serious side effects. Let's examine some of these serious and sometimes fatal side effects.

TOLERANCE   When a drug is used or abused regularly, the body may develop a **tolerance** to it. Tolerance causes the body to need increasingly larger amounts of the drug to get the same effect that was originally produced. This is exactly what happens to people who abuse drugs. They soon discover that they must take more of the drug each time in order

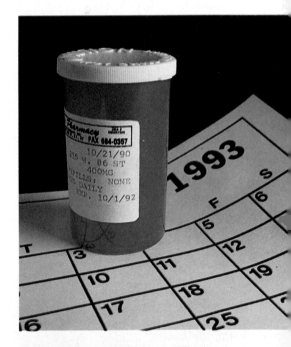

Figure 9–3 *Notice the expiration date on this container of pills. Using a medicine after its prescription has expired is an example of drug misuse. What is a prescription drug?*

Drugs and Daphnia

1. With your teacher's help, place a *Daphnia* (water flea) in the depression on a depression slide.

2. Cover the slide with a coverslip and place the slide under a microscope.

3. Use the low-power objective to observe the *Daphnia*. You should be able to clearly see the *Daphnia*'s heart beating.

4. Calculate the average heart rate per minute of the *Daphnia*.

5. Remove the coverslip and with a dropper, place one drop of cola in the depression. Replace the coverslip and observe the *Daphnia* again.

6. Calculate the average heart rate per minute again.

Was there a difference in heart rate after the cola was added? If there was a difference, what may have caused it?

■ What does this investigation tell you about cola?

to get the same feeling they did in the beginning. Tolerance can cause people to take too much of a drug—a problem that can lead to overdose and even death.

DEPENDENCE   Some drugs produce a dependence, or a state in which a person becomes unable to control drug use. Dependence can be psychological (sigh-kuh-LAHJ-ih-kuhl), physical, or both. In all cases, dependence changes the way the body functions, and it can seriously damage a person's health.

Psychological dependence is a strong desire or need to continue using a drug. When people become psychologically dependent on a drug, they link the drug with specific feelings or moods. When the drug's effect wears off, so does the feeling.

Drug abusers who are psychologically dependent on a drug often believe they can stop using the drug if they want to. Unfortunately, stopping drug abuse once a person is psychologically dependent is not easy and may require a doctor's care.

Physical dependence occurs when the body becomes used to a drug and needs the drug to function normally. This type of dependence generally takes time to develop and usually occurs as tolerance builds. Physical dependence is sometimes referred to as an addiction.

WITHDRAWAL   A person who is physically dependent on a drug such as heroin needs to take the drug at least three to four times a day. Miss a dose and the body begins to react: The nose runs, the eyes tear. Miss several doses and the body reacts more violently: chills, fever, vomiting, cramps, headaches, and body aches. In time, the muscles begin to jerk wildly, kicking out of control. This is the beginning of **withdrawal**, or stopping the use of a drug.

Figure 9–4 *In this anti-crack wall mural, an artist describes his attitude toward drug abuse. These children express their views during an anti-drug rally. What types of dependence can result from drug abuse?*

Although it takes a few days, the most painful symptoms of heroin withdrawal pass. However, heroin abusers are never entirely free of their need for the drug. In fact, far too many heroin abusers who have "kicked the habit" return to the drug again unless they receive medical, psychological, and social help.

Figure 9–5 *People take drugs for many reasons. One reason is to escape from personal problems.*

9–1 Section Review

1. What is a drug? Compare prescription and over-the-counter drugs.
2. What is drug misuse? Drug abuse?
3. Compare psychological and physical dependence.

Critical Thinking—*You and Your World*
4. How might you convince someone not to use drugs?

9–2 Alcohol

Alcohol is a drug. In fact, alcohol is the oldest drug known to humans. Egyptian wall writings, which are among the oldest forms of written communication, show pictures of people drinking wine. It was not until the Egyptian writing symbols were decoded, however, that the meaning of some of the wall paintings was revealed. Their message warned of the dangers of alcohol abuse. **The abuse of alcohol can lead to the destruction of liver and brain cells, and it can cause both physical and psychological dependence.**

How Alcohol Affects the Body

Unlike food, alcohol does not have to be digested. Some alcohol, in fact, is absorbed directly through the wall of the stomach into the bloodstream. If the stomach is empty, the alcohol is absorbed quickly, causing its effects to be felt almost immediately. If the stomach contains food, the alcohol is absorbed more slowly. Upon leaving the

Focus on this question as you read.

▶ *What effects does alcohol have on the body?*

Figure 9–6 *This Egyptian wall painting, painted thousands of years ago, shows how grapes were gathered to make wine.*

FIND OUT BY WRITING

Figure 9–7 *As this diagram illustrates, alcohol can cause harmful effects throughout the body. What effect does alcohol have on the brain?*

stomach, the alcohol enters the small intestine, where more of it is absorbed.

After the alcohol is absorbed, it travels through the blood to all parts of the body. As the alcohol in the blood passes through the liver, it is changed into carbon dioxide and water. Carbon dioxide and some water are released from the body by way of the lungs. Most of the water, however, passes out of the body as perspiration and urine.

Because the liver can convert only a small amount of alcohol at a time into carbon dioxide and water, much of the alcohol remains unchanged in the blood. When the alcohol reaches the brain, it acts as a **depressant**. A depressant is a substance that slows down the actions of the central nervous system (brain and spinal cord). Perhaps this seems confusing to you if you have noticed that people who drink do not seem to be depressed at all. Rather, they seem quite energetic.

The reason for this false sense of energy is that alcohol initially affects the part of the brain that controls judgment and self-control. At the same time, alcohol makes people become more relaxed and unafraid. The net result is that the controls people put on their emotions are reduced, causing them to behave in ways they would never normally consider. Thus, people may seem quite stimulated during this time.

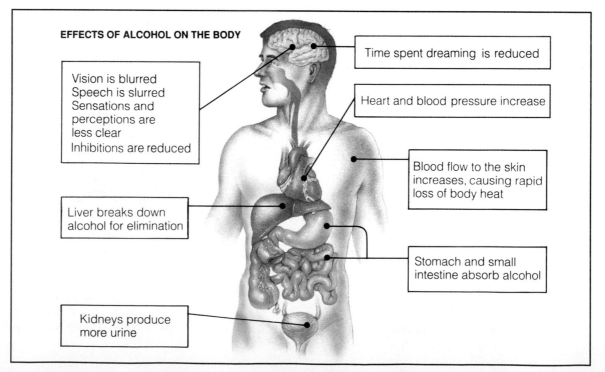

Figure 9–8 *Blood alcohol concentration, or BAC, is a measure of the amount of alcohol in the bloodstream per 100 mL of blood. The BAC is expressed as a percentage. The higher the BAC, the more powerful the effect of alcohol on the brain. What type of behavior occurs if the BAC is 0.1 percent?*

But if people continue to drink, the alcohol in their blood begins to affect other areas of the brain. Soon the areas that control speech and muscle coordination are affected. A person may slur words and have trouble walking. More alcohol can lead to a state of total confusion as more of the brain is affected. Often a person loses consciousness. Sometimes the areas of the brain controlling breathing and heartbeat are affected. Such an overdose of alcohol is life threatening.

Alcohol and Health

For most people, the moderate use of alcohol does not result in health problems. Drinking large amounts of alcohol on a daily basis, however, can cause health problems. Prolonged alcohol abuse may cause mental disturbances, such as blackouts and hallucinations (seeing or hearing things that are not really there). It can also damage the linings of the stomach and small intestine. The risk of cancer of the mouth, esophagus, throat, and larynx is increased among alcohol abusers. Continued use of alcohol also causes cirrhosis (suh-ROH-sihs) of the liver. Cirrhosis is a disease in which liver cells and the connective tissue that hold the cells together are damaged by the heavy intake of alcohol. The damaged liver cells and connective tissue form scar tissue, which interferes with the liver's ability to perform its normal functions. Figure 9–9 shows the difference in appearance between a normal liver and a liver with cirrhosis. Cirrhosis is responsible for about 13,000 deaths in America every year.

The abuse of alcohol can lead to **alcoholism**. Alcoholism is an incurable disease in which a person is physically and psychologically dependent on alcohol. A person who has the disease is called an alcoholic. An alcoholic needs both medical and psychological help. The aid of organizations such as Alcoholics Anonymous is also important in helping alcoholics

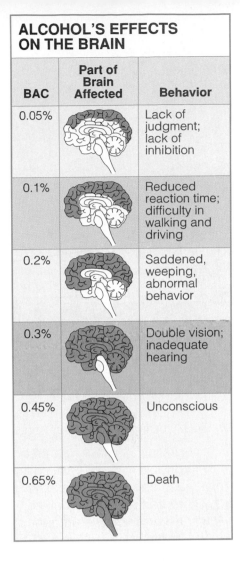

ALCOHOL'S EFFECTS ON THE BRAIN

BAC	Part of Brain Affected	Behavior
0.05%		Lack of judgment; lack of inhibition
0.1%		Reduced reaction time; difficulty in walking and driving
0.2%		Saddened, weeping, abnormal behavior
0.3%		Double vision; inadequate hearing
0.45%		Unconscious
0.65%		Death

Figure 9–9 *Long-term alcohol use destroys liver cells. Notice the differences in appearance of a normal liver (left), one that has some fatty deposits due to alcohol abuse (center), and one that is consumed by cirrhosis (right).*

overcome their problems. There are even organizations for the relatives of the 10 million or more alcoholics in this country. One, called Alateen, is for the children of people who have an alcohol problem.

Knowing about the damage that alcohol does to the body and the brain, one would think alcohol abusers would stop drinking. Unfortunately, withdrawal from alcohol can be very difficult. Like other drug abusers, alcoholics may suffer from withdrawal symptoms when they try to stop drinking. About one fourth of the alcoholics in the United States experience hallucinations during withdrawal.

CONNECTIONS

"Bad Breath?"

You have probably seen television programs in which a person suspected of driving while intoxicated is stopped by police and asked to exhale into a breath analyzer. A breath analyzer is a device that determines the amount of alcohol in the body.

The first breath analyzer, which consisted of an inflatable balloon, was developed in the late 1930s by the American doctor Rolla N. Hager who called it a "Drunkometer." Today, most breath analyzers in use are electronic. That is, they are powered by *electric currents* (flow of charged particles). About the size of a television remote-control device, an electronic breath analyzer contains a fuel cell that works like a battery. A person exhales into the breath analyzer, and the air is pulled into the fuel cell through a valve. There the air comes in contact with a small strip of positively charged platinum. This strip is in contact with a disk containing sulfuric acid. The platinum changes any alcohol that might be present to acetic acid. When this happens, particles of platinum lose electrons and an

electric current is set up in the disk. The electric current then flows from the positively charged platinum particles to the negatively charged particles on the other side of the disk.

The more alcohol the breath contains, the stronger the electric current. A weak electric current or no electric current produces a green light, indicating that a person's breath contains little or no alcohol. A stronger current produces an amber light, showing that a person's breath contains some alcohol. A very strong electric current produces a red light, meaning that a person's breath contains a lot of alcohol. In the case of either an amber light or a red light, a person has failed the breath test. The person needs to be tested further to determine exactly how much alcohol the body contains.

9–2 Section Review

1. How does alcohol affect the body?
2. What is alcoholism?

Critical Thinking—*You and Your World*
3. Why is driving after drinking dangerous?

9–3 Tobacco

In 1988, the Surgeon General (chief medical officer in the United States Public Health Service) warned that the nicotine in tobacco products is as addictive (habit-forming) as the illegal drugs heroin and cocaine. This report was the fifth on the effects of smoking tobacco to come from the Surgeon General's office. The first report, which was issued in 1964, declared that cigarette smoking causes lung cancer, heart disease, and respiratory illnesses. In 1972, the Surgeon General issued the first report to suggest that secondhand (passive) smoke is a danger to nonsmokers. A 1978 report warned pregnant women that smoking could affect the health of their unborn children. This report also stated that smoking could prevent the body from absorbing certain important nutrients. In 1982, cigarette smoking was named as the single most preventable cause of death in the United States. Four years later, another report published the results of studies linking secondhand smoke to lung cancer and respiratory diseases in nonsmokers. Despite all these warnings, our nation still has millions of tobacco smokers!

Guide for Reading

Focus on this question as you read.

▶ *What effects does tobacco have on the body?*

Some Harmful Chemicals in Tobacco Smoke
acetaldehyde
acetone
acetonitrile
acrolein
acrylonitrile
ammonia
aniline
benzene
benzopyrene
2,3 butadione
butylamine
carbon monoxide
dimethylamine
dimethylnitrosamine
ethylamine
formaldehyde
hydrocyanic acid
hydrogen cyanide
hydrogen sulfide
methacrolein
methyl alcohol
methylamine
methylfuran
methylnaphthalene
nicotine
nitric oxide
nitrogen dioxide
phenol
pyridine
toluene

Figure 9–10 *Smoking at any age is dangerous. In addition to the harmful substances listed in the chart, about 4000 other substances are inhaled when smoking cigarettes. Why do people smoke cigarettes?*

Up in Smoke

1. Place a few pieces of tobacco in a test tube. Using some cotton, loosely plug up the mouth of the test tube.

2. With your teacher's permission, use a Bunsen burner to heat the test tube until the tobacco burns completely. **CAUTION:** *Be very careful when working with a Bunsen burner.*

3. Allow the test tube to cool before removing the cotton plug.

Describe the appearance of the cotton plug before and after the investigation. Which substance in tobacco smoke was collected in the cotton?

■ Design an investigation in which you determine whether a brand of cigarettes that is advertised as low in tar really is.

Figure 9–11 *There is a significant difference between the walls of the bronchus of a nonsmoker (right) and those of a smoker (left). This difference can often be fatal. The large grayish-green objects are cancer cells.*

Effects of Tobacco

Why is smoking so dangerous? When a cigarette burns, about 4000 substances are produced. Many of these substances are harmful. Some of these substances are listed in Figure 9–10. Although 10 percent of cigarette smoke is water, 60 percent is made of poisonous substances such as nicotine and carbon monoxide. Nicotine, as you have just read, is an addictive drug. Once in the body, nicotine causes the heart to beat faster, skin temperature to drop, and blood pressure to rise. Carbon monoxide is a poisonous gas often found in polluted air. Yet even the most polluted air on the most polluted day in history does not contain anywhere near the concentration of carbon monoxide that cigarette smoke does!

The remaining 30 percent of cigarette smoke consists of tars. Tars are probably the most dangerous part of cigarette smoke. As smoke travels to the lungs, the tars irritate and damage the entire respiratory system. Unfortunately, this damage is particularly serious in the developing lungs of teenagers.

Tobacco and Disease

Cigarette smoking causes damage to both the respiratory system and the circulatory system. Long-term smoking can lead to lung diseases such as bronchitis (brahng-KIGH-tihs) and emphysema (ehm-fuh-SEE-muh). These diseases are often life threatening. In addition, a heavy smoker has a twenty-times-greater chance of getting lung cancer than a nonsmoker has.

In addition to lung irritation, smoking also increases heartbeat, lowers skin temperature, and causes blood vessels to constrict, or narrow. Constriction of blood vessels increases blood pressure and makes the heart work harder. Heavy smokers are twice as likely to develop some forms of heart disease than are nonsmokers.

The Surgeon General's 1982 report not only named cigarette smoking as the single most preventable cause of death in the United States, it also contained a long list of cancers associated with smoking. In addition to lung cancer, the report named cancer of the bladder, mouth, esophagus, pancreas, and larynx. In fact, at least one third of all cancer deaths may be caused by smoking.

Not everyone who experiences the harmful effects of cigarette smoking has chosen to smoke. Many people are passive, or involuntary, smokers. A passive smoker is one who breathes in air containing the smoke from other people's cigars, pipes, or cigarettes. If one or both of your parents smoke, you probably have been a passive smoker all your life. As you may already know, passive smoking can be extremely unpleasant. It can cause your eyes to burn, itch, and water, and it can irritate your nose and throat.

What is even more important, however, is that passive smoking is harmful to your health. Recent research shows that nonsmokers who have worked closely with smokers for many years suffer a decrease in the functioning of the lungs. Other studies show that infants under the age of one year whose mothers smoke have twice as many lung infections as infants of nonsmoking mothers.

THIS IS A SMOKE-FREE BUILDING

Figure 9–12 *Because passive smoking is harmful, some companies have made their buildings totally smoke free.*

9–3 Section Review

1. What effects does tobacco smoking have on the body?
2. What is nicotine? Tar?

Critical Thinking—*You and Your World*

3. What factors do you think influence someone to use tobacco?

FIND OUT BY CALCULATING

Cigarette Smoking

In 1980, there were 54 million smokers in the United States. If these people smoked 630 billion cigarettes each year, approximately how many cigarettes did each person smoke in a year? In a month?

9–4 Commonly Abused Drugs

As you have already learned, drugs are substances that have an effect on the body. The specific effects differ with the type of drug. Some drugs affect the circulatory system, whereas others affect the respiratory system. The most powerful drugs, however, are those that affect the nervous system and change the user's behavior.

For the most part, drugs that affect the nervous system are the drugs that are most commonly abused. **Some commonly abused drugs include inhalants, depressants, stimulants, hallucinogens** (huh-LOO-sih-nuh-jehnz)**, and opiates** (OH-pee-ihtz)**.** In this section you will learn about the effects these drugs have on the body.

Inhalants

Drugs that are inhaled to get a desired effect are called **inhalants**. Because inhalants are able to enter the bloodstream directly through the lungs, they affect the body quickly.

Typically, people abuse inhalants to get a brief feeling of excitement. One such example of inhalant abuse is glue sniffing. After the effects of inhaling the fumes have worn off, the abuser often has nausea, dizziness, loss of coordination, blurred vision, and a headache. Some inhalants do permanent damage to the brain, liver, kidneys, and lungs. Continued abuse can lead to unconsciousness and even death.

Other examples of inhalants include nitrous oxide, amyl nitrite (AM-ihl NIGH-tright), and butyl (BYOO-tihl) nitrite. Nitrous oxide, which is more commonly known as "laughing gas," is used by dentists as a painkiller because it causes the body to relax. Long-term abuse of nitrous oxide can cause psychological dependence and can damage the kidneys, liver, and bone marrow. Both amyl nitrite and butyl nitrite cause relaxation, light-headedness, and a burst of energy. As with nitrous oxide, abuse of these drugs can cause psychological dependence and certain circulatory problems.

Figure 9–13 *Because products such as paint thinner give off dangerous fumes, their labels contain warnings for their use in well-ventilated rooms.*

COMMONLY ABUSED DRUGS

Type of Drug	Examples	Basic Action on Central Nervous System	Psychological Dependence	Physical Dependence	Withdrawal Symptoms	Development of Tolerance
Opiates and related drugs	Heroin Demerol Methadone	Depressant	Yes, strong	Yes, very fast development	Severe but rarely life-threatening	Yes
Barbiturates	Phenobarbital Nembutal Seconal	Depressant	Yes	Yes	Severe, life-threatening	Yes
Tranquilizers (minor)	Valium Miltown Librium	Depressant	Yes	Yes	Yes	Yes
Alcohol	Beer Wines Liquors Whiskey	Depressant	Yes	Yes	Severe, life-threatening	Yes, more in some people than in others
Cocaine	As a powder Crack	Stimulant	Yes, strong	Yes	Yes	Possible
Cannabis	Marijuana Hashish	Ordinarily a depressant	Yes, moderate	Probably not	Probably none	Possible
Amphetamines	Benzedrine Dexedrine Methedrine	Stimulant	Yes	Possible	Possible	Yes, strong
Hallucinogens	LSD Mescaline Psilocybin	Stimulant	Yes	No	None	Yes, fast
Nicotine	In tobacco of cigarettes, cigars; also in pipe tobacco, chewing tobacco	Stimulant	Yes, strong	Yes	Yes	Yes
Inhalants	Nitrous oxide Amyl nitrite Butyl nitrite	Depressant	Yes	No	None	No

Figure 9–14 *This chart lists some of the commonly abused drugs. What type of drug is nicotine?*

Depressants

Earlier you read that alcohol is a depressant. Depressants slow down or decrease the actions of the nervous system. Two other commonly abused depressants are the powerful barbiturates (bahr-BIHCH-er-ihts) and the weaker tranquilizers (TRAN-kwihl-ighz-erz). Usually, these drugs are taken in pill form.

Because depressants calm the body and can bring on sleep, doctors once prescribed them for people who had sleeping problems or suffered from

Figure 9–15 *When people take drugs such as barbiturates in combination with alcohol, the results are often fatal. Why?*

Figure 9–16 *Under the influence of amphetamines, an orb-weaver spider weaves an irregular web. What type of drug is an amphetamine?*

nervousness. But depressants, particularly barbiturates, cause both physical and psychological dependence. Withdrawal from barbiturate abuse is especially severe and can result in death if done without medical care. And because a tolerance to depressants builds up quickly, a person must continue to take more and more of the drug. This can lead to an overdose, which can lead to death. When barbiturates are used with alcohol, the results are often fatal because the nervous system can become so slowed down that even breathing stops.

Stimulants

While depressants decrease the activities of the nervous system, **stimulants** increase these activities. Caffeine, a drug in coffee, is a stimulant. However, caffeine is a mild stimulant. Far more powerful stimulants make up a class of drugs called amphetamines (am-FEHT-uh-meenz).

Today, the legal use of amphetamines is limited. Yet many people abuse amphetamines illegally. They seek the extra pep an amphetamine pill may bring. Long-term amphetamine abuse, however, can lead to serious psychological and physical problems. Perhaps no side effects are more dramatic than the feelings of dread and suspicion that go hand in hand with amphetamine abuse.

A stimulant that has been increasingly abused in recent years is cocaine. Cocaine comes from the leaves of coca plants that grow in South America. Cocaine may be injected by needle but is usually inhaled as a powder through the nose. In time, the lining of the nose becomes irritated from the powder. If abuse continues, it is not uncommon for cocaine to burn a hole through the walls of the nose.

Psychological dependence from cocaine abuse is so powerful that the drug is difficult to give up. Long-term cocaine abuse can lead to the same mental problems as those of amphetamine abuse.

Within the last 10 years, a very dangerous form of cocaine known as crack has become popular. Unlike cocaine, crack is smoked. Once in the body, crack travels quickly to the brain, where it produces an intense high. This high, however, wears off quickly, leaving the user in need of another dose. Crack is

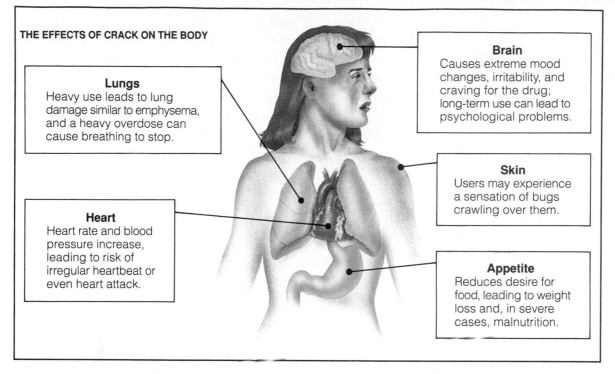

THE EFFECTS OF CRACK ON THE BODY

Lungs
Heavy use leads to lung damage similar to emphysema, and a heavy overdose can cause breathing to stop.

Brain
Causes extreme mood changes, irritability, and craving for the drug; long-term use can lead to psychological problems.

Skin
Users may experience a sensation of bugs crawling over them.

Heart
Heart rate and blood pressure increase, leading to risk of irregular heartbeat or even heart attack.

Appetite
Reduces desire for food, leading to weight loss and, in severe cases, malnutrition.

Figure 9–17 *Crack is an extremely powerful form of cocaine. What effects does crack have on the brain?*

among the most addictive drugs known. A crack user can become hooked on the drug in only a few weeks. Figure 9–17 shows some effects that crack has on the body.

Marijuana

Another drug that is usually smoked is **marijuana**. Marijuana is an illegal drug made from the flowers and leaves of the Indian hemp plant. The effects of marijuana are due mainly to a chemical in the plant known as THC. The THC in marijuana affects different people in different ways. And the effects are often hard to describe once they have passed.

Some users of marijuana report a sense of well-being, or a feeling of being able to think clearly. Others say that they become suspicious of people and cannot keep their thoughts from racing. For many, marijuana distorts the sense of time. A few seconds may seem like an hour, or several hours may race by like seconds.

Research findings now point to a variety of possible health problems caused by marijuana. Like alcohol, marijuana slows reaction time and is the direct cause of many highway accidents. Marijuana seems to have an effect on short-term memory. Heavy users

Figure 9–18 *Marijuana is an illegal drug made from the flowers and leaves of the Indian hemp plant. What chemical in marijuana is responsible for its effects?*

often have trouble concentrating. And there can be no doubt that marijuana irritates the lungs and leads to some respiratory damage. It may surprise you to learn that smoking marijuana harms the lungs more than smoking tobacco does. Long-term abuse of marijuana produces psychological dependence but does not seem to lead to physical dependence. Withdrawal symptoms usually do not occur, but heavy users may suffer sleep difficulties and anxiety.

Hallucinogens

All **hallucinogens** are illegal. Hallucinogens are drugs that alter a user's view of reality. Abusers of hallucinogens cannot tell what is real and what is not. They may also experience memory loss and personality changes, and they may not be able to perform normal activities.

The strongest hallucinogen is LSD. The effects of LSD are unpredictable—it can either stimulate or depress the body. Abusers commonly see colorful pictures. A person may report seeing sound and hearing color. Solid walls may move in waves. Not all hallucinations are pleasant, however. Some people experience nightmarelike "bad trips" in which all sense of reality is lost. Fears are heightened, and a feeling of dread overcomes the user. During this time, accidental deaths and even suicide are not uncommon. A small percentage of abusers do not recover from an LSD experience for months and have to be hospitalized.

The hallucinogen called PCP or "angel dust" was originally developed as an anesthetic (painkilling substance) for animals. PCP may be smoked, injected, sniffed, or eaten. PCP can act as a stimulant, depressant, or hallucinogen. PCP abusers often engage in violent acts and some have even committed suicide.

Opiates

Some of the most powerful drugs known are the **opiates**, or painkilling drugs. Opiates, which are produced from the liquid sap of the opium poppy plant, include opium, morphine, codeine, paregoric (par-uh-GOR-ihk), and heroin. With the exception of

Figure 9–19 *A close-up of a ripe poppy pod shows some of the opium-containing juice oozing out (left). The roundish yellow structure in the middle of the poppy flower is the pod (right).*

heroin and opium, all opiates can legally be used under a doctor's supervision.

In addition to causing a strong physical and psychological dependence, there are other dangers of opiate abuse. The most obvious to nonabusers is the antisocial behavior of people who have a strong need for the drug heroin but no money with which to buy it illegally. Such abusers become trapped in a world from which they cannot escape without help. And the longer they use heroin, the longer they are likely to suffer the dangers of its abuse. For example, most abusers risk an overdose. And overdoses often lead to death. In addition, life-threatening diseases such as AIDS and hepatitis can be transmitted by sharing needles. In their weakened condition, heroin abusers are no match for such serious diseases.

9–4 Section Review

1. Compare the effects a depressant and a stimulant have on the body.
2. Describe the effect hallucinogens have on the body.

Critical Thinking—*You and Your World*
3. You are at a party where drugs are being used. What should you do?

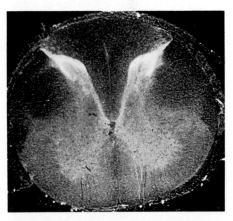

Figure 9–20 *The bright spots in this cross section of the spinal cord are opiate receptors. Opiate receptors are those areas where opiates attach to nerve cells.*

Laboratory Investigation

Analyzing Smoking Advertisements

Problem

How are advertisements used to convince people to smoke or not to smoke?

Materials *(per group)*

> magazines
> paper

Procedure

1. Choose two or three different types of magazines. Glance through the magazines to find advertisements for and against cigarette smoking.

2. On a sheet of paper, make a chart like the one shown. Then, for each advertisement you found, fill in the information in the chart. In the last column, record the technique that the advertisement uses to attract the public to smoke or not to smoke. Examples of themes used to attract people to smoke are "Beautiful women smoke brand X"; "Successful people smoke brand Y"; "Brand Z tastes better." Examples of themes used to stop people from smoking are "Smoking is dangerous to your health"; "Smart people do not smoke"; "If you cared about yourself or your family, you would not smoke."

Observations

1. Were there more advertisements for or against smoking?
2. Which advertising themes were used most often? Least often?

Analysis and Conclusions

1. Which advertisements appealed to you personally? Why?
2. In general, how are the advertising themes that are used related to the type of magazine in which the advertisements appear?
3. **On Your Own** Repeat the procedure, but this time look for advertisements for and against drinking alcohol. Compare the way in which drinking alcohol is advertised to the way in which smoking cigarettes is advertised.

Magazine	Advertisements for Smoking *(specify brand)*	Advertisements Against Smoking *(specify advertisement)*	Theme

Study Guide

Summarizing Key Concepts

9–1 What Are Drugs?

▲ A drug is any substance that has an effect on the body.

▲ Tolerance, dependence, and withdrawal are serious dangers of drug abuse.

▲ Tolerance causes the body to need increasingly larger amounts of the drug to get the same effect originally produced.

▲ Psychological dependence is a strong desire or need to continue using a drug. Physical dependence, or addiction, occurs when the body becomes used to a drug and needs it to function normally.

▲ Withdrawal is stopping the use of a drug.

9–2 Alcohol

▲ The abuse of alcohol can lead to destruction of liver and brain cells and can cause both physical and psychological dependence.

▲ In the brain, alcohol acts as a depressant and slows down the actions of the central nervous system.

▲ Treatment for alcoholism includes medical and psychological help.

9–3 Tobacco

▲ Cigarette smoking causes damage to both the respiratory system and the circulatory system.

▲ Cigarette smoke contains poisonous substances such as nicotine, carbon dioxide, and tars.

▲ Cigarette smoking is the most important cause of lung cancer. Cigarette smoking irritates the lining of the nose, throat, and mouth; increases heartbeat; lowers skin temperature; and constricts blood vessels.

▲ Passive smokers are those people who breathe in air containing smoke from other people's cigars, cigarettes, and pipes.

9–4 Commonly Abused Drugs

▲ Some commonly abused drugs include inhalants, depressants, stimulants, hallucinogens, and opiates.

▲ Inhalants are drugs that are inhaled to get a desired effect.

▲ Depressants are drugs that decrease the actions of the nervous system.

▲ Stimulants speed up the actions of the nervous system.

▲ The effects of marijuana are due mainly to a chemical called THC. Like alcohol, marijuana slows down reaction time.

▲ Hallucinogens are drugs that produce hallucinations.

▲ Opiates, which are produced from the opium poppy, are used as painkillers.

Reviewing Key Terms

Define each term in a complete sentence.

9–1 What Are Drugs?
drug
drug abuse
tolerance
psychological dependence
physical dependence
withdrawal

9–2 Alcohol
depressant
alcoholism

9–4 Commonly Abused Drugs
inhalant
stimulant

marijuana
hallucinogen
opiate

Chapter Review

Content Review

Multiple Choice

Choose the letter of the answer that best completes each statement.

1. Which requires no prescription?
   a. barbiturate
   c. amphetamine
   b. tranquilizer
   d. aspirin
2. Which is not an example of drug misuse?
   a. buying an over-the-counter drug
   b. taking an illegal drug
   c. taking more of a drug than the amount prescribed by a doctor
   d. taking a drug prescribed for someone else
3. Alcohol acts as a(an)
   a. stimulant.
   c. hallucinogen.
   b. opiate.
   d. depressant.
4. Alcohol mainly affects the
   a. heart.
   c. brain.
   b. muscles.
   d. stomach.
5. Which system does bronchitis, a disorder aggravated by smoking, affect?
   a. respiratory
   c. digestive
   b. circulatory
   d. nervous

6. An addictive drug found in tobacco products is
   a. tar.
   c. nicotine.
   b. THC.
   d. heroin.
7. An example of an inhalant is
   a. THC.
   b. a barbiturate.
   c. codeine.
   d. nitrous oxide.
8. Barbiturates are
   a. opiates.
   b. hallucinogens.
   c. depressants.
   d. stimulants.
9. Crack is classified as a(an)
   a. stimulant.
   c. depressant.
   b. opiate.
   d. hallucinogen.
10. Heroin is a(an)
    a. stimulant.
    c. depressant.
    b. opiate.
    d. hallucinogen.

True or False

If the statement is true, write "true." If it is false, change the underlined word or words to make the statement true.

1. The deliberate misuse of drugs for uses other than medical ones is known as <u>drug abuse</u>.
2. <u>Physical dependence</u> is also known as addiction.
3. The abuse of alcohol can lead to <u>alcoholism</u>.
4. Cirrhosis affects the <u>lungs</u>.
5. The most dangerous part of cigarette smoke is <u>carbon dioxide</u>.
6. <u>Amphetamines</u> and barbiturates are examples of depressants.
7. LSD belongs to a group of drugs known as <u>opiates</u>.

Concept Mapping

Complete the following concept map for Section 9–1. Refer to pages H8–H9 to construct a concept map for the entire chapter.

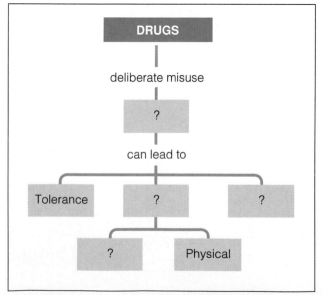

Concept Mastery

Discuss each of the following in a brief paragraph.

1. Explain how any drug can be abused.
2. It has been said that no one is ever cured of drug dependence. Explain why.
3. Why is alcohol considered a depressant?
4. What are dependence, withdrawal, and tolerance?
5. List the six commonly abused drugs. Describe the effect each has on the body.
6. How does an alcoholic differ from those who drink occasionally?
7. Describe the substances in cigarette smoke and their effects on the body.
8. List and describe some of the disorders that can result from smoking.
9. Compare psychological dependence and physical dependence.

Critical Thinking and Problem Solving

Use the skills you have developed in this chapter to answer each of the following.

1. **Applying facts** What precautions would you take when working with paint thinner?
2. **Applying concepts** Explain why heroin abusers need medical help while they are going through withdrawal.
3. **Relating facts** Almost 30 percent of the people in the United States smoke. Explain why people smoke even when they know the dangers.
4. **Making comparisons** Compare cocaine and crack.

5. **Relating cause and effect** How is cigarette smoke related to respiratory and circulatory problems?
6. **Relating concepts** Cigarette smoke is harmful to nonsmokers as well as to smokers. Explain this statement.
7. **Expressing an opinion** What are some ways in which people who abuse drugs can be discouraged from doing so?
8. **Applying concepts** Explain the meaning of this old Japanese proverb: "First the man takes a drink, then the drink takes a drink, then the drink takes the man!"
9. **Making inferences** In what ways are drug abuse and criminal acts related?
10. **Using the writing process** Imagine you are a parent. Write a letter to your child in which you try to discourage your child from experimenting with drugs.

Ask Claire Veronica Broome about her work at the Centers for Disease Control in Atlanta, Georgia, and she is apt to break into a grin. "It's very exciting," she says, "because the answers you get are practical." Along with other scientists on her team, Dr. Broome travels to different locations to study outbreaks of disease.

One of the most confusing cases this "disease detective" has ever solved was an outbreak of listeriosis in Halifax, Nova Scotia. Listeriosis is a disease that affects membranes around the brain. This disease is caused by a type of bacterium called *Listeria monocytogenes*. Often the disease affects the

CLAIRE VERONICA BROOME:
DISEASE DETECTIVE

elderly. However, it can infect an infant before it is born. In fact, it was an epidemic of listeriosis in newborn infants that brought this case to Dr. Broome's attention.

Before going to Halifax, Dr. Broome gathered as much data on listeriosis as possible. She discovered that the bacteria that cause listeriosis were identified as a cause of human disease in 1929. At that time, it was learned that the bacteria live in soil and can infect animals. But as late as the 1980s, no one was certain how the bacteria are transmitted to unborn humans.

When Claire Broome and her team of researchers arrived in Halifax, they set to work reviewing hospital records and talking to physicians about past occurrences of listeriosis. Soon, they discovered the hospital in Halifax was experiencing an epidemic.

Dr. Broome compared two groups of people. The mothers of infants born with listeriosis made up one group. Mothers who gave birth to healthy babies made up the second group. People in both groups were interviewed. Dr. Broome collected data that covered several months of the new mothers' lives before they gave birth. Dr. Broome soon noticed a definite trend. The women with sick babies had eaten more cheeses than the women with healthy babies. Could the cheese have been contaminated by the bacteria that made the babies ill?

During her research, Dr. Broome became aware of another case of listeriosis. This case occurred in a Halifax man who had not spent time in a hospital. After examining the contents of the man's refrigerator, Dr. Broome added coleslaw to her list of possible transmitters of listeriosis. She reasoned that coleslaw is made from uncooked cabbage and cabbage grows in soil—a place in which listeria bacteria had already been discovered. Careful chemical analysis revealed that listeria bacteria were present in the coleslaw found in the sick man's refrigerator.

Dr. Broome and her team traced some of the contaminated coleslaw to a cabbage farm.

▲ In her laboratory, Dr. Broome uses a computer to analyze data about epidemics.

They found that the farmer used sheep manure to fertilize the cabbage. When the sheep were tested, they were also found to contain the listeria bacteria.

Now it was time for Dr. Broome to interview the mothers of the sick babies again. Not surprisingly, she found that many of them had eaten coleslaw during the time they were carrying their child. Later, Dr. Broome discovered that the bacteria that causes listeriosis can also live in milk and milk products, including cheese.

What made the packaged coleslaw and the milk products a good environment for bacteria to live in? Actually, it was the refrigerator in which these foods were stored that contributed to this disease outbreak. Refrigerators are used to keep foods from spoiling quickly. However, *Listeria monocytogenes* can survive, and even multiply, in cold temperatures. Even under proper storage conditions, the coleslaw and the cheese contained enough bacteria to make people ill.

The mystery of the Halifax listeriosis outbreak was solved. This case was closed. Dr. Broome returned to her office in Atlanta, but she barely had time to unpack before she was off to discover the cause of another "mystery" disease.

★ ARE AMERICANS ★ OVEREXERCISING?

ne summer day in 1984, 13-year-old Rory Bentley left his home for his daily 6-mile jog through Carlisle, Massachusetts. On this particular day, however, Rory never made it back home. After jogging, he collapsed and died on the sidewalk in front of his house. Although he was only 13 and a veteran of many races, Rory died from heart failure.

Less than two months before Rory died, a motorcyclist found the body of a man lying on a country road in Vermont. The dead man was identified as James Fixx, the 52-year-old author of *The Complete Book of Running*. Fixx died of a heart attack during one of his daily 20-mile jogs.

Deaths such as these have led Americans to question the value of vigorous exercise, and running in particular. Soon after these incidents occurred, many magazines began publishing articles warning runners of the dangers of too much exercise. Doctors, medical writers, athletic directors, and others have recently expressed doubt over whether exercise is always good and whether more exercise is always better. In fact, doctors recently have reported many more patients with exercise-related injuries. For example, shin splints, a condition in which the shin tendons peel away from the bone, have become much more common since the exercise boom began. One cause of shin splints is running on hard surfaces.

Even grade school and high school athletics may be getting out of hand. Some scientists point out that young people can suffer serious long-term effects from too much ex-ercise. For example, overdoing running or other sports can stunt growth by damaging the flexible tissue that surrounds the bones.

Adults, too, can be victims of serious problems caused by exercise, doctors say. Among the most serious to female runners is the loss of calcium in the body. This loss can eventually damage the spine and other bones. Muscles and tendons can also be damaged—sometimes causing lasting joint problems.

Nutrition experts have discovered a rise in what they call "eating disorders" among amateur runners and others who exercise a great deal. Such people tend to undereat out of fear that they'll lose their trim, athletic look. In doing so, they deprive their bodies of essential proteins, vitamins, and minerals. In the most serious cases, heart muscles are weakened and fatal heart attacks can occur.

RUNNERS, RUNNERS EVERYWHERE

Despite the recent warnings, however, there appears to be little decrease in the popularity of exercise. The jogging craze began in the mid-1970s, and there seems to be no shortage of runners today. There's hardly a place where runners are not a common sight. A few years ago, a 1-mile run by an amateur runner was considered special. But today's runners regularly run 3, 5, or more miles.

But running is just one part of the exercise boom. People exercise in their homes, their offices, and in their health clubs or gyms. These people learn their exercises from

▶ **Off and running—toward better health or serious injury?**

▲ **More and more men and women of all ages are exercising in their homes, offices, and gyms. Should everyone do this? And how much exercise is good for a person? Scientists, sports health experts, and doctors have different opinions.**

a variety of books, records, videocassettes, TV programs, and magazine articles. Not only are more people exercising, but there has been an increase in the amount of exercising that individuals do.

THE BIG QUESTION

Should exercise be avoided? To begin with, there is strong evidence that people who exercise regularly are much less likely to have heart attacks, develop high blood pressure, and suffer from diseases related to old age. One study of nearly 17,000 Harvard University graduates showed that there were twice as many heart attacks among those who did *not* exercise as there were among those who exercised regularly. Another study of about 6000 men and women aged 20 to 65 who exercised showed fewer people with high blood pressure. Some of the researchers said that regular exercise also helped rid the body and mind of stress and anxiety, which can cause health and psychological problems.

Those who favor regular exercise and see running as a definite health benefit are not stopped by "horror stories" such as the sudden deaths of Rory Bentley and James Fixx. They argue that carelessness and not the ex-

ercise itself is to blame in most cases of injury or death. People with a family history of heart disease should be careful not to overdo their exercise and, in fact, should exercise only under a doctor's care. When that is done, exercise is healthy.

SOME TIPS ON EXERCISING

People should warm up before strong exercise, avoid overdoing exercise, and cool down slowly afterward. People should also eat the proper foods, wear correct shoes, and learn the rules of the sport they are playing.

Picking the right exercise and the right amount of it for you is the key rule. "We think that people need a prescription for exercise just as they need a prescription for a drug," said a sports health expert. "While there is a sport for everyone, not everyone can play each and every sport."

Studies indicate that even if exercise does have some risks and drawbacks, lack of exercise is even worse. Statistics seem to show that more Americans die from sitting around than from running around. But are too many Americans running around too much, too far, and too often? What do you think?

THE BIONIC BOY

FROM: *Dr. R. K. Smith, Moon Base Alpha, Crater Village (6M14Y14)*
TO: *Evelyn Washington, Futura Center, Dakotas (1/ZM-43BY)*
DATE: *06/14/2071*

Dear Evelyn:

T hank you so much for your last interspace message. Both your Aunt Mary and I are thrilled that you want to be a doctor of medicine. It is an ancient and wonderful profession. We are also pleased because you will be the fourth doctor in our family. It's a tradition that goes back over one hundred and fifty years! I recall my father telling me that our family helped develop the first vaccines against cancer in the early 1990s!

You asked what it was like "being a doctor in the old days." The year I started treating people, 2006, seems like yesterday. I was a new physician then, and I wanted to set up a small-town practice. The town I chose, Chesterville, was so old-fashioned that it still had push-button telephones.

Chesterville turned out to be a good choice. Beth and Mike played on the same spaceball team as many of the children I treated, and Aunt Mary was a Scoutmaster. I still

smile when I think back to how excited the kids were when we took them to the first Undersea Colony in the Atlantic Ocean.

But what I remember most clearly was a terrible accident. A group of children were on their way home from the learning center. As they were crossing the main intersection on the moving sidewalk, an old gravity-car lost its automatic steering. A crash occurred, and Tommy, a boy of only 14, was thrown through a plate-glass window. Tommy suffered terrible damage to his muscles and skin, and his lungs were destroyed as well. Fortunately, by then—the early part of the twenty-first century—we had learned how to replace all destroyed body parts with artificial parts. Since you want to be a doctor, Evelyn, I thought I'd tell you a little more about how we performed surgery on Tommy.

It might be interesting if I told you a little about artificial body parts. During an important period of research, 1960 to 1990, scientists tried to perfect transplant techniques. That is, they would take organs from one person and put them into the body of another person to help that person live. By the time I was born in 1976, doctors had learned how to transplant skin, hearts, livers, lungs, kidneys, and bone tissue.

Unfortunately, in most cases, the organs would not live in the new body for very long—even with the use of special drugs.

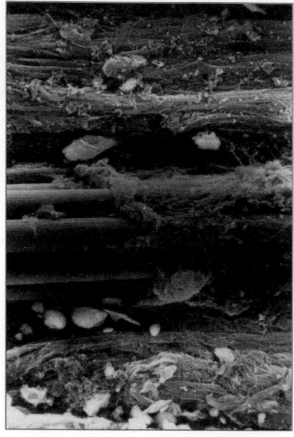

▲ Carbon fibers, implanted in ligaments, strengthen injured limbs and become part of the living system.

The reasons are complicated, and you will learn about them in time. However, the main reason has to do with the fact that the body "thinks" that living tissues, cells, or organs not of its own making must be destroyed. Even though a transplanted human heart, for example, may work perfectly, the body will use all its defenses to destroy it.

So, as early as 1950, scientists began to experiment with special metals, plastics, and filters that could be used to replace real body parts. I think I know what you must be thinking. Why wouldn't the body try to destroy these artificial hearts, livers, and lungs? The simplest answer is that the body doesn't "think" the plastic part is dangerous.

By 1965, doctors were using metal and plastic parts to replace hip and finger joints. With further research, they learned to build organs that could work just like the real thing for short periods of time. A few years after I was born, the first artificial heart was put inside a man. It worked for only a few weeks. Now, of course, the heart transplant lasts indefinitely! But the big news toward the end of the twentieth century was the making of artificial parts that would, in time, become living parts. The body's own cells would slowly grow around it and in it until it was alive!

Now back to Tommy. After he was brought into our emergency center, our examination showed that his lungs were damaged beyond repair. Also, the muscles in his left arm were destroyed, and he had several broken bones.

A set of artificial lungs was hooked up to Tommy's windpipe, or trachea. The hookup was done with a special "glue." The amazing thing about this glue was that the cells of the body grew over and around it, making new tissue. In a few months, this body glue actually became part of the body's tissue.

The artificial lungs looked a lot like large, gray sponges. When we attached these artificial organs to the chest wall, they moved in and out with the diaphragm and chest muscles, just like real lungs. As you know, our lungs are needed to help us take in oxygen and get rid of carbon dioxide. Real lungs work because tiny blood vessels, or capillaries, surround the air sacs, or alveoli, of the lung and carry gases back and forth. Our artificial lungs were made so that Tommy's own capillaries would grow into the channels in the spongy material.

▼ Artificial lungs would be made of spongy material so they could move as a person breathes.

As I mentioned before, a great deal of the boy's arm muscle was destroyed during the accident by glass. We had to rebuild his arm using a new substance called Bionic Jelly. This jelly was made from plastic fibers that could be molded into any shape we wanted. The jelly could get bigger and smaller just like real muscle when the arm moved. We glued the ends of the fake muscle to the bones of the arm using our special glue. Then we hooked up the nerve endings to a pea-sized computer in the jelly itself. The arm looked and worked like the real thing.

Why do I remember Tommy? Because it was just so amazing to me, as a young doctor, to see how far science had come.

Now, at the age of 95, I look back at our achievements with pride. Science is wonderful, and I am glad you want to take part in it. I hope to be at your medical school graduation, which should be on my 110th birthday!

Love,
Uncle Bill

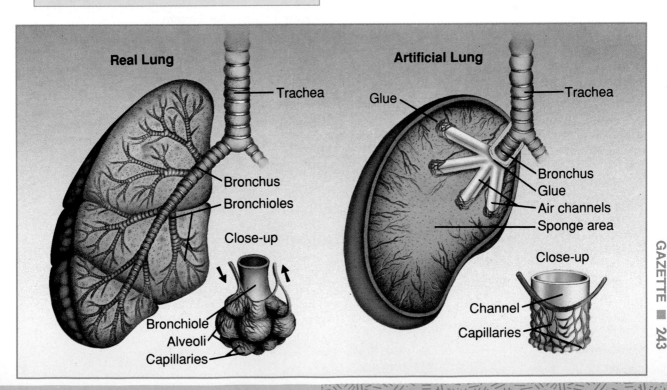

For Further Reading

> If you have been intrigued by the concepts examined in this textbook, you may also be interested in the ways fellow thinkers—novelists, poets, essayists, as well as scientists—have imaginatively explored the same ideas.

Chapter 1: The Human Body

Asimov, Isaac. *Fantastic Voyage.* New York: Bantam.

Platt, Kin. *The Boy Who Could Make Himself Disappear.* New York: Dell.

Swift, Jonathan. *Gulliver's Travels.* New York: Penguin Books.

Chapter 2: Skeletal and Muscular Systems

Blume, Judy. *Deenie.* New York: Bradbury Press.

Savitz, Harriet May. *Run, Don't Walk.* New York: Signet Vista Books.

Chapter 3: Digestive System

Atwood, Margaret. *The Edible Woman.* New York: Warner Books.

Dacquino, V. T. *Kiss the Candy Days Goodbye.* New York: Delacorte Press.

Levenkron, Steven. *The Best Little Girl in the World.* New York: Warner Books.

Silone, Ignazio. *Bread and Wine.* New York: Atheneum.

Chapter 4: Circulatory System

Arnold, Elliott. *Blood Brother.* Lincoln, NE: University of Nevada Press.

McCullers, Carson. *The Heart Is a Lonely Hunter.* Boston: Houghton.

Paterson, Katherine. *Jacob Have I Loved.* New York: Crowell.

Chapter 5: Respiratory and Excretory Systems

Myers, Walter Dean. *Hoops.* New York: Delacorte Press.

Winthrop, Elizabeth. *Marathon Miranda.* New York: Holiday House.

Chapter 6: Nervous and Endocrine Systems

Keller, Helen. *The Story of My Life.* New York: Watermill Press.

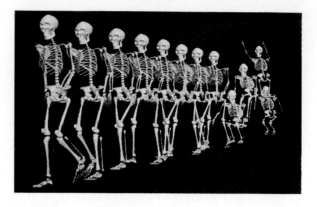

Pomerance, Bernard. *The Elephant Man.* New York: Grove-Weidenfield.

Young, Helen. *What Difference Does It Make, Danny?* New York: Andre Deutsch.

Chapter 7: Reproduction and Development

Eyerly, Jeanette. *He's My Baby Now.* New York: J. B. Lippincott Co.

Zindel, Paul. *The Girl Who Wanted a Boy.* New York: Bantam Books.

Chapter 8: Immune System

Crichton, Michael. *Five Patients: The Hospital Explained.* New York: Avon Books.

Gunther, John. *Death Be Not Proud.* New York: Harper and Row.

Hoffman, Alice. *At Risk.* London: MacMillan.

Lipsyte, Robert. *The Contender.* New York: Harper.

Chapter 9: Alcohol, Tobacco, and Drugs

Abbey, Nancy and Ellen Wagman. *Say No to Alcohol.* Santa Cruz, CA: Network Publications.

Anonymous. *Go Ask Alice.* Englewood Cliffs, NJ: Prentice Hall.

Newman, Susan. *It Won't Happen to Me: True Stories of Teen Alcohol & Drug Abuse.* New York: Putnam.

Scott, Sharon. *How to Say No and Keep Your Friends, Peer Pressure Reversal.* Amherst, MA: Human Resource Development Press.

Ward, Brian. *Smoking and Health.* New York: Watts.

The metric system of measurement is used by scientists throughout the world. It is based on units of ten. Each unit is ten times larger or ten times smaller than the next unit. The most commonly used units of the metric system are given below. After you have finished reading about the metric system, try to put it to use. How tall are you in metrics? What is your mass? What is your normal body temperature in degrees Celsius?

Commonly Used Metric Units

Length   The distance from one point to another

meter (m)   A meter is slightly longer than a yard.
1 meter = 1000 millimeters (mm)
1 meter = 100 centimeters (cm)
1000 meters = 1 kilometer (km)

Volume   The amount of space an object takes up

liter (L)   A liter is slightly more than a quart.
1 liter = 1000 milliliters (mL)

Mass   The amount of matter in an object

gram (g)   A gram has a mass equal to about one paper clip.

1000 grams = 1 kilogram (kg)

Temperature   The measure of hotness or coldness

degrees   0°C = freezing point of water
Celsius (°C)   100°C = boiling point of water

Metric–English Equivalents

2.54 centimeters (cm) = 1 inch (in.)
1 meter (m) = 39.37 inches (in.)
1 kilometer (km) = 0.62 miles (mi)
1 liter (L) = 1.06 quarts (qt)
250 milliliters (mL) = 1 cup (c)
1 kilogram (kg) = 2.2 pounds (lb)
28.3 grams (g) = 1 ounce (oz)
$°C = 5/9 \times (°F - 32)$

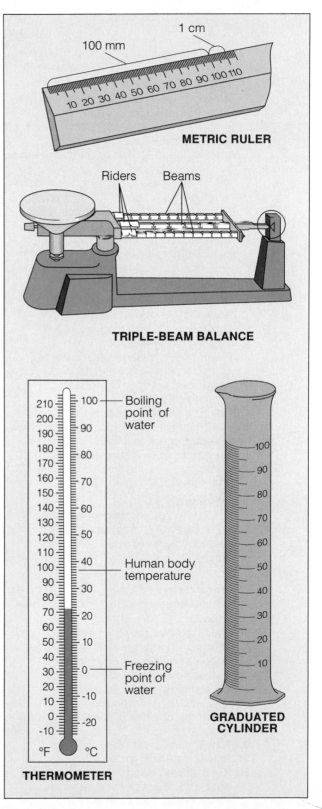

METRIC RULER

TRIPLE-BEAM BALANCE

THERMOMETER

GRADUATED CYLINDER

Glassware Safety

1. Whenever you see this symbol, you will know that you are working with glassware that can easily be broken. Take particular care to handle such glassware safely. And never use broken or chipped glassware.
2. Never heat glassware that is not thoroughly dry. Never pick up any glassware unless you are sure it is not hot. If it is hot, use heat-resistant gloves.
3. Always clean glassware thoroughly before putting it away.

Fire Safety

1. Whenever you see this symbol, you will know that you are working with fire. Never use any source of fire without wearing safety goggles.
2. Never heat anything—particularly chemicals—unless instructed to do so.
3. Never heat anything in a closed container.
4. Never reach across a flame.
5. Always use a clamp, tongs, or heat-resistant gloves to handle hot objects.
6. Always maintain a clean work area, particularly when using a flame.

Heat Safety

Whenever you see this symbol, you will know that you should put on heat-resistant gloves to avoid burning your hands.

Chemical Safety

1. Whenever you see this symbol, you will know that you are working with chemicals that could be hazardous.
2. Never smell any chemical directly from its container. Always use your hand to waft some of the odors from the top of the container toward your nose—and only when instructed to do so.
3. Never mix chemicals unless instructed to do so.
4. Never touch or taste any chemical unless instructed to do so.
5. Keep all lids closed when chemicals are not in use. Dispose of all chemicals as instructed by your teacher.

6. Immediately rinse with water any chemicals, particularly acids, that get on your skin and clothes. Then notify your teacher.

Eye and Face Safety

1. Whenever you see this symbol, you will know that you are performing an experiment in which you must take precautions to protect your eyes and face by wearing safety goggles.
2. When you are heating a test tube or bottle, always point it away from you and others. Chemicals can splash or boil out of a heated test tube.

Sharp Instrument Safety

1. Whenever you see this symbol, you will know that you are working with a sharp instrument.
2. Always use single-edged razors; double-edged razors are too dangerous.
3. Handle any sharp instrument with extreme care. Never cut any material toward you; always cut away from you.
4. Immediately notify your teacher if your skin is cut.

Electrical Safety

1. Whenever you see this symbol, you will know that you are using electricity in the laboratory.
2. Never use long extension cords to plug in any electrical device. Do not plug too many appliances into one socket or you may overload the socket and cause a fire.
3. Never touch an electrical appliance or outlet with wet hands.

Animal Safety

1. Whenever you see this symbol, you will know that you are working with live animals.
2. Do not cause pain, discomfort, or injury to an animal.
3. Follow your teacher's directions when handling animals. Wash your hands thoroughly after handling animals or their cages.

Appendix C

One of the first things a scientist learns is that working in the laboratory can be an exciting experience. But the laboratory can also be quite dangerous if proper safety rules are not followed at all times. To prepare yourself for a safe year in the laboratory, read over the following safety rules. Then read them a second time. Make sure you understand each rule. If you do not, ask your teacher to explain any rules you are unsure of.

Dress Code

1. Many materials in the laboratory can cause eye injury. To protect yourself from possible injury, wear safety goggles whenever you are working with chemicals, burners, or any substance that might get into your eyes. Never wear contact lenses in the laboratory.

2. Wear a laboratory apron or coat whenever you are working with chemicals or heated substances.

3. Tie back long hair to keep it away from any chemicals, burners and candles, or other laboratory equipment.

4. Remove or tie back any article of clothing or jewelry that can hang down and touch chemicals and flames.

General Safety Rules

5. Read all directions for an experiment several times. Follow the directions exactly as they are written. If you are in doubt about any part of the experiment, ask your teacher for assistance.

6. Never perform activities that are not authorized by your teacher. Obtain permission before "experimenting" on your own.

7. Never handle any equipment unless you have specific permission.

8. Take extreme care not to spill any material in the laboratory. If a spill occurs, immediately ask your teacher about the proper cleanup procedure. Never simply pour chemicals or other substances into the sink or trash container.

9. Never eat in the laboratory.

10. Wash your hands before and after each experiment.

First Aid

11. Immediately report all accidents, no matter how minor, to your teacher.

12. Learn what to do in case of specific accidents, such as getting acid in your eyes or on your skin. (Rinse acids from your body with lots of water.)

13. Become aware of the location of the first-aid kit. But your teacher should administer any required first aid due to injury. Or your teacher may send you to the school nurse or call a physician.

14. Know where and how to report an accident or fire. Find out the location of the fire extinguisher, phone, and fire alarm. Keep a list of important phone numbers—such as the fire department and the school nurse—near the phone. Immediately report any fires to your teacher.

Heating and Fire Safety

15. Again, never use a heat source, such as a candle or burner, without wearing safety goggles.

16. Never heat a chemical you are not instructed to heat. A chemical that is harmless when cool may be dangerous when heated.

17. Maintain a clean work area and keep all materials away from flames.

18. Never reach across a flame.

19. Make sure you know how to light a Bunsen burner. (Your teacher will demonstrate the proper procedure for lighting a burner.) If the flame leaps out of a burner toward you, immediately turn off the gas. Do not touch the burner. It may be hot. And never leave a lighted burner unattended!

20. When heating a test tube or bottle, always point it away from you and others. Chemicals can splash or boil out of a heated test tube.

21. Never heat a liquid in a closed container. The expanding gases produced may blow the container apart, injuring you or others.

22. Before picking up a container that has been heated, first hold the back of your hand near it. If you can feel the heat on the back of your hand, the container may be too hot to handle. Use a clamp or tongs when handling hot containers.

Using Chemicals Safely

23. Never mix chemicals for the "fun of it." You might produce a dangerous, possibly explosive substance.

24. Never touch, taste, or smell a chemical unless you are instructed by your teacher to do so. Many chemicals are poisonous. If you are instructed to note the fumes in an experiment, gently wave your hand over the opening of a container and direct the fumes toward your nose. Do not inhale the fumes directly from the container.

25. Use only those chemicals needed in the activity. Keep all lids closed when a chemical is not being used. Notify your teacher whenever chemicals are spilled.

26. Dispose of all chemicals as instructed by your teacher. To avoid contamination, never return chemicals to their original containers.

27. Be extra careful when working with acids or bases. Pour such chemicals over the sink, not over your workbench.

28. When diluting an acid, pour the acid into water. Never pour water into an acid.

29. Immediately rinse with water any acids that get on your skin or clothing. Then notify your teacher of any acid spill.

Using Glassware Safely

30. Never force glass tubing into a rubber stopper. A turning motion and lubricant will be helpful when inserting glass tubing into rubber stoppers or rubber tubing. Your teacher will demonstrate the proper way to insert glass tubing.

31. Never heat glassware that is not thoroughly dry. Use a wire screen to protect glassware from any flame.

32. Keep in mind that hot glassware will not appear hot. Never pick up glassware without first checking to see if it is hot. See #22.

33. If you are instructed to cut glass tubing, fire-polish the ends immediately to remove sharp edges.

34. Never use broken or chipped glassware. If glassware breaks, notify your teacher and dispose of the glassware in the proper trash container.

35. Never eat or drink from laboratory glassware. Thoroughly clean glassware before putting it away.

Using Sharp Instruments

36. Handle scalpels or razor blades with extreme care. Never cut material toward you; cut away from you.

37. Immediately notify your teacher if you cut your skin when working in the laboratory.

Animal Safety

38. No experiments that will cause pain, discomfort, or harm to mammals, birds, reptiles, fishes, and amphibians should be done in the classroom or at home.

39. Animals should be handled only if necessary. If an animal is excited or frightened, pregnant, feeding, or with its young, special handling is required.

40. Your teacher will instruct you as to how to handle each animal species that may be brought into the classroom.

41. Clean your hands thoroughly after handling animals or the cage containing animals.

End-of-Experiment Rules

42. After an experiment has been completed, clean up your work area and return all equipment to its proper place.

43. Wash your hands after every experiment.

44. Turn off all burners before leaving the laboratory. Check that the gas line leading to the burner is off as well.

Glossary

Pronunciation Key

When difficult names or terms first appear in the text, they are respelled to aid pronunciation. A syllable in SMALL CAPITAL LETTERS receives the most stress. The key below lists the letters used for respelling. It includes examples of words using each sound and shows how the words would be respelled.

Symbol	Example	Respelling
a	hat	(hat)
ay	pay, late	(pay), (layt)
ah	star, hot	(stahr), (haht)
ai	air, dare	(air), (dair)
aw	law, all	(law), (awl)
eh	met	(meht)
ee	bee, eat	(bee), (eet)
er	learn, sir, fur	(lern), (ser), (fer)
ih	fit	(fiht)
igh	mile, sigh	(mighl), (sigh)
oh	no	(noh)
oi	soil, boy	(soil), (boi)
oo	root, tule	(root), (rool)
or	born, door	(born), (dor)
ow	plow, out	(plow), (owt)

Symbol	Example	Respelling
u	put, book	(put), (buk)
uh	fun	(fuhn)
yoo	few, use	(fyoo), (yooz)
ch	chill, reach	(chihl), (reech)
g	go, dig	(goh), (dihg)
j	jet, gently, bridge	(jeht), (JEHNT-lee), (brihj)
k	kite, cup	(kight), (kuhp)
ks	mix	(mihks)
kw	quick	(kwihk)
ng	bring	(brihng)
s	say, cent	(say), (sehnt)
sh	she, crash	(shee), (krash)
th	three	(three)
y	yet, onion	(yeht), (UHN-yuhn)
z	zip, always	(zihp), (AWL-wayz)
zh	treasure	(TREH-zher)

active immunity: immunity in which a person's own immune system responds to the presence of an antigen

adolescence: stage of development that begins at age 13 and ends at age 20

adrenal: endocrine gland on top of each kidney that produces the hormone adrenaline

adulthood: stage of development that begins at age 20 and lasts the rest of a person's life

AIDS: Acquired Immune Deficiency Syndrome; disease in which certain cells of the immune system are killed by a virus called HIV

alcoholism: incurable disease in which a person is physically and psychologically dependent on alcohol

allergy: reaction that occurs when the body is overly sensitive to certain substances called allergens

alveolus (al-VEE-uh-luhs): grapelike clusters of round sacs in the lungs; site of gas exchange

amino acid: building block of protein

amniotic (am-nee-AHT-ihk) **sac:** fluid-filled sac that cushions and protects the developing baby

antibody: protein produced by the immune system in response to an antigen

antigen: invading organism or substance that triggers the action of an antibody

anus: opening at the end of the rectum through which solid wastes are eliminated

artery: blood vessel that carries blood away from the heart

atherosclerosis (ath-er-oh-skluh-ROH-sihs): thickening of the inner wall of an artery

atrium (AY-tree-uhm): upper heart chamber

axon: taillike fiber that carries messages away from the cell body

bone: structure that makes up the body's skeleton

brain: main control center of the central nervous system

bronchus (BRAHNG-kuhs): tube that branches off from the trachea and enters the lung

Calorie: amount of energy needed to raise the temperature of 1 kilogram of water by 1 degree Celsius

cancer: noninfectious disease in which the body's own cells multiply uncontrollably

capillary: tiny, thin-walled blood vessel that connects an artery to a vein

capsule: cup-shaped part of the nephron

carbohydrate: energy-rich nutrient found in foods such as vegetables and grain products

cardiac muscle: muscle tissue found only in the heart

cardiovascular (kahr-dee-oh-VAS-kyoo-ler) **disease:** disease that affects the heart and blood vessels

cartilage: dense, fibrous, flexible connective tissue

cell: building block of living things

cell body: largest part of the neuron, which contains the nucleus

cerebellum (ser-uh-BEHL-uhm): part of the brain that controls balance and coordinates muscle activity

cerebrum (SER-uh-bruhm): largest part of the brain; controls the senses, thought, and conscious activity

childhood: stage of development that begins at about 2 years of age and continues until the age of 13

cochlea (KAHK-lee-uh): snail-shaped tube in the inner ear from which nerve impulses are carried to the brain

cornea: transparent protective covering of the eye

dendrite: threadlike structure in the neuron that carries messages to the cell body

depressant: substance that slows down the actions of the brain and spinal cord

dermis: bottom layer of the skin

diabetes mellitus (digh-uh-BEET-eez muh-LIGHT-uhs): noninfectious disease in which the body either secretes too little insulin or is not able to use the insulin that is does secrete

diaphragm (DIGH-uh-fram): dome-shaped muscle that aids in breathing

disease: sickness or illness

dislocation: injury in which a bone is forced out of its joint

drug: substance that has an effect on the body

drug abuse: deliberate misuse of a drug for a use other than a medical one

eardrum: membrane in the ear that vibrates when struck by sound waves

effector: muscle cell or gland cell that is stimulated by a motor neuron

egg: female sex cell; ovum

embryo (EHM-bree-oh): developing baby from the second to the eighth week of development

enzyme: chemical substance that helps control chemical reactions

epidermis: top layer of the skin

epiglottis (ehp-uh-GLAHT-ihs): small flap of tissue that closes over the trachea (windpipe)

esophagus (ih-SAHF-uh-guhs): tube that carries food to the stomach

excretion: process by which wastes are removed from the body

Fallopian (fuh-LOH-pee-uhn) **tube:** structure through which an egg travels from the ovary to the uterus; oviduct

fat: nutrient that supplies the body with energy and also helps support and cushion the vital organs in the body

fertilization: process by which a sperm nucleus and an egg nucleus join

fetus (FEET-uhs): developing baby from the eighth week to birth

fibrin (FIGH-brihn): chemical that forms a net across cut in a blood vessel to trap blood cells and plasma

fracture: break in a bone

hallucinogen (huh-LOO-sih-nuh-jehn): illegal drug that alters an abuser's view of reality

hemoglobin (HEE-muh-gloh-bihn): iron-containing protein found in red blood cells

homeostasis (hoh-mee-oh-STAY-sihs): process by which the delicate balance between the activities occurring inside the body and those occurring outside is maintained

hormone (HOR-mohn): chemical messenger produced by an endocrine gland

hypertension: high blood pressure

hypothalamus (high-poh-THAL-uh-muhs): endocrine gland at base of brain that provides a link between the nervous system and the endocrine system

immunity (im-MYOON-ih-tee): resistance to a disease-causing organism or a harmful substance

infancy: stage of development that lasts from 1 month to about 2 years of age

infectious (ihn-FEHK-shuhs) **disease:** disease transmitted by disease-causing microorganisms

inflammatory (ihn-FLAM-uh-tor-ee) **response:** body's second line of defense against invading organisms, in which fluid and white blood cells leak from blood vessels into tissues

inhalant: drug that is inhaled

interferon: substance produced by body cells when they are attacked by viruses

interneuron: type of neuron that connects sensory and motor neurons

iris: circular, colored portion of the eye

islets (IGH-lihts) **of Langerhans** (LAHNG-er-hahns): small group of cells in the pancreas that produce the hormones insulin and glucagon

joint: place where two bones meet

kidney: main excretory organ

large intestine: organ in the digestive system in which water is absorbed and undigested food is stored

larynx (LAR-ihngks): voice box; organ that contains the vocal cords

lens: part of the eye that focuses light rays coming into the eye

ligament: connective tissue that holds bones together

liver: organ that produces bile

lung: main respiratory organ

marijuana: illegal drug that is made from the leaves and flowers of the Indian hemp plant

marrow: soft material found within bone

medulla (mih-DUHL-uh): part of the brain that controls involuntary actions

menstrual (MEHN-struhl) **cycle:** monthly cycle of change that occurs in the female reproductive system

mineral: nutrient that helps maintain the normal functioning of the body

motor neuron: type of neuron that carries messages from the brain and spinal cord to an effector

negative-feedback mechanism: mechanism by which the production of a hormone is controlled by the amount of another hormone

nephron (NEHF-rahn): microscopic chemical filtering factory in the kidneys

nerve impulse: electrical and chemical signals that travel across a neuron

neuron: nerve cell

noninfectious disease: disease not caused by disease-causing microorganisms

nose: organ through which air enters the respiratory system

nutrient (NOO-tree-ehnt): usable portion of food

opiate: pain-killing drug produced from the opium poppy

organ: group of different tissues that have a specific job

organ system: group of organs that work together to perform a specific job

ovary (OH-vuh-ree): endocrine gland that produces female hormones; female sex gland

ovulation (ahv-yoo-LAY-shuhn): process by which the follicle in the ovary releases the egg

pancreas (PAN-kree-uhs): organ that produces pancreatic juice and insulin

parathyroid: endocrine gland embedded in the thyroid that produces a hormone which controls the level of calcium in the blood

passive immunity: immunity that is gotten from another source

pepsin: enzyme produced by the stomach that digests proteins

peristalsis (per-uh-STAHL-sihs): waves of muscular contractions that move food through the digestive system

physical dependence: effect of drug abuse that occurs when the body becomes used to a drug and needs it to function normally

pituitary (pih-TOO-uh-ter-ee): endocrine gland located below the hypothalamus that controls many body processes

placenta (pluh-SEHN-tuh): structure through which a developing baby receives food and oxygen from its mother

plasma: fluid portion of the blood

platelet: cell fragment that aids in blood clotting

protein: nutrient that is used to build and repair body parts; made of amino acids

psychological (SIGH-kuh-lahj-ih-kuhl) **dependence:** effect of drug abuse in which a person has a strong desire or need to continue using a drug

ptyalin (TIGH-uh-lihn): enzyme in saliva that breaks down some starches into sugars

puberty (PYOO-ber-tee): beginning of adolescence

pupil: small opening in the middle of the eye

receptor: special cell that receives information from its surroundings

rectum: end of the large intestine

red blood cell: cell that carries oxygen throughout the body

reflex: simple response to a stimulus

respiration: energy-releasing process that is fueled by oxygen

retina (REHT-'n-uh): inner layer of the eye on which an image is focused; contains the light-sensitive rods and cones

rheumatoid (ROO-muh-toid) **arthritis:** disabling disease that affects the skin, lungs, and joints

semicircular canal: tiny canal in inner ear that is responsible for the sense of balance

sensory neuron: type of neuron that carries messages from the receptors to the brain or spinal cord

skeletal muscle: muscle tissue that is attached to bone and moves the skeleton

skin: outer covering of the body

small intestine: digestive organ in which most digestion takes place

smooth muscle: muscle tissue responsible for involuntary movement

sperm: male sex cell

spinal cord: provides the link between the brain and the rest of the body

sprain: injury in which ligaments are torn or stretched

stimulant: substance that speeds up the actions of the brain and spinal cord

stimulus: change in the environment

stomach: J-shaped digestive organ that connects the esophagus to the small intestine

synapse (SIHN-aps): tiny gap between two neurons

tendon: connective tissue that attaches bone to muscle

testis (TEHS-tihs): endocrine gland that produces male hormones; male sex gland

thymus (THIGH-muhs): endocrine gland that is responsible for the development of the immune system

thyroid: endocrine gland located in the neck that produces a hormone which controls how quickly food is burned up

tissue: group of similar cells that perform the same function

tolerance: effect of drug abuse in which the body needs increasingly larger amounts of the drug to get the same effect that was originally produced

trachea: windpipe; carries air from the nose to the lungs

umbilical (uhm-BIHL-ih-kuhl) **cord:** cordlike structure that connects the fetus to the placenta

ureter (yoo-REET-er): tube that carries urine from a kidney to the urinary bladder

urethra (yoo-REE-thruh): tube through which urine leaves the body

urinary bladder: muscular sac that stores urine

uterus (YOOT-er-uhs): pear-shaped organ in which a fertilized egg develops into a child; womb

vaccination (vak-sih-NAY-shuhn): process by which an antigen is deliberately introduced to stimulate the immune system

vein: blood vessel that carries blood to the heart

ventricle: lower heart chamber

villus (VIHL-uhs): fingerlike structure that lines the small intestine through which food is absorbed into the bloodstream

vitamin: nutrient that helps regulate growth and normal body functioning

vocal cord: fold of tissue stretched across the larynx that vibrates with the movement of air to form sounds

white blood cell: cell that defends the body against invading organisms

withdrawal: stopping the use of a drug

zygote (ZIGH-goht): fertilized egg

Index

Credits

Cover Background: Ken Karp
Photo Research: Natalie Goldstein
Contributing Artists: Warren Budd Assoc., Ltd.; Fran Milner; Function Thru Form
Photographs: **4** left: Calvin Larsen/Photo Researchers, Inc.; right: Mary Kate Denny/Photoedit; **5** left: Lee Wardle/Sports File; center: Obremski/Image Bank; right: Dan McCoy/Rainbow; **6** top: Bill Longcore/Photo Researchers, Inc.; center: A. Upitis/Image Bank; bottom left: Granger Collection; bottom right: USDA; **7** top: Stuart Franklin/Sygma; center: Art Siegel; bottom: David Madison/Duomo Photography, Inc.; **8** top: Lefever/Grushow/Grant Heilman Photography; center: Index Stock Photography, Inc.; bottom: Rex Joseph; **10** top: David Madison Photography; bottom: Chris Jones/Stock Market; **11** David Madison/Duomo Photography, Inc.; **12** and **13** Dr. R. P. Clark & M. Goff/Science Photo Library/Photo Researchers, Inc.; **14** Richard Hutchings/Photoedit; **16** left: M. P. Kahl/DRK Photo; right: David Phillips/Visuals Unlimited; **17** top: Dwight Kuhn Photography; bottom: Michael Webb/Visuals Unlimited; **18** Alfred Pasieka/Science Photo Library/Photo Researchers, Inc.; **19** Veronika Burmeister/Visuals Unlimited; **20** top left: Bruce Iverson/Visuals Unlimited; top right: Cabisco/Visuals Unlimited; center: Robert E. Daemmrich/Tony Stone Worldwide/Chicago Ltd.; bottom left: Dwight Kuhn Photography; bottom right: Don Fawcett/Visuals Unlimited; **23** top left, right, and bottom left: Dan McCoy/Rainbow; **27** Tony Duffy/Allsport; **28** and **29** Leonard Kamsler; **30** Seltzer/OSU/Dan McCoy/Rainbow; **31** Tom McHugh/Photo Researchers, Inc.; **32** Biophoto Associates/Photo Researchers, Inc.; **33** Prof. Aaron Polliack/Science Photo Library/Photo Researchers, Inc.; **34** From TISSUES AND ORGANS: A TEXT-ATLAS OF SCANNING ELECTRON MICROSCOPY by Richard G. Kessel and Randy H. Kardon. Copyright © 1979 by W. H. Freeman and Company. Reprinted by permission.; **35** top left: © Lennart Nilsson, BEHOLD MAN, Little, Brown and Company; top right: © Lennart Nilsson, THE INCREDIBLE MACHINE, National Geographic Society; bottom: Dan McCoy/Rainbow; **36** Tim Davis/David Madison Photography; **38** top left: Dwight Kuhn Photography; bottom left: Steven J. Krasemann/DRK Photo; bottom right: Brooks Dodge/Sports File; **40** left: Eric Grave/Photo Researchers, Inc.; center: Triarch/Visuals Unlimited; right: Michael Abbey/Photo Researchers, Inc.; **41** Ken Karp; **43** Bruce Curtis/Peter Arnold, Inc.; **44** left: Photo Researchers, Inc.; right: Princess Margaret Rose Orthopaedic Hospital/Science Photo Library/Photo Researchers, Inc.; **45** right and bottom: © Lennart Nilsson, THE INCREDIBLE MACHINE, National Geographic Society; **49** left and right: Biophoto Associates/Science Source/Photo Researchers, Inc.; **50** and **51** NASA; **52** top and bottom: USDA; **53** top left: Tony Freeman/Photoedit; top right: Myrleen Ferguson/Photoedit; bottom left: David Young-Wolff/Photoedit; bottom right: Don & Pat Valenti/F/Stop Pictures, Inc.; **54** CNRI/Science Photo Library/Photo Researchers, Inc.; **56** top left: L. Morris/Photoquest, Inc.; top right: Wolfgang Kaehler; bottom: Kristen Brochmann/Fundamental Photographs; **59** left: Guido Alberto Rossi/Image Bank; right: A. Upitis/Image Bank; **63** Howard Sochurek Inc.; **64** top left and bottom: © Lennart Nilsson, BEHOLD MAN, Little, Brown and Company; top right: Omikron/Science Source/Photo Researchers, Inc.; **65** L. V. Bergman & Associates; **66** top and bottom: Lennart Nilsson, THE INCREDIBLE MACHINE, National Geographic Society, © Boehringer Ingelheim International GmbH; **69** © Lennart Nilsson, THE INCREDIBLE MACHINE, National Geographic Society; **70** top and bottom left: L. V. Bergman & Associates; bottom right: © Lennart Nilsson, THE INCREDIBLE MACHINE, National Geographic Society; **71** John McGrail; **72** top: Tony Duffy/Allsport; bottom: Robert Rathe/Folio, Inc.; **73** Derik Murray/Image Bank; **77** Nancy Coplon; **78** and **79** David Wagner/Phototake; **80** CNRI/Science Photo Library/Photo Researchers, Inc.; **82** Lennart Nilsson, THE INCREDIBLE MACHINE, National Geographic Society, © Boehringer Ingelheim Internationl GmbH; **84** top: Philippe Plailly/Science Photo Library/Photo Researchers, Inc.; bottom: VU/SIU/Visuals Unlimited; **86** R. G Kessel and R. H. Kardon; **87** © Lennart Nilsson, BEHOLD MAN, Little, Brown and Company; **90** top: NIBSC/Science Photo Library/Photo Researchers, Inc.; bottom left: Lennart Nilsson, THE INCREDIBLE MACHINE, National Geographic Society, © Boehringer Ingelheim International GmbH; bottom right: Bill Longcore/Photo Researchers, Inc.; **91** top: © Lennart Nilsson, THE INCREDIBLE MACHINE, National Geographic Society; bottom left: CNRI/Science Photo Library/Photo Researchers, Inc.; bottom right: Lennart Nilsson, THE INCREDIBLE MACHINE, National Geographic Society, © Boehringer Ingelheim International GmbH; **92** Lennart Nilsson, THE INCREDIBLE MACHINE, National Geographic Society, © Boehringer Ingelheim International GmbH; **94** © Lennart Nilsson, THE INCREDIBLE MACHINE, National Geographic Society; **96** and **97** Lennart Nilsson, THE INCREDIBLE MACHINE, National Geographic Society, © Boehringer Ingelheim International GmbH; **99** Alexander Tsiaras/Science Source/Photo Researchers, Inc.; **101** Simon Fraser, Hexham General/Science Photo Library/Photo Researchers, Inc.; **102** Ken Karp; **105** Dan McCoy/Rainbow; **106** and **107** Tim Davis/Duomo Photography, Inc.; **108** left: Michael Fogden/DRK Photo; right: Peter Veit/DRK Photo; **110** top: Art Siegel; bottom: Lennart Nilsson, THE INCREDIBLE MACHINE, National Geographic Society, © Boehringer Ingelheim International GmbH; **111** Chet Childs/Tony Stone Worldwide/Chicago Ltd.; **112** top and bottom: Dr. G. Paul Moore; **113** left: Jack Vartoogian; right: Myrleen Ferguson/Photoedit; **114** © Lennart Nilsson, THE INCREDIBLE MACHINE, National Geographic Society; **115** CNRI/Science Photo Library/Photo Researchers, Inc.; **116** top: Paul J. Sutton/Duomo Photography, Inc.; bottom: NASA; **119** L. V. Bergman & Associates; **120** CNRI/Science Photo Library/Photo Researchers, Inc.; **121** top: © Lennart Nilsson, THE INCREDIBLE MACHINE, National Geographic Society; bottom: David York/Medichrome/The Stock Shop; **123** left: Veronika Burmeister/Visuals Unlimited; right: Obremski/Image Bank; **124** top left: P. Bartholomew/Gamma-Liaison, Inc; top right: Biophoto/Photo Researchers, Inc.; bottom: © Lennart Nilsson, BEHOLD MAN, Little, Brown and Company; **125** Eric Reynolds/Adventure Photo; **130** and **131** Alan Goldsmith/Stock Market; **132** top: David Madison/Duomo Photography, Inc.; bottom left: Mary Kate Denny/Photoedit; bottom right: Bob Daemmrich Photography; **133** left: Johnny Johnson/DRK Photo; right: Bob Daemmrich/The Image Works; **134** Michael Abbey/Photo Researchers, Inc.; **135** © Lennart Nilsson. THE INCREDIBLE MACHINE, National Geographic Society; **136** CNRI/Science Photo Library/Photo Researchers, Inc.; **138** Bill Longcore/Photo Researchers, Inc.; **141** CNRI/Science Photo Library/Photo Researchers, Inc.; **142** © Lennart Nilsson, THE INCREDIBLE MACHINE, National Geographic Society; **145** left: Randy Trine/DRK Photo; right: Andrew McClenaghan/Science Photo Library/Photo Researchers, Inc.; **146** © Lennart Nilsson, BEHOLD MAN, Little, Brown and Company; **147** top: Jesse Simmons Photo; bottom left: © Lennart Nilsson, BEHOLD MAN, Little, Brown and Company; bottom right: © Lennart Nilsson, THE INCREDIBLE MACHINE, National Geographic Society; **149** © Lennart Nilsson, BEHOLD MAN, Little, Brown and Company; **150** top: © Lennart Nilsson, BEHOLD MAN, Little, Brown and Company; bottom: © Lennart Nilsson, THE INCREDIBLE MACHINE, National Geographic Society; **151** top left: John Zoiner/Stock Boston, Inc.; top right: Hank Morgan/Rainbow; bottom: Garry Gay/Image Bank; **152** top: © Lennart Nilsson, BEHOLD MAN, Little, Brown and Company; bottom: Nathan Benn/Woodfin Camp & Associates; **154** top: Synaptek Scientific Products, Inc./Science Photo Library/Photo Researchers, Inc.; bottom: © 1991 Bill Redic; **158** © Lennart Nilsson, THE INCREDIBLE MACHINE, National Geographic Society; **160** Martin M. Rotker; **166** and **167** Michael Tcherevkoff/Image Bank; **168** left: Animals Animals Stock/Animals Animals/Earth Scenes; right: David W. Hamilton/Image Bank; **169** top: John Giannicchi/Science Source/Photo Researchers, Inc.; bottom: Dr. G. Schatten/Science Photo Library/Photo Researchers, Inc.; **170** Dr. Ram Verna/Phototake; **172** Bob Daemmrich/The Image Works; **174** © Lennart Nilsson, THE INCREDIBLE MACHINE, National Geographic Society; **175** top left: © Lennart Nilsson, A CHILD IS BORN, Dell Publishing Company; top right: © Lennart Nilsson, BEHOLD MAN, Little, Brown and Company; bottom left and bottom right: © Lennart Nilsson, THE INCREDIBLE MACHINE, National Geographic Society; **179** Howard Sochurek Inc.; **180** Mickey Pfleger; **181** left: Niki Mareschal/Image Bank; center: Richard Hutchings/Photo Researchers, Inc.; right: Edward Lettau/FPG International; **182** top: Bob Daemmrich Photography; bottom: W. Rosin Malecki/Photoedit; **183** Bill Hess/National Geographic Magazine; right: Bob Daemmrich Photography; **184** left: Janeart Ltd./Image Bank; right: Don Hamerman/Folio, Inc.; **185** Karen Leeds/Stock Market; **190** and **191** Larry Mulvehill/Photo Researchers, Inc.; **192** left: K. G. Murti/Visuals Unlimited; right: © Lennart Nilsson, National Geographic Society; **193** top: © Lennart Nilsson, THE INCREDIBLE MACHINE, National Geographic Society; center and bottom: Lennart Nilsson, THE INCREDIBLE MACHINE, National Geographic Society © Boehringer Ingelheim International GmbH; **194** Lennart Nilsson, THE INCREDIBLE MACHINE, National Geographic Society, © Boehringer Ingelheim International GmbH; **195** Gabe Palmer/Stock Market; **196** top: E. D. Getzoff, J. A. Tainer, A. J. Olson of the Scripps Research Institute; bottom: Lennart Nilsson, National Geographic Society, © Boehringer Ingelheim International GmbH; **198** Bob Daemmrich/The Image Works; **200** top left: Manfred Kage/Peter Arnold, Inc.; top right: Robert Dudzic/F/Stop Pictures, Inc.; bottom left: Dick Canby/DRK Photo; bottom right: Dr. Jeremy Burgess/Science Photo Library/Photo Researchers, Inc.; **201** left: Lennart Nilsson, National Geographic Society, © Boehringer Ingelheim International GmbH; right: Stuart Franklin/Sygma; **202** top: Lennart Nilsson, National Geographic Society, © Boehringer Ingelheim International GmbH; bottom: Susan Van Etten/Photoedit; **203** left and right: CNRI/Science Photo Library/Photo Researchers, Inc.; **204** top left: Don Smetzer/Tony Stone Worldwide/Chicago Ltd.; top center: © Lennart Nilsson, THE INCREDIBLE MACHINE, National Geographic Society; top right: G. I. Bernard/Animals Animals/Earth Scenes; bottom: Dr. Willy Burgdorfer/Rocky Mountain Laboratories; **205** top: Lennart Nilsson, National Geographic Society, © Boehringer Ingelheim International GmbH; bottom: CNRI/Science Photo Library/Photo Researchers, Inc.; **206** top: © Lou Lainey/1984 Discover Publications; bottom: Lennart Nilsson, National Geographic Society, © Boehringer Ingelheim International GmbH; **207** Lennart Nilsson, National Geographic Society, © Boehringer Ingelheim International GmbH; **208** Lee Wardle/Sports File; **209** Tom & Pat Leeson/Photo Researchers, Inc.; **214** and **215** Bobby Holland/Reader's Digest Foundation; **216** left: Michael P. Gadomski/Photo Researchers, Inc.; right: Benn Mitchell/Image Bank; **217** top: The University Museum, University of Pennsylvania; bottom: Ken Karp; **218** left: Tony Savino/Sipa Press; right: Bruce Delis/Gamma-Liaison, Inc; **219** top: Richard Hutchings/Photo Researchers, Inc.; bottom: Granger Collection; **221** A. Glauberman/Science Source/Photo Researchers, Inc.; **222** Stacy Pick/Stock Boston, Inc.; **223** Richard Hutchings/Photo Researchers, Inc.; **224** Lennart Nilsson, THE INCREDIBLE MACHINE, National Geographic Society, © Boehringer Ingelheim International GmbH; **225** Calvin Larsen/Photo Researchers, Inc.; **226** Ken Karp; **228** top: Ken Karp; center: Edward S. Ross/Phototake; bottom: Howard Sochurek Inc.; **229** Fred Lombardi/Photo Researchers, Inc.; **230** David Alan Harvey/Woodfin Camp & Associates; **231** top left: Walter H. Hodge/Peter Arnold, Inc.; top right: Michael Hardy/Woodfin Camp & Associates; bottom: National Institutes of Health; **235** Wesley Bocxe/Photo Researchers, Inc.; **236** Grant Heilman/Grant Heilman Photography; **237** Centers for Disease Control; **239** UPI/Bettmann; **240** Charles Gupton/Stock Boston, Inc.; **242** Dr. Jack Ricci, Department of Orthopaedic Research, New Jersey Medical School; **244** Seltzer/OSU/Dan McCoy/Rainbow; **248** Dick Canby/DRK Photo; **253** Dwight Kuhn Photography